For Rowan Gibbs

BLOCKBUSTER!

Lucy Sussex was born in New Zealand and now lives in Melbourne. She has edited four anthologies, including *She's Fantastical*, shortlisted for the World Fantasy Award. Her award-winning fiction includes books for younger readers and the novel *The Scarlet Rider*. She has published five short-story collections and is the author of *Women Writers and Detectives in Nineteenth-Century Crime Fiction: The Mothers of the Mystery Genre*.

BLOCK BUSTER!

FERGUS HUME & THE MYSTERY OF A HANSOM CAB

TEXT PUBLISHING

MELBOURNE AUSTRALIA

The Text Publishing Company
Swann House
22 William Street
Melbourne Victoria 3000
Australia
textpublishing.com.au

First published in 2015 by The Text Publishing Company

Plate section: John Irvine images from the collection of the Toitū Otago Settlers Museum. Trischler photographs courtesy of David Green. Alice Cornwell photograph from the collection of Tony Rackstraw. Cyril R. Hallward illustration from Fergus Hume's *When I Lived in Bohemia* (Bristol: Arrowsmith, 1892). Maria L. Kirk illustration from Fergus Hume's *The Chronicles of Fairy Land* (Philadelphia: J. B. Lippincott Co., 1911). Caricatures from Melbourne *Punch* and New Zealand *Land and Sea* magazines.

Book design by W. H. Chong and Imogen Stubbs
Typeset by J & M Typesetting
Printed in Australia by Griffin Press

National Library of Australia Cataloguing-in-Publication entry
Creator: Sussex, Lucy, 1957- author.
Title: Blockbuster! : Fergus Hume and the mystery of a hansom cab /
          by Lucy Sussex.
ISBN: 9781922147943 (paperback)
          9781922148940 (ebook)
Subjects: Hume, Fergus, 1859-1932. Mystery of a hansom cab.
          Detective and mystery stories, Australian.
Dewey Number: A823.2

'The Mystery of a Hansom Cab? Now there's a murky story…'
Jeff Prentice, book historian and publisher

CONTENTS

THE DARK AVENUE

Melbourne, 2012

A fine spring day, perfect for walking outdoors with a television researcher. Our destination: the mean streets of crime-fiction history. We met at the Scots Church corner of Collins Street, where Fergus Hume's 1886 novel *The Mystery of a Hansom Cab* begins. From there we walked a block to Chinatown, scouting locations, and then to Little Lonsdale Street, where I stood against an antique brick wall and talked to camera.

In Hume's time Lonsdale Street was the red-light district of Melbourne town. It would become even more infamous as the possible hiding place of the Colonial Parliament's mace, stolen in 1891. 'Lilly Lon', as Little Lonsdale Street was known, was even worse, an unsewered and unlit slum. Now it rises high, with upmarket apartment buildings. Few signs remain of its desperate past, though the 2002 Casselden Place archaeological excavation unearthed rich detritus, century-old sin: bottles, crockery, coins and rarest of all, the remains of imported pessaries, Victorian contraceptives. Besides these artefacts exists a literary record: the seediest scenes of Hume's novel.

Little may remain physically of Lilly Lon the slum, but what of ghostly traces? Victorians were ardent spiritualists, holding seances and supporting a thriving trade in photographs where phantasms appeared alongside the living, macabre family portraits. Arthur Conan Doyle, Fergus Hume's great crime-writing rival, was fascinated by such things. But the twenty-first-century camera completely fails to capture any uproarious ghosts frolicking nearby. Neither does it show a quieter spectre: an unobtrusive man in coat and bowler hat, with a thick waxed moustache, walking the street and taking notes.

Hume was a flâneur, a term defined by Baudelaire as 'a person who walks the city in order to experience it'. To stroll through Melbourne today is to experience both its present and its past, and Hume's experience of the city is accessible to us still. Through *Hansom Cab* we saunter into a lost place, Marvellous Melbourne, a glorious if short-lived boom town of the 1880s. Hume would write three novels with this setting, his Melbourne Trilogy.

Hansom Cab begins with a hidden, personal joke, dependent upon architecture and locale. Although he was born in England Hume was a Scot by inheritance, with Glaswegian parents. When Hume was a child his family emigrated to Dunedin, New Zealand, a city founded by settlers belonging to the Free Church of Scotland, bastions of Calvinist morality. Dunedin is a Presbyterian town, with the values of piety, good works and sobriety.

Hume would encounter Scots Presbyterians again in Melbourne. Their neo-Gothic church, built by Nellie Melba's father, was a spiritual and physical landmark: the spire was the tallest structure in the city during the last decades of the nineteenth century. In using the Scots Church as the starting point for a novel that descends into some seamy depths—sex, murder, drugs—Hume cocked a snook at the sect, and by implication its members, who included some of the richest and most powerful men in Melbourne.

The action proper of the novel starts with Malcolm Royston, a hansom-cab driver plying the streets at 1 a.m. on Friday, in search of fares. The late July night is beautifully still and clear, stars and moon shining bright despite the gas streetlighting. No doubt it is cold, yet the temperature is never mentioned. Hume had come from Dunedin, whose winters are icy: Melbourne to him would have been balmy in comparison.

Royston drives his horse down Collins Street. He passes the 1865 Burke and Wills memorial statue, the first public monument in Melbourne, now translocated slightly downhill, at the corner of Collins and Swanston Streets. At Russell Street he is hailed by a man in a fawn coat supporting another, staggering drunk. This scene—minus the detail that both men on the footpath sport evening dress, white tie and tailcoats—is repeated every night in Melbourne, though now with motorised cabs rather than horse-drawn vehicles.

Royston turns his cab, in the process passing another church: the Independent (Congregational) Church, now St Michael's Uniting Church, across the road from Scots. Hume had been christened in a Congregational Church, in Worcester, England. Presbyterian and Congregational had their theological differences, wider than the width of a colonial street, but both were fiery temperance activists, bitterly opposed to alcohol. Situating public drunkenness in their vicinity, at the beginning of a crime novel, was quite outrageous—as Hume would well have known.

The hansom successfully hailed, the drunk and his companion embark, and Royston receives his destination: St Kilda. Horse pulls hansom and humans down Collins Street, turning left into Swanston Street and continuing down St Kilda Road. To recreate the feel of a nineteenth-century cab ride on this route today is to play tourist, sitting self-consciously in the back of a coach and pair as cars, trams and bikes shoot by, in the case of the latter dangerously close to the clopping hooves.

The tourism operators do not use hansom cabs, opting for the larger, more regal open landaus or barouches. A comparison in terms of size and style might be between a Cadillac and a Smart Car. The hansom cab accommodates two passengers at most. It is light and speedy, could be pulled by a single horse, and has a low centre of gravity, enabling neat turns. For the increasingly crowded urban streets of the late 1800s, they were the perfect vehicle.

It is almost impossible to envisage Hume's St Kilda Road. These days it is never a dark avenue, nor truly deserted, not even after midnight when the trams cease their noisy progress back and forth. Trams do not feature in *Hansom Cab*, which sets it firmly in 1885, as they were introduced to Melbourne the following year. The closest modern Melbourne gets to *Hansom Cab*'s street- and soundscape is when the tourist carriages return to their floats, or the police horses plod back to their barracks in South Melbourne. Yet in 1886, the city was only a few decades away from bushrangers in St Kilda Road, or bullock drays mired in the mud of the Central Business District. Fifty years prior, not even a village had existed.

In the book the fatal cab journey continues down St Kilda Road, past the belvedere tower of Government House, which would later figure in the background of the original cover, and Melbourne Grammar, then called the Church of England Grammar School. Another icon of respectability to include in his novel, another institution to annoy!

At this point Royston is instructed to stop. The man in the fawn coat departs the cab, paying a much appreciated half sovereign. Lighting a cigarette, he heads back towards the city on foot. In those peripatetic days, with no cars and few bicycles, a walk from the school back to the city would not seem unusual, nor long. Royston does not question it, chirruping his horse onwards. With the passengers reduced to one, Royston continues down St Kilda Road, as he had been instructed. At the junction, he asks his remaining passenger for directions. Receiving no answer, he clambers down from his seat, and opens the door, finding a man not dead drunk, but dead, with a handkerchief tied over his mouth. A practical man, Royston drives to St Kilda police station to report the crime, his vehicle a temporary hearse. A doctor would testify that the handkerchief had been soaked in chloroform: once used as an anaesthetic, but here a murder weapon, inducing cardiac or respiratory arrest.

And so the novel begins, with the creation of a mystery. Who is the dead man in the cab? Why was he murdered? And who is the guilty man in the fawn coat? It is the classic form of the whodunnit, a literary form that developed over the course of the nineteenth century. It derived from popular newspaper reportage, the depiction of a detective investigation *as it happens*, in daily instalments: the discovery of a murder; suspects identified; clues and leads followed, until the story concludes with the guilty party revealed.

Hume stated in a preface to *Hansom Cab* that he wrote the book to draw attention to his theatre writing. What he did not anticipate was that he had something very rare on his hands: a genuine literary blockbuster. Upon publication in late 1886 the book quickly became a local sensation, for which extraordinary sales figures were cited: five thousand copies sold of the first edition, with up to twenty-five thousand copies sold in Australasia in less than a year. At the time the population of Melbourne was between three-hundred and four-hundred thousand, and literacy was by no means universal. The book was then taken to England by a consortium named for the project, the Hansom Cab Publishing Company. Here even more extraordinary sales figures were achieved, with the book rapidly selling half a million copies, something unprecedented for the new publishing genre of detective fiction. It was adapted for theatre widely; it had a book-length parody; silent film versions appeared in 1911 (from Amalgamated Pictures, whose members Tait, Johnson and Gibson were the makers of pioneering feature *The Story of the Kelly Gang*), 1915 (Eliot Stannard, UK) and 1925 (Arthur Shirley), all lost; radio serials were broadcast, as well as television adaptations, including the 2012 telemovie.[1] There were even criminal consequences: the novel inspired fraudulent impersonations and a reported copycat murder.

Not least, it made Hume famous, and led to a career which would include more than a hundred books.

Most people know little about Hume beyond his debut novel's success, and the fact that he sold his copyright to the Hansom Cab Publishing Company for £50, disbelieving that a book from the colonies could have major overseas success. *How to Write a Bestseller and Not Become Rich* might have been the title of his autobiography, had he written one. Yet he and his novel had a huge influence.

The story behind *The Mystery of a Hansom Cab* is complex: a tale of a publishing genre; of readership; of the morals of an era and its dark secrets; of a great city in full boom, and the financial crash which followed, to which Hume was indirectly but also intimately linked. It has never been told before. Only recently has substantial information emerged about *Hansom Cab* and its writer, enough to construct a lengthy narrative. However, *Blockbuster!* is not a biography of a man, more the biography of a book: how a genuine publishing phenomenon was created—and its wide-reaching consequences.

So much information about Hume is missing, from family photographs to publishing records, that the temptation is to delve into his many books in search of clues: the biographical fallacy, which can ensnare too many writers whose subject is creative lives, where the action is on the page or in the head. Here be dangers, for authors are tricksy beasts. As Hume's villain Gaston Vandeloup observes in *Madame Midas*, language 'was given to us to conceal our thoughts'.[2] Isherwood may have famously proclaimed that 'I am a camera', but only the dullest of realists—'looker-putters', to use a term from amateur art circles—depict life as it exactly is. Others embellish, or if treating something private and profound, invert or disguise it. Only rarely can something so obscured be revealed by a biographer.

Blockbuster! is not a cradle-to-grave literary biography. Nor is it replete with plot summaries of Hume's many works, although their titles and sometimes quotations from them open each chapter. A full biography might yet be written: the digitisation of nineteenth-century records is progressing at such a pace that, during the writing of this book, new information about Hume and his times has emerged almost daily. Inevitably, more will come to light after this manuscript's deadline. But there will always be gaps, for Hume was a private person, leaving no diaries nor even many surviving letters. The approach here is by nature impressionistic. But it tells a story, a bibliographic mystery, one in which life intertwines with the subject matter of crime almost inextricably.

In searching for the truth behind Hume the forms and terminology of the crime genre are appropriate. He had an important role in establishing detective fiction as a publishing category, being one of the most influential crime writers of all time. Yet Hume himself is a mystery: what led a young man from the colonies to write the biggest-selling crime novel of the nineteenth century, and one of the most important Australian books ever? *The Mystery of a Hansom Cab* has never been out of print. At this point another query, another crime-narrative form, comes into play: howdunnit? How could a small-press publication, from the edge of the British Empire, conquer the international market? And finally: howcatchem? How can we, in the twenty-first century, capture and understand a lost past?

We cannot summon the ghost of Hume from the bricks of Little Lonsdale Street, or riding down St Kilda Road in a phantom hansom cab. But it is possible to excavate, like the archaeologists in Casselden Place, and find the clues to an enduring mystery, that of Fergus Hume and his blockbuster.

1

THE MAN WITH A SECRET

England, 1861

It was about eleven o'clock, and Myles Desmond sat in his sitting-room scribbling an article for a society journal, called 'Asmodeus', published for the express purpose of unroofing people's houses, and exposing to the world their private life. [...]

When the door opened he glanced up and saw that the new-comer was not a friend, but a tall, grey man whom he did not know. Myles paused with his pen in his hand, and waited for his visitor to speak, looking at him interrogatively meanwhile.

Mr. Dowker—for of course it was he—closed the door carefully, and advancing to the table, introduced himself in two words: 'Dowker—detective!'

THE PICCADILLY PUZZLE[3]

Hume was an author of whose life little can be directly detected from his novels. His secrets are well-hidden, yet sometimes it is possible to perceive allusive games. In *The Piccadilly Puzzle* (1889), his fifth novel, Hume introduces a young man living in London's Bohemian quarter, who writes for a scandal sheet, like Melbourne's *Table Talk*, for which Hume worked briefly. So far, so semi-autobiographical, but unlike his hero Hume was never suspected of murder. Rather he is guilty of a pun, in which he shows off his knowledge of Latin.

The Piccadilly Puzzle was a cheaply produced book, what we would now term a pulp. Not all of its wide readership had been educated in the classical languages, something usually reserved for men, like Hume, from the middle class and upwards. Only this select group would have understood the allusion: Myles and Dowker, writer for a muckraking journal and detective, have the same job.

The pair are linked via the etymology of the word detective, a curious history involving a demon from Hell. Our current understanding of the word, as a profession, or referring to a publishing genre, is relatively recent. Once it meant something entirely different. What happened was that a Latin word *detegere* (*de+tegere*, the Latin for roof), a word formed along the same lines as de-compose, de-populate, was borrowed into mediaeval English. There, the language being a fluid and multilingual hybrid, it met a synonym: *unroof* (from the German *hrof*, a roof). Roofers tending not to know Latin, the Germanic word kept its meaning. Detective instead mutated semantically. Few now would associate de-roofing with the police, but the verb 'to detect' originated in *detegere*—a detective raises the roof, figuratively.

How lifting the roof came to refer to detection is almost as complex as a mystery novel. The first signs of change came in middle and early modern English, with detect coming to mean uncovering, or a revelation. In the 1600s, a demon entered this etymological story: Asmodeus, a figure as old as the Talmud. He featured in a 1641 novel by Spanish writer Luis Vélez de Guevara, *El Diablo Cojuelo* (*The Lame Devil*). Guevara's Asmodeus is a comic troublemaker, imprisoned in a bottle. A student releases him and is repaid with a series of fantastic adventures. Asmodeus lifts the roofs off Madrid houses to show what is happening inside, a source of much happy satire. He detects, revealing guilty secrets—as if he was a modern private eye or police investigator.

Guevara's flight of fancy caught the imagination, and detective

Asmodeus featured in literature for the next two centuries. In chapter forty-seven of Charles Dickens' *Dombey and Son* (1848) a plea is made: 'Oh for a good spirit who would take the house-tops off, with a more potent and benignant hand than the lame demon in the tale, and show a Christian people what dark shapes issue from amidst their homes...'

With 'what dark shapes', Dickens nails an anxiety of his age. Victorian culture was sex-segregated, the men active in the wide world and women relegated to the domestic sphere, where they reigned as passive angels in the house. But safe as the home might seem, it could conceal dark secrets: sexual abuse, particularly of female servants; infanticide; drunkenness; and drug addiction, with opium readily available in everything from patent medicine to baby pacifiers.

Dickens would interview the first English detectives of the future Scotland Yard, just as the word became linked to the police. They fascinated him, with their power for revealing the secrets of all hearts and the miseries behind the facade of respectability—such as Dickens' own. To lift the roofs off the domestic sanctum was to release monsters, as notorious crimes of the era revealed. In the Road Murder of 1860 the privacy of a middle-class family was violated, as much by the press as by a monstrous crime: a small boy was murdered by someone in the household and dropped down a privy. Such cases provided work for detectives, lawyers, journalists—and vicarious thrills for the reading public.

Dickens and his friend Wilkie Collins speculated 'whodunnit' about the Road Murder and Collins included details from it in his bestselling 1868 novel, *The Moonstone*. Here he followed a trend: from the true crime of the era, revealed by police investigation and displayed in the newspapers, came the source matter for the new genre of detective fiction, still in the process of formation, and lacking an official name.

A bigger player also raised the roofs. Despite the privacy of the Victorian home, the modern bureaucratic state required the gathering of information, however quotidian. Every decade, a de-roofing of Victorian England would occur through the Census. Now digitised and searchable online, it provides a wealth of biographical information about the lives of ancestors—and even detective writers.

Consider the census of 1861, taken on the night of 7 April: across the nation the roofs were raised on every house, revealing the lives of the people within. From city terraces to county mansions to humble hovels, all were presented for scrutiny, and recorded for posterity. Lost trades appear: straw-plaiters, death-hunters (itinerant sellers of murder broadsheets), colporteurs (ditto, of books). Also are found, in these days before contraception, large households: a Paterfamilias, dear Mamma, grandparents, bachelor uncles and spinster aunts, a passel of children, and the servants who kept the domestic realm functioning.

If we seek to play Asmodeus, then this census is a perfect place to snoop. It reveals secrets and lies—in particular regarding two of the major crime writers of the century. In London can be found Wilkie Collins, aged thirty-six, who gave his occupation as non-practising barrister and author of fiction. Collins had just reached bestseller status, writing in a genre dubbed by the press 'Sensation'. The label denoted popular fictions featuring murder and bigamy (common in those days of rare and expensive divorces). In content Sensation novels are full of crime, and some works, such as Collins' *The Moonstone*, also contain the detective mystery structure.

Collins had his own personal mystery, into which the census-taker intruded: he 'lived in sin' with Caroline Graves. Embarrassed into the semblance of respectability, the pair declared themselves married on the census form. Also sensational in life as well as fiction was Collins' great rival, Mary Braddon, found in Essex with her lover, publisher John Maxwell. In the census Mary and her mother Fanny are listed as Maxwell's visitors, but Mrs Braddon was hardly a chaperone. Maxwell was married, with a wife he could not divorce due to her insanity, a real-life Mrs Rochester. While the couple waited for her to die, Braddon would produce a string of bestselling Sensation novels and six children with Maxwell. Like Collins and Graves, the couple hid their private life from the reading public, the fans of 'Miss Braddon's' novels.

Such were the secrets of one generation of Victorian crime writers. The next generation, too young to have secrets yet, can also be found in the 1861 census. Here are listed two small boys of Celtic heritage (Irish and Scot), both born in 1859: Arthur Conan Doyle on 22 May and Ferguson Wright Hume on 8 July. Both would devour the works of Collins and Braddon, then follow their literary idols into the developing genre of detective fiction.

The census shows the Doyles living in Edinburgh. While no photographs are known to survive of the infant Hume, they do of young Doyle with his older sister Annette and two dolls. He wears a scowl, a lank bob and a flouncy frock. In the Victorian era children were not differentiated in dress until about the age of four, when boys were shorn of their long locks and put into breeches. Hume would have worn similar drag.

The Doyles had moved to Scotland; the Humes had moved from Glasgow to the English Midlands. They were of far humbler origins, with Fergus's grandfather, Robert Hume, a roof slater. His father was scarcely better, class-wise, being a madhouse attendant at the Royal Glasgow Asylum, Gartnavel.

In the early nineteenth century this institution was at the forefront of reform in the treatment of lunacy. Previously, as Gartnavel patient James Frame wrote, 'the maniac's doom was suffocation in a dark, damp, filthy cell, fit only for a habitation for rats.'[4] Now more humane approaches were preferred: the patients' restraints were removed and they were treated sympathetically, with their mental and physical health closely supervised. Work as occupational therapy was adopted, along with entertaining diversions in the form of music, dance and theatre. This treatment, termed moral management, had positive results—something forgotten by the twentieth century, with its enthusiasm for ECT and psychotropic drugs. From moral management came the notion that madness need not be permanent. The afflicted could experience remission, temporary in the case of King George III, or total cure.

Frame noted: 'There are few positions in life which necessitate more wear and tear of mind and body than that of an attendant upon the insane who conscientiously performs his duty.'[5] These words apply to young James Hume, who entered Gartnavel as an apprentice attendant. He was tough, principled and enterprising. Moral management he learnt on the job, and he would apply its precepts successfully for decades and in two hemispheres.

James Hume worked at Gartnavel from his teens. He got married in 1851, aged twenty-eight, to Mary Fergusson, aged twenty-six. Only their eldest child, Sara, was born in Scotland, for James Hume got a new job at the Worcester County Pauper and Lunatic Asylum, in the village of Powick. In 1858 the Asylum had three hundred and fifty patients. Hume was effectively third in charge, after the Superintendent and the Assistant Medical Officer, both men better educated but younger than him.

Fergus Hume was born in Powick. Home births were the Victorian norm. If medical attention was needed for the birth beyond a midwife, the asylum's two doctors could have been summoned, a luxury beyond the reach of most working-class mothers. The census showed the asylum's staff and their families living on the premises. A fact stranger than fiction: Fergus Hume was born in a lunatic asylum.

That part of his biography he discarded when famous: a secret he might privately allude to in his fiction, but never divulge. A huge stigma attached to mental illness. It blighted lives, not only those personally affected, but also their family, via the belief in hereditary transmission: in *Jane Eyre* Bertha Rochester inherited her madness.

The Powick Asylum was a county charity, but nonetheless even paupers had privacy and discretion assured in the census. Patients are identified by their initials, and only the staff of the asylum and their families have their full names and details listed.

James Hume, aged thirty-eight, was Clerk and Steward, an important administrative role. He and Mary had five children: Sara Jane Hume, aged nine, Elizabeth F. Hume, aged seven, and Mary W. Hume, aged five, of school age, and so described as scholars. The two sons were younger: James E. (Edward) W. Hume, three, and Fergus W. Hume, one.

The Superintendent of the Asylum, Dr James Sherlock, had a wife and four children, also maintaining four servants. William Hinch, the bachelor second-in-command of the Asylum, had a housemaid. The lower-class Humes relied on family for the hard domestic work: Elizabeth Fergusson, Mrs Hume's younger sister, lived with the family as housekeeper.

Both Collins and Braddon wrote madhouse scenes, though they were unfamiliar with the subject, and their work evinces no great research nor fine detail. In contrast, Fergus Hume had personal knowledge of the mad. He grew up with his father's charges: drunks suffering from delirium tremens (DTs), the terrifying stage of alcoholism characterised by intense hallucinations; patients with tertiary syphilis; women with puerperal fever (post-natal depression or psychosis); paranoiacs; depressives, and so on.

Such was a uniquely useful upbringing for a crime writer—and the knowledge was shared by Arthur Conan Doyle. For him also it was a secret to be elided, for his father Charles suffered from an alcoholism so severe he would be committed. Like Fergus Hume, young Doyle knew about insanity: the year after the census Charles Doyle drank himself into his first attack of DTs, the 'blue devils'. As his wife Mary would record, 'for nearly a year he had to be on half pay and for months he cd only crawl and was perfectly idiotic, could not tell his own name. Since then he has been from one fit of dipsomania to another.'[6]

But in 1861, the two children were secure, the babies of their families, the centres of attention. As the census-takers took their leave in the chill spring evening, already darkening, the households prepared for the night. Dolls, balls, slates, primers were laid aside for the night. The families gathered together for a chapter of the Bible, prayers. Two little boys were unbuttoned from their frocks, dressed in their nightshirts and put to bed. Lullabies were sung, and as their eyelids drooped, the bedside candles were extinguished.

One day these infants would be competitors in a tough game of literary fame, writing tales of bloody murder and detection. But for the moment they slept peacefully, each as full of potential as an egg.

2

CRAZY-QUILT

Dunedin, New Zealand, 1860s

'Crazy-quilt! Crazy-quilt!' Thus was Hunston meditating. 'That's what we called him at school; and no wonder, with his patch-work mind, all fits and starts and silly impulsiveness.'

CRAZY-QUILT[7]

A crazy-quilt is a Victorian patchwork formed of random scraps of fabric, with no pattern to it, no repeating motifs. It is also the title of a 1919 Fergus Hume novel—referring to the hero, who gained the nickname at Rugby School. He is described as a Celt with 'a patch-work mind'. Another autobiographical allusion, to an actual school nickname of Fergus Hume? He was a Celt, went to a rugby-playing school and lived in a madhouse. Sadly, no, for crazy-quilts were a fad of the 1880s, too late for Hume, whose schooldays were two decades earlier.

Nonetheless the quilt is an image relevant to the biographical search for Hume. Quilts are made of the fabric of lives, of the stuff of recollection: here is your father's old shirt, offcuts from your sister's best dress. In searching through the records for such scraps of memory, a personality takes shape, the making of a creative mind. Birth, christening records, the census: these are the earliest chronological records of young Fergus. What happened next was a dramatic relocation, which utterly changed the Hume family's fortunes. 'I belong to New Zealand,' Hume would write in a preface to *Hansom Cab*, and that was the place that made him, the home where he grew to man's estate.

To get to the other side of the world in the mid-nineteenth century required a sea voyage that could take months. Those who migrated to the Antipodes in this era were almost unimaginably brave by our cosseted standards. They left behind everything familiar and ventured into the unknown on a boat that might get wrecked, might never reach its destination.

For those travelling to the Australasian colonies, there was a degree of safeguard, of governmental care. The British Empire had a vested interest in getting its subjects to their destination, the lands to be colonised, alive and healthy. Many were even subsidised to make the voyage, termed 'assisted' immigrants—known in the twentieth century as 'ten-pound Poms'. Lessons had been learnt about mass migration over the seas, first from slavery, then the rather less lethal convict experience. A ship's doctor was provided and even those in steerage, the cheapest passage, received plain but nourishing food. By contrast the shorter Atlantic run to the former English colony of America was a free-enterprise market, with shipowners unregulated or policed as to the level of provisions, standards of safety and accommodation on board. As a result far more passengers died or fell ill than did during the longer Australasian voyages.

Fergus Hume immigrated to Dunedin, in New Zealand's South Island, as a small child. The catalyst for the family's departure from England occurred the month after the 1861 census was taken. For some ten years the Antipodes had meant to the English goldfields, first in New South Wales and then Victoria. Across the Tasman Sea, the New Zealanders eyed their landscape and wished for something similar, with the consequent huge influx of immigrant miners. In 1861 the Otago Provincial Council offered £1000 reward to the discoverer of a viable goldfield. Tasmanian Gabriel Read accepted the challenge and in late May discovered a cache of gold. Proving that miners can on occasion be poetic he would write: 'I shovelled away about two-and-a-half feet of gravel, arrived at a beautiful soft slate, and saw the gold shining like the stars in Orion on a dark, frosty night.'

The consequent rush became the biggest in New Zealand history, swelling the population of the South Island and making Otago's fortune. The news made headlines in England. James Hume was forty, a father of five, and an intelligent, sensible man. Did he have hopes of golden riches? Or did he note that a colony swollen with gold would also provide opportunities for advancement? Another attractive factor was that Dunedin, the urban centre most benefiting from the South Island gold finds, had been founded by Scots Presbyterian settlers, men and women similar to James and Mary Hume.

The first Europeans in Otago had been whalers, intermarrying with the Ōtākou Māori from the 1820s. In 1848 three hundred members of the Free Church of Scotland arrived, their spiritual leader Reverend Thomas Burns, pious nephew of the poet Robert. The link is commemorated by a statue of Robert Burns in Dunedin's central square, the Octagon, famously with his back to the Church (although of England rather than Scotland: behind Burns is St Paul's Anglican Cathedral). Like Burns Fergus Hume wrote verse; he too would turn his back on orthodoxy, the Kirk which dominated Dunedin.

Christchurch, to the north, and at that time yet to gain fame as an earthquake zone, had been deliberately created as an Anglican settlement. The Presbyterians intended a new Edinburgh in the South. Indeed the new city was named after the Celtic name for Edinburgh, a suggestion from a literary man, Scots publisher William Chambers. As Fergus Hume wrote in his novel *The Fever of Life*, whose heroine is of Māori descent, and very proud of Dunedin: it was 'the new Edinburgh with the old name, not the old Edinburgh with the new name.'[8]

Dunedin is hilly, with the world's steepest street; cool, both in terms of weather and culture. The dominant architecture is Victorian Gothic Revival, accompanied by a strong tradition of education and the arts. Today Dunedin is largely a college town, but during the 1800s it was New Zealand's biggest and richest city. From 1861 it had the first daily newspaper in New Zealand, the *Otago Daily Times* (known as the *Oddity*), which still survives. Fergus Hume might have grown up in a remote part of the British Empire, but Dunedin was a very rich cultural milieu.

The Scots valued education. James Hume had little more than what we would term primary-school learning, with additional auto-didacticism. He could read and write, with occasional misspellings, and was good with numbers. His sons would get the best education available, attending the first secondary school in Dunedin, Otago Boys' High (founded 1863). Their next destination was the University of Otago, the first in New Zealand (founded 1871). The daughters would have attended private schools for girls, typically offering a narrower range of education than boys' schools, although two of the Misses Hume did study music at an advanced level.

Education, particularly for Scots immigrants to the colonies, where society was relatively fluid and opportunities for advancement could be found, was the pathway to higher social status. In London a journalist would describe Fergus Hume as 'an Australian gentle-man—at least by education', making an important class distinction.[9] Without the education, young Hume was no gentleman. With it, doors were open to him, at least in Dunedin.

James Hume emigrated first, working his way out as assistant ship's purser on the *Ben Lomond* with three hundred other emigrants. On the way one passenger died and an apprentice fell fatally from the yardarm—considering the perils of the voyage, it was a minor death toll. He arrived in Dunedin on 19 January 1863; his family followed later, although their arrival is missing from the migration records, which are not exhaustive for the period.

For genteel emigrants, the wilderness and rudimentary settlements of New Zealand came as a shock. But James Hume was tough, inured to poor conditions from his working-class background. He found work as a bookkeeper with Whittingham Bros, wholesalers. Here he established his good repute amongst similar sober-minded, hard-working Scots. Into this community he fitted perfectly.[10]

The chance for advancement came quite quickly. Emigration, for those not mentally tough, is dangerous to the psyche; and there were some for whom the other side of the world was a useful dumping-place. A Dunedin writer, describing madness as 'this worst of all the ills that flesh is heir to', complained of 'the shameful extent to which weak-minded and mentally impaired persons have been deported from the Home country by their relatives or others, and shunted on to the colony'.[11]

As the population swelled, twenty-five per cent of the Otago Hospital's admissions comprised the insane. By 1863 they needed separate housing. Robert Drysdale, Superintendent of the Lunatic Asylum, resigned—and James Hume was uniquely qualified for the job, with his decades of madhouse experience. The new job significantly raised his income and social status. The salary was £150 and his wife, Mary, was the Matron, at £60—by 1870 the pay for the two positions had been raised to £350 and £100. The Otago Provincial Surgeon, Dr Edward Hulme, lived nearby, at Hulme House, which still stands, though the asylum is gone, its grounds now the playing fields of Otago Boys' High School. He had studied at the Paris hospital that was the home of moral management, the Salpêtrière.[12]

By 1872 the Dunedin Asylum was the largest in New Zealand, with close to two hundred inmates. It formed a little kingdom for James Hume—his son would describe the asylum-keeper's role as being a 'local potentate'.[13] The asylum had its own bowling green (the first in Dunedin), bakehouse (which also supplied the hospital and jail), vegetable gardens and piggery. The women had distaff chores, sewing, cleaning, cooking. The male patients that were tractable laboured on the grounds, taming a steep and gullied waste. They could also be lent out to build roads: the citizens of Melrose, a settlement outside Dunedin, were so pleased with the result that they imported from Melbourne a billiard table worth £120 and presented it to the asylum. Other successes were noted in the newspapers: after ten years, of the nearly seven hundred patients admitted, sixty-five per cent had been discharged as cured, nine per cent died, and twenty-six per cent proved incurable.[14]

Despite these achievements, the asylum was not a high priority for the Provincial Government. It rapidly became crowded, drainage and sewerage presented constant problems, and conditions for refractory patients were particularly poor. The Hume family lived in 'less of an asylum than a prison',[15] surrounded by the mentally disturbed. To grow up in this milieu was to learn about difference and its toleration—something reflected in Fergus Hume's writing, with its expressed sympathy for outsiders.

The children had an odd upbringing, even by Victorian standards. Both parents essentially worked from home, but had very long hours. Mary Hume was mother and madhouse matron—something counter to the middle-class ideal of the domestic angel. Either their aunt Janet Fergusson, who had also emigrated, or the eldest daughter Sara, now a teenager, kept house for the family in their asylum quarters.

A reporter visited the asylum in 1868, and described the Female Day Room:

> There were about twenty women present. Several of them were standing near the fire, perfectly happy, as it appeared, under its exhilarating influence. There were others, however, who seemed afraid of letting the play of the fire

light reach their features, who shaded their faces with their hands, and paid no attention to the merry chatterings of their companions. Others wandered up and down the room in an apparently angry mood, as if oppressed by some insufferable injustice. There were several who seemed disposed to be excessively friendly, and proclaimed their perfect sanity over and over again; there were others whose silence and despondent gaze could not fail to enlist the sympathy of the most callous.[16]

He found the sight moving and disturbing, but it was something to which the Hume family were inured.

In 1867 Mary Hume died. James Hume, keeping the madhouse in the family, appointed her sister as the hospital matron. Janet would continue in the role successfully for several decades. Hume did not remarry: his work schedule interfered with socialising, let alone courting. Not many women would have taken on life in an asylum, either. Henceforth James Hume's life seemed to comprise almost exclusively his work.

Conditions improved with the acquisition of Park House, a boarding house next to the asylum. It would house the Superintendent and his family, yet even then escaping the job was impossible: private patients, who could pay for extra comfort and care, as well as 'others who are quiet and recovering',[17] lived with the Humes. These mad lodgers surely created stress for the family: in asylums minor or major acts of violence are common between the unstable, and towards their carers. The family home was not a private place, not least as being part of a public institution it was subject to visits from the asylum Inspectors.[18]

James Hume was 'a man of an exceedingly kind and firm disposition',[19] genuinely concerned with the care of his charges. These qualities, along with thrift and practicality, are revealed by several volumes of his official diary, which survive from the early years of the asylum. The diary begins:

Thurs Nov 10th 1864

No of patients males 30, females 18 Household 9

The inmates had for dinner today. Meat Soup & Vegetables. Received Superintendents Order (per Provincial Treasury) to remove post & Rail fencing at present round the Military Barracks for Asylum use—

The grounds can now be enclosed and a great boon will be conferred by enabling the patients to cultivate a Garden the produce of which will materially assist the economy of the Institution and at the same time assist the recovery of the patients.[20]

The asylum menu was nourishing but not fancy: broth, meat and vegetables, steak pie. At Christmas inmates and staff were served a festive meal: roast beef and plum pudding. The health of the patients was noted, their progress or decline. At 10 p.m. Hume inspected the wards, ensuring all inmates were tucked into bed and comfortable. Only then would he retire to his office to do paperwork. His day had begun at six, and he might be roused during the night as well.

On 15 November the first death was recorded, of a married woman suffering from puerperal fever. Cause: exhaustion, and from refusing food and stimulants. Other particularly difficult inmates included a flasher, who regularly exposed himself; a man who habitually tore his bedding and clothes or smeared them with excrement; and a woman who spat, constantly.

Such people were, to quote an 1879 New Zealand Lunatic Asylum report, 'persons of disordered passions and bereft of self-control'. But the report's wording goes further, into the Victorian unmentionable: asylum patients were prone to 'the abominable vices', the euphemism for same-sex practices.[21] At the time no real conception of a homosexual identity existed: the 'vices' were what people did, rather than something that defined them. Though sodomy was a recognised, even capital, offence it was relatively rarely prosecuted, being hard to prove unless caught in the act. Gross indecency between men would not become a criminal offence until the 1885 Labouchère Amendment—whose first prominent victim would be Oscar Wilde, ten years later.

While inmates undoubtedly encountered 'abominable vices' even in the most moral and well-ordered asylums like Hume's their committal was usually for other reasons. Most of the Otago patients were single males with alcohol problems. Dr Hulme would claim in 1874 that seventy per cent of current admissions, and fifty per cent of inmates, were due to drink.[22] Most often they arrived in the throes of delirium tremens, grounds for committal in Otago. Inside they would dry out, and then be released into the community, to reoffend, and be recommitted.

Even if Fergus Hume had not been reared as a Presbyterian and teetotaller (something in which he persisted), the Otago inmates would have been an object lesson in the perils of drink. He would comment in his novel *Across the Footlights*, 'No one can save a dipso-maniac.'[23] Arthur Conan Doyle's father, Charles, would sell household goods or break into his children's money boxes to get money for liquor. By his forties, he was pensioned off from his work, developing epilepsy and then dementia. In 1885 he was admitted to Montrose Royal Asylum. A photo survives of Charles Doyle among his fellow inmates, clutching a sketchbook—all apparently content under the regime of moral management, a doctrine that stretched from Scotland to the Antipodes.[24]

James Hume did have some challenges that were uniquely colonial. He now had Chinese patients, housed in a separate ward to protect them from the other inmates.[25] He also dealt with those damaged by the Australian transportation system: ex-convicts who had 'hopped over the ditch' in search of Otago's gold. And stranger stuff. One lunatic:

mentally has many delusions—Such that he can brew excellent beer from New Zealand flax—he is surrounded by Spirits of hundreds of people that he killed—That pieces of Stone & Clay that he occasionally brought in from the Suburbs of Dunedin was rich Quartz—and all he required was a good [crushing] Machine to produce plenty of Gold—[26]

Another patient was noteworthy in the diary when he 'commenced Singing again (a favorite amusement when in good health)'. The inmate, known as the Frenchman, would have been impossible to ignore: 'He was an excellent vocalist and had a superb voice of great volume, and was wont daily to walk the grounds and ring out his melodies in his own language to the pleasures of passers by.' That indicates a music professional, even operatic—a possible explanation as to how Mary and Bessie Hume, the daughters of the madhouse, became opera singers. Did the Frenchman notice they had voices good enough for professional training? It could have begun with small girls singing along, leading to informal voice instruction, then James Hume being persuaded to pay for lessons from a less erratic teacher. Even a very strict Presbyterian—and some in Dunedin felt that musical instruments in church was Popery—could not object to a cappella singing.[27]

In any case music was therapeutic, an important aspect of moral management. Powick Asylum had its own band, comprised of the attendants, something taken so seriously by the management that they hired a musical director in the 1870s—the young Edward Elgar. Gartnavel's Frame recalled that 'music had almost a magical influence over insanity…Concerts far excel any other description of amusement that can be introduced in the asylum in the universality of their application.'[28]

The Dunedin Asylum did not have a band, but it did have an excellent piano, purchased through a charity drive.[29] James Hume's brother Marcus, a gifted amateur musician who had also immigrated to Dunedin, would visit with his brass bands and the Coloured Opera Troupe (blackface minstrels). Even such un-Presbyterian activities as dancing featured at the Dunedin asylum on Friday evenings. On Sundays, though, the music at the asylum comprised hymns, as ministers visited from the various denominations, catering to the inmates' spiritual needs. The Keeper and his family attended the Protestant service.

Fergus himself is recorded as a pianist of ability, playing Chopin waltzes for relaxation.[30] More important for him was another of moral management's cultural therapies: the theatre. Drama in the 1800s madhouse is popularly regarded in terms of *Marat/Sade* by Peter Weiss, famously filmed by Peter Brook—an orgy of alienation and violence. What Sade's plays in Charenton asylum were actually like is unknown, but as moral management was developing in France during this period, the madhouse drama can be surmised as being unobjectionable, tending to the popular and good fun. Both the South Island asylums featured amateur theatre. In Dunedin, performances took place in a building, erected in 1868, which served as a combined amusement hall and chapel. It had a 'very handsome stage', and the piano, where the Misses Hume presided. Even the scene-painting was contributed by a professional, from the nearby Princess Theatre.[31]

While the audiences were usually made up of the patients, the asylum staff and their respective families, the general theatre-going public attended benefit performances. The shows were advertised in the newspapers, tickets were sold, and 'the entertainments assumed at one time almost the appearance of social gatherings'. James Hume provided supper for the performers, including bread, cheese and alcohol ('best bottled'). He might be a Presbyterian, but he was not rigid with regard to those outside the sect. On one memorable occasion a joke was played, with soap substituted for the cheese in a sandwich, a schoolboy jape.[32]

Several amateur troupes performed, the Luna and the Sheridan Dramatic Club. The latter, active from 1872 until the asylum relocated in the 1880s, included several future newspaper editors, including C. C. Whittington, the chief comic actor. The connection was probably Marcus Hume, who moonlighted as musical director of the Press Dramatic Club, journalistic amateurs. Whittington was a favourite performer of the patients, as he featured plenty of eating and drinking in his roles. It was he who ate the soap sandwich, frothing at the mouth.

Some classics were played, such as the duel scene from Sheridan's *The Rivals*, but mostly the repertoire was light (no *King Lear*), entertaining, even 'low': farces and burlesques. In the 2012 television version of *Hansom Cab*, actress Rosanna Moore performs in the modern understanding of the word burlesque, with red corsets and sexy feather fans. But in the 1800s it meant comedy, pantomimes for grown-ups, full of dreadful puns. Burlesques were often parodies, such as the 1865 *Burlesque of Frankenstein* (a genuine title, by Australian writer George Isaacs), which did not involve the monster performing a striptease. But it would have featured scantily clad women for the day: girls in tights, playing male roles.

Burlesques at the asylum were no doubt very proper, with nary an ankle exposed. The Sheridan Dramatic Club did include several respectable young misses, whose career would be marriage, not 'women of the stage'—then regarded as disreputable, not without reason. James Hume's daughters were restricted to the piano.[33] The boy Fergus can be imagined sitting beside his sisters, turning the pages of the sheet music, or in the audience with his family, laughing and applauding.

The theatre was an irruption of fun and colour into the asylum, where otherwise settled routine ruled. James Hume's life was 'difficult and jading'[34]—a round of patients in, out, incurable, trouble with drains, the contractor who supplied bread sacked for inferior product, inmates taken for walks, the occasional escape, a near confla-gration averted in 1865, those going into remission released. Outside, Dunedin grew from Wild West settlement to stately colonial city, complete with tramways. New Zealand did experience unrest during this time—the second Taranaki war. As a consequence Dunedin had tattooed Māori warriors working as prisoners of war on road-building and other civic projects. It little affected James Hume, within his enclosed world at the asylum.

And what of Fergus? As an adult, he reportedly suffered from bouts of illness, suggesting that he was a delicate child. He was also isolated. The Dunedin Asylum was not exactly the sort of place to which parents would welcome him taking his schoolfriends home to play—though for more adventurous children there would be a frisson from the presence of the mad. The rearing of this boy, after his mother's death and his aunt's full-time employment as asylum matron, would have been the responsibility of his older sisters. They shared interests in music, and probably encouraged his dandy dress-ing. He was educated, along with his brother James, at the Middle District School, both boys being top scholars. Indeed, Fergus's first mention in the press occurred when he was ten and awarded the special prize of a writing desk.[35]

The written records survive, fragments of the quilt. There are also visual traces, of the parents and possibly the children, held in the collection of the Toitū Otago Settlers Museum. James Hume's status in Dunedin had increased to the extent that he and Mary somehow found the time to sit for portraits attributed to the artist John Irvine, another expatriate Scot. Irvine painted colonial worthies, and was skilled at his work, with an insight into character. The couple he depicted are not the attendants upon the mad of popular fiction, such as *Jane Eyre*'s Grace Poole, who is described as hard-featured and commonplace. Far from being coarsened by their job, the Humes appear genteel—in the case of Mary, even refined. She does not look like a woman whose work might involve physical violence at the hands of her charges.

The pair wear sober garb, conventionally middle-class. James, looking like a practical man of business, has a fringe of beard, but is surprisingly fresh-faced, with brown hair and penetrating grey eyes. It must have been a good likeness, for photographs of Fergus show the same brow and hairline, the same shape of the eyes. He inherited, though, his mother's darker hair. Mary is delicate-featured, with the pink-and-white complexion of a Victorian porcelain doll. Her black hair is looped back in a simple but becoming style of the 1860s. She wears a plain black dress, with a white collar, adorned only by a large gold brooch at her throat and a long gold chain—Otago gold, something she could never have been able to afford in England.

The paintings were more than a business transaction, however artistic, for Irvine painted the custodians for his only son, William, who had been admitted to the lunatic asylum in 1863, an incurable inmate. Another painting by Irvine depicts Park House, the Superintendent's residence, later demolished when Otago Boys' High took over the madhouse site. The scene is far less formal than his earlier work, with the composition probably influenced by photography and painted with a looser, lighter style that suggests Impressionism. It shows a pleasant, even semi-rural setting: houses with established trees and gardens, in the background a low grassy hill. The painting is signed by Irvine and an inscription on its back, though hard to read, seems to indicate that he presented it to the Misses Hume on New Year's Day, 1876.

Three children appear in the foreground, quick oil sketches, playing in a garden. They seem a later addition, to improve the composition: the garden fence is clearly visible through the figure of the one boy, as if he were a ghost.[36] One girl, seated, wears a dark dress; a standing girl, in pink, picks flowers. They appear unfinished, rough shapes only. Their gaze is directed to the central figure, a smaller boy in retroussé profile. He is natty, wearing a dark jacket, white collar, olive-drab waistcoat and knickerbockers. The outfit is completed by a straw boater, bright red stockings and a red flower in his buttonhole. While the two girls are little more than shapes in skirts, this child is more of a portrait, a specific boy. Given that Fergus Hume was known as a dandy, his middle-schoolfellow Isaac Selby recalling 'Furgi' as 'always well dressed', it might be wondered if this image is a portrait of his younger self.[37] Are the two girls then his sisters—included as a bonus with the representation of the family home?

A boy with a red buttonhole. If this is Fergus Hume, then he is a decided character, the personality coming through clearly, even in an oil sketch.

3

A COLONIAL BANSHEE

Dunedin, 1870s

'You don't like the colonies?'
   'Divil a bit. Oi've not met a single ghost of any consequence here. There's no ruins to haunt an' hathens like yoursilf don't belave in us.'

'A COLONIAL BANSHEE'[38]

In winter 1877 Otago held its first fancy-dress ball, under the auspices of the Dunedin Football (Rugby) Club. The two hundred attend-ees donned costumes ranging from the fantastic—Bo-Peep and Bluebeard—to characters from recent novels. James Hume's five children went with their uncle Marcus, Steward at the hospital. He and James Hume Jr wore military uniform, in Marcus's case probably from the Artillery Band, a brass ensemble he conducted and led.[39]

The girls and eighteen-year-old Fergus were more exotic, indeed operatic, in their costumes. 'Miss' Sara Hume was the title character from *La Traviata*, in a 'white silk dress trimmed with pearls, lace, and crimson camellias'. Bessie Hume went as the flamboyant Elvira, from *The Rose of Castille*, in orange 'silk dress, black velvet Spanish jacket, silver fringed mantilla, crimson and orange roses'. Mary Hume was Margherita from *Faust* (most likely Gounod's opera) in a white-and-blue 'merino dress, tanned leather satchel and shoes'. Fergus's garb is not described, but his character was Elvino, a rich farmer, from Bellini's pastoral *La Sonnambula*. No doubt it was a natty ensemble.[40]

Even with Uncle Marcus as chaperone, it was daring for young Presbyterian misses to dress up as opera heroines in Victorian Dunedin. Worse still, Sara and Mary's characters were fallen women. The girls obviously had no fear of parental disapproval. Outside the asylum gates, they were away from their father's scrutiny. Even within, James Hume Sr spent little time with his family. That same year the Inspector of Asylums reported:

> The Keeper is manifestly overworked; he has a large amount of clerking work, most of which he does after 11 pm., and he is often at work until 1.30 in the morning. He sleeps in his office, so as to be constantly on hand when wanted. He has never had a week's holiday since he entered on duty [twelve years earlier] and is frequently not off the premises for three months at a time.[41]

Even when James Hume got out into the lush green countryside of Otago it was on madhouse business. He and Alexander Cairns, Inspector of Works, were sent to investigate a new site for the asylum at Seacliff. They got lost in the bush on a warm and humid day, 'the two gentlemen, who were by no means of light build' spending three hours tramping in circles. The joke in this account is on Hume and Cairns, but tellingly both are described as gentlemen—so far had the son of a slater ascended the social scale.[42]

As the report on the ball shows, the young Humes socialised with their uncle, who was only eight years older than Sara Hume. If James Hume aspired to middle-class respectability, then Marcus Hume aspired to the arts: he took early retirement from the hospital and became involved in ventures ranging from business to music to journalism. With his amateur ensemble the Coloured Opera

Troupe (a spinoff of the Artillery Band), he could fill the Princess Theatre.[43] He also wrote songs. A musical uncle with links to the newspapers was useful in a family where the girls were opera-mad and the youngest son aspired to writing. Nellie Melba, who also had a Presbyterian father, had to fight his opposition to women performing in public. Marcus Hume is a lively shadow, but that all three of his nieces became music teachers, and Bessie and Mary Hume sang opera onstage, indicates his importance as an ally. The girls got their wish; but it was Fergus who achieved the greatest success.

For his secondary education, Fergus Hume had gone no further than next door: Otago Boys' High School was in the process of being built beside the asylum. It would, in later years, be jokingly described as 'the mad school'. OBHS required an entrance examination, no problem for the Hume boys, who had already shone at primary school. Fergus was, outwardly at least, a dutiful son, and therefore not likely to fall into bad company, despite the school having rowdy pupils. It was complained that they climbed on the roof, tore off the slates 'and put them on the chimneys, cut the water pipes…' From the school it was only a short step to sneak into the asylum, to gawk at the inmates or steal from the fruit trees.[44]

Fergus enrolled at the school in 1873, the total enrolment being just over a hundred pupils. He was a Scot, like most of the students, but had the social disadvantages of his madhouse background and his bookish, artistic, non-sporty interests. 'A perfect candidate for bullying, in a school with a proud tradition in that area,' was a comment made to me by a former Dunedin resident.

Fergus Hume may have encountered an antipodean Flashman, but his education was not Tom Brown's schooldays. Otago followed the Scottish rather than English model. The curriculum was practical, emphasising the sciences, useful for James, who would become an engineer and surveyor. Fergus had more inclination for the classic matter of the English public school, Greek and Latin. OBHS would later be famous for its rugby. Indeed the first game of rugby in Otago was played in 1871, between the school and the University, with the forty-year-old Foundation Professor of Classics, George Sale (a genuine Rugby School old boy), taking the field. Even the school's rector, Australian Stuart Hawthorne, played. Like the first recorded game of Australian Rules it was something of a rabble, ending in a draw. Nonetheless it was a portent of games to come, on the playing fields that had been partly smoothed by James Hume's inmates and Māori prisoners of war.

An anonymous Old Boy recollected a typical 1874 school day:

> On arrival the first object was to get a place on the tennis court. If unsuccessful then some other form of amusement was looked for. In the winter time football was played across the upper end of the ground. The rules were chiefly Association, with some innovations from the Victorian game [Australian Rules], and all games were played 'big side,' of course. In the mornings the players took up sides by arrangement of captains or mutual consent. If football did not claim the attention, there was occasionally some forgotten lesson or exercise to be done with the assistance of a chum who had done it, or a stamp-swapping to be carried out. On the ringing of the bell the whole School assembled in the Hall, where the religious exercise for the day was performed. One of the elder boys read aloud an allotted portion of the Scripture, and the Rector recited a prayer; then each form filed off to its own room. [After two hours of lessons] at 11.25 there was given a five minutes interval—utilised for tennis by the fortunate who secured one of the two courts—in football or the refined 'goosey' by the others. At 12.25 the bell gives the signal for the 'dinner hour.' The earlier part of this is occupied in the consumption of luncheon or in a visit to the town, but the boys begin to collect again about

one o'clock, and the usual amusements begin. At one time many of the boys went boating in hired boats at this hour, but that form of amusement disappeared—it was too costly, both in money and time, as it regularly involved an 'impop' [penalty] for being late...Keeping in was not much resorted to, however, and the usual impositions were given out to be done at home. Under Mr Hawthorne the whole School was detained until 5 o'clock for a week, in a vain attempt to discover who cut certain initials (not his own) in large size in the School wall. The regular punishment at this time was the square and square root and cube and cube root. All offences were visited with so many figures, and they were graded according to heinousness.[45]

If anything of the schoolboy Fergus can be gleaned from this account, it is probably as a 'stamp-swapper': stamp collecting was an interest of his.[46] Or else he was the conscientious 'chum' who helped with the forgotten homework. That the 'impops' involved mathematical problems can be ascribed to Rector Hawthorne's preference for sparing the rod and pleasing the practical Scots parents.

James Hume came to Dunedin to better himself, and succeeded. His sons would achieve even more: their destination was the new University of Otago, whose grey buildings edged with white Oamaru stone were appearing around the river Leith. The Hume boys would be professional men: James, a surveyor, Fergus, a lawyer. However, Fergus, though studious—Nigel Molesworth would have called him a swot—had other ideas. He wanted to be an author.

For those of an artistic bent, a sympathetic teacher can be crucial. The Misses Hume studied with Signor Carmini Morli, ex of the touring Simonsen Opera Troupe, who settled in the South Island. Fergus Hume had two possible mentors. The charismatic Professor George Sale, who taught both Classics and Literature, has been cited in Hume's life;[47] but before him Rector Hawthorne seems equally significant.

At the middle school, Isaac Selby recalled Hume as writing good essays, but 'I never thought of him writing books of imagination.'[48] It seems the fanciful side of the boy emerged later, at OBHS. Hume told journalists his writing began after reading *The Count of Monte Cristo* at the age of fifteen. The book reappears in his fiction: as a boy the hero of his novel *When I Lived in Bohemia* discovers the book in the family attic. He thus gains 'the greatest delight of his life' but also 'a severe whipping for precocity' from his father. Such would not have been the reaction of Rector Hawthorne, nicknamed 'Prickly'. A man of Irish Anglican background but Australian training, Hawthorne believed in the classical education, but also promoted sport and reading. His innovations included a library run by senior boys, elected by the pupils.[49]

Another Old Boy recalled him:

> Mr Stuart Hawthorne…was an exceedingly earnest and conscientious man, whose main effort was to inculcate in the boys a high standard of conduct and morality. I am sure that every boy who ever read the Sixth Book of the *Aeneid* with him will remember the earnestness with which he dwelt on the famous line, '*Non ignara mali miseris succurrere disco*.' ['Not unacquainted with misfortune, I have learned to assist the wretched.'] This line served him as a text—other lines were used as they came, but this one I remember most vividly—whereon to hang a disquisition and an appeal…
> Most of the Old Boys will remember the gesture of physical pain with which the Rector received a false quantity. He used to shrink as if he were avoiding an awkward blow.[50]

Hawthorne is considered by Rory Sweetman, historian of OBHS, to have been a remarkable educationalist. It was Hawthorne's ill luck that his charges did poorly in the first university scholarship examinations. He was castigated in the press and subject to an official inquiry. His health collapsed: he resigned, and died in 1875.

It was not only the school that connected Hawthorne with the Humes. In 1872 the Rector married language teacher Madame Marie Willeby, the only daughter of Dr Angel of Paris. She had come to New Zealand the previous year an army widow, with a young son, Charles (b. 1865). She may have been nothing of the sort, since her first husband apparently cannot be traced. It was not only the mad who were sent out to the colonies, to occupy space in James Hume's asylum; the inconvenient, illegitimate or compromised went as well. Also dubious seem claims Marie was a governess for the future Queen Mary (b. 1867). Charles Willeby would later marry into the Hume family.[51]

Fergus's ambitions were literary and Willeby's were musical— both were young men living at the edge of the British Empire, who followed their artistic dream to London. But first they were obliged to earn their keep in New Zealand. Willeby practised music while working as a Wellington insurance clerk. Hume worked his way through the University of Otago as a clerk in the legal practice of Sievwright and Stout, which included George Mondy, his father's friend.

Robert Stout was an outstanding lawyer and politician, a leader of freethinking (that is, secular and rational) beliefs in Dunedin, contrary to the influence of the Kirk. He was active in debates on religion and morality. His career would include a knighthood, and being both colonial Premier and Chief Justice of New Zealand. He would also act for the Hume family in a court case. *Hansom Cab*'s lawyer-detective Calton was drawn from life, Hume claimed. Clearly he observed a brilliant trial lawyer closely. Stout he knew the best.[52]

The Sievwright-Stout practice had a varied clientele, with work ranging from conveyancing to criminal law—excellent material for a detective writer. Not that Fergus had thought of writing crime; in

Dunedin, what writing he did in his spare time was poetry, drama or reviewing, although he did produce one novella in the Sensation genre. Here he gained the habit of sheer hard work, maintaining a job and his studies while also following his loves of writing and the theatre.

What sort of man was the young Fergus Hume? If we could follow him on a typical day, as he left the asylum grounds and headed towards the law courts or the university, we would have seen a dark-haired man, not tall, tending to the stocky. Most noticeable would be his dandy styling: a bowler or wide-awake hat on his head, moustache curled with wax, high stiff collar above a starched shirt, diamond studs (paste), a well-tailored jacket and waistcoat, buttoned gloves, tight trousers, and patent leather boots. If he could get one, a gardenia buttonhole was 'indispensable'. From 1883, while still a student, Fergus Hume also sported a George II guinea on his watch-chain, bought from a pawn shop with his first writing pay (£1/-, for a book review in the *Oddity*). A caricature from 1888, when he was famous, shows him dapper, with cane and cigarette: he is recorded as a great smoker.[53]

Contemporaries described Hume as a Dunedin 'dude', the term being quite the reverse of the modern meaning. Willeby was a similar dandy. The most common term used was masher. It signified a love of dress and the theatre, meeting in fashionable handkerchiefs for males comprising 'lawns and silks of a new hue, called "Elephant's breath," [light grey] with a picture printed in the corner of the wearer's favourite stage artiste'. The look shaded into the aestheticism of Oscar Wilde. Being a masher was not much more than a young man's fashion statement, a Teddy Boy or Mod without the violence. As such, they were the object of jokes, and more: the contrarian journalist Eliza Lynn Linton decreed the masher effeminate and 'of the fringe between the sexes'.[54]

A tale told with variations about Hume is that he regarded the street as a public place for discussions or arguments. He was remembered by a Dunedin contemporary as ready to talk at length, 'on any given subject'. It indicates a mind moving at fever pitch, desperate for intellectual comradeship. Some may have ducked for cover when they saw him; he 'was considered a bit of a bore'. Once the topic was really arcane: metempsychosis, the transmigration of the soul. Hume could have encountered the—hardly Presbyterian—concept from Plato, in his classical Greek studies, or from Poe's stories. But it was a persistent notion throughout his life. In an article on Gilbert and Sullivan's operas, which he adored, he wrote: 'No one now-a-days—at least, not openly—is a convert to the doctrine.' But covertly? Did he himself feel like an old soul, or else someone born into the wrong body? There seems more here than the dislocation of the colonial, or the usual adolescent sense of being a misfit.[55]

Hume was part of the scenery of Dunedin, accepted despite his father's employment, a colourful peacock against the Presbyterian black. He could rebel by dressing showily, showing off his interest in the philosophically abstruse, and the arts.

Soon he would start to show of just what he was capable.

4

THE FATAL SONG

Dunedin, 1880s

It seemed, therefore, as though Kitty had found her vocation, and would develop into an operatic star, but fate intervened, and Miss Marchurst retired from the stage, which she had adorned so much.

MADAME MIDAS[56]

Even before the dawn of the new decade, life at the madhouse began to change. Crowding and maintenance issues meant a new site would have to be found. That would disrupt both patients and staff, but otherwise little deviation could be foreseen from the path into which James Hume had settled: respectable prosperity, with the anticipation of his sons as professional men, his daughters marrying well.

The Misses Hume had different ideas. Their enthusiasm for opera propelled them onto the stage—central and singing, as opposed to politely accompanying asylum amusements on the piano. They had a mentor in Signor Carmini Morli, who in 1878 showcased his students in a highly successful series of concerts. The programme was ambitious: Grand Opera, including Verdi's *Il Trovatore*, sung in Italian, with Bessie and Mary the female leads. Fergus, as musical little brother and opera fan, was not a performer, but could hardly have been uninvolved as his sisters practised, with Morli or at the madhouse piano.

Making an opera debut with Verdi was risky in a city that, though remote, had sophisticated musical tastes and was *au fait* with the latest compositions. But it worked: the younger Miss Humes became instant Dunedin stars. Indeed Mary Hume would later make the claim that she and Bessie were the first local women to sing on the concert platform in New Zealand.[57]

It is possible that the favourable reception had some orchestration from Marcus Hume, whose hats included music criticism, but he could not write all the reviews. While Mary, the soprano, received some critiques of her technique, nobody in the newspapers had anything but praise for Bessie. Her role of Azucena the gypsy required a strong voice and dramatic flair, and she acquitted herself superbly. Her contralto voice would be described as unequalled for 'volume, culture, expression and range'—not only in Dunedin, but the world.[58]

For the next few years Bessie and Mary would feature in Dunedin performance at the very top of the amateur level. They followed a similar path to Nellie Melba in Australia, playing charitable benefits, which could be justified as for a good cause, even if it happened to be the Catholic cathedral. They also supported visiting professional singers and filled concert venues in their own right.

In 1881 Morli moved to Christchurch. The Hume sisters had received the best training available in the colonial city and now needed to travel for further musical education. In early 1882 they took the steamship to England, spending a year away. Here they followed local precedent: teenage Jennie West, a Dunedin piano prodigy, who had been taken by her father to study in London. The Humes were mature women, in their late twenties, not needing a chaperoning parent even had James Hume spared the time. The cost was considerable, but the pay from concerts and music teaching could be saved. Possibly Marcus Hume assisted them. He also travelled north, not to study, but seeking pastures new, work-wise. Marcus is recorded as being in the 'Old Country' later that year, taking the opportunity to feast on fine musical fare, and likely reuniting proudly with his musical nieces.[59]

James Hume could not have helped, or even hindered, for that year he was busy fighting for his professional life. Both the two major asylums in the South Island, in Dunedin and Sunnyside in Christchurch, had been capably run, with humane and innovative treatment of the inmates. The Superintendents had shown great ability, but neither were qualified doctors—and a government decision had been made to have only medical men in charge of the public asylums. Both Sunnyside's Edward Seager and Hume lost their jobs.

Seager and his wife, Esther, the matron, stayed at Sunnyside unhappily for some years before being asked to retire, Seager an embittered man. In Dunedin, James Hume was demoted to house steward, similar to his post at Powick before his emigration two decades before. His salary was reduced, and he left in June 1882. The same issue of the *Otago Witness* that reported his farewell presentation also listed Fergus as passing his solicitor's law examination. Sorrow, and joy, at least for James Hume. Though nearly sixty, he remained vigorous, enterprising and resourceful. He had a plan, in which practicality mixed with a soupçon of revenge.[60]

James Hume petitioned for compensation at a Superintendent's level of salary, which was refused. Yet, canny as ever, he was able to proceed without the extra money. Joining forces with his sister-in-law, Matron Janet Fergusson, and Dr E. W. Alexander, who had worked with the Dunedin asylum, Hume created a rival establishment. He and Alexander bought ninety acres of land on the outskirts of the city and built a private asylum, the first in the colony. Ashburn Hall opened in October 1882, with Hume and Janet resident keepers, and Alexander the visiting doctor. They gained better conditions, an idyllic country setting, and less crowding: the licence was for forty patients only. 'It is a lovely spot, and there is nothing in the cheery-looking block of buildings and picturesque surroundings to suggest the idea of a home for the insane'. Hume was so highly regarded that his wealthier patients followed him, paying for the privilege: two and a half guineas a week.[61]

Fergus would write a tribute to his father, in the description of a private asylum in *The Silent House in Pimlico* (1900):

> The grounds were large, and well laid out in flower gardens and orchards; and as it was Dr. Jorce's system to allow his least crazy patients as much liberty as was possible, they roamed at will round the grounds, giving the place a cheerful and populated look. The more violent inmates were, of course, secluded; but these were well and kindly treated by the doctor. Indeed, Jorce was a very humane man and had a theory that more cures of the unhappy beings under his care could be effected by kindness than by severity.
>
> His asylum was more like a private hotel with paying guests than an establishment for the retention of the insane, and even to an outside observer the eccentricities of the doctor's family—as he loved to call them—were not more marked than many of the oddities possessed by people at large. Indeed, Jorce was in the habit of saying that 'There were more mad people in the world than were kept under lock and key,' and in this he was doubtless right. However, the kindly and judicious little man was like a father to those under his charge and very popular with them all. Anything more unlike the popular conception of an asylum than the establishment at Hampstead can scarcely be imagined.

Even with a London setting, and writing after James' death, Fergus disguised his father, with only his methods and penetrating grey eyes drawn from life. It was another of his allusive asides, for only those who had known James in Dunedin to recognise.[62]

*

Ashburn Hall would not be home for the Hume children, who were grown and largely independent. Fergus was preparing for the bar and scribbling away. Three pieces of his juvenilia are known from this time and they show sophisticated interests, a product of his locale. Dunedin might be geographically distant, but it was well read. The town was bookish—the libraries, whether of the University or the Dunedin Athenaeum and Mechanics' Institute, had excellent holdings, and subscriptions to the best English magazines. Even the Dunedin asylum acquired reading matter, books and illustrated journals for the inmates.[63]

The precocious youth found press publication early. Here he had connections, via the Sheridan players and the Press Dramatic Club. Uncle Marcus Hume could not have been musical director of the latter without belonging to the fourth estate, if so following the common practice of using a pseudonym. In an obituary he was even said to have started a penny daily newspaper in Dunedin. Fergus Hume would claim his first paid writing was a book review when he was eighteen, which would have been in 1877. However, as the book he reviewed first appeared in 1882, his memory erred—or else he deliberately chose to forget his juvenilia. At least two other publications preceded the review.[64]

Shortly after the opening of Ashburn Hall, from November to December 1882, Fergus Hume's *Professor Brankel's Secret: A Psychological Story* appeared. It was serialised in Dunedin's weekly *Saturday Advertiser*, for which it was 'specially written', implying a commission. This newspaper, founded in 1877, went through a variety of names and amalgamations. In a court case of early 1882, Marcus Hume was named as a director of the company.[65] Thus Fergus Hume's first publication was likely achieved via nepotism; small wonder he later elided it from his early history.

This novella concerns a German professor researching alchemy. In an old book he discovers a secret formula enabling time travel. But it only deals with the past: the rest of the formula, for futuristic travel, is hidden in another volume. So ensues a thrilling tale of bibliographic pursuit, with drug-taking and attempted virgin sacrifice. It showcases a melodramatic sensibility that is exquisitely over the top (although certainly no stranger than some of Arthur Conan Doyle's early efforts, which featured alchemy and paranormal phenomena). *Brankel*'s genre was both Gothic and Sensational—hardly something that a lawyer just short of qualifying for the bar would have published under his own name. At the very least, the pious readers of Dunedin might have wondered at the sanity of the madhouse-keeper's son, already known as an eccentric.

James Hume was no supporter of his son's writing. In Fergus's novel *When I Lived in Bohemia*, which despite its London setting is strongly autobiographical, the following appears. It has the regretful ring of truth:

> Alas! he was so very respectable, my poor father, that the lame feet of my halting verse entered like iron into my soul; therefore, resorting to strong measures, he perched me on the giddy height of an office stool, with the laudable intention of breaking short my courting of the draggle-tailed Muse, and converting me into a dry-as-dust lawyer.[66]

A correspondent to the *Bulletin*, who signed himself Cobbler, provides more direct evidence. He clearly knew the Humes in Dunedin well, and also seemed to be a music critic, for he had a professional recall of Bessie Hume's voice. Indeed, it was Cobbler who said he had heard no contralto to compare with hers. It seems likely that this writer was Uncle Marcus Hume, who at one stage of his long and interesting life co-owned a shoemaking business in Dunedin.[67] Cobbler wrote that Fergus had 'a weakness for scribbling, to which his father strongly objected'. He claims an agreement was made between father and son, by which Fergus first qualified as a lawyer but was then free to try literature afterwards.

Another source agrees that Fergus had scant enthusiasm for the law:

> Oh, bless your soul, Hume was a jolly good fellow, who could sing a jolly good song, and write one too; none of your greenery-yallery [Wildean] aspirers after the infinite. He certainly *did* go on a little about Keats, who to my mind wrote fearful bosh…But having been to school with him I can assure you his masters never knew they had a genius in the schoolroom. To be sure he was not very fond of the law, but he did his work like a man; and what a jolly oyster supper he gave us when he was admitted.[68]

The comment appears in the context of a satirical article, jokingly ascribing *Hansom Cab* to Sir Robert Stout. Humorous it may be but it does seem based on fact: Hume's love of music and his songwriting, which he would do later with Willeby; his essential conservatism as a poet; his capacity for sheer hard work.

In early February 1883, Hume was admitted to the bar—newsworthy in the *Saturday Advertiser*, the paper that had published *Brankel*.[69] The bargain fulfilled, a lawyer in the Hume family, Fergus quickly and publicly staked his literary claim. That same day his name appeared in the Dunedin press in an entirely different context.

The local newspapers had excellent local and international coverage, with a direct cable connection since 1872. When Richard Wagner died on 13 February 1883, in New York, the news reached Dunedin early on the 15th and made the papers that day. On the 16th Fergus Hume, perhaps after a night around the piano with his sister Sara and some Wagner sheet music, wrote a commemorative ode. It was topical, if very conventional—and fare for the press. The poem appeared in the *Evening Star*, on Saturday 17 February.

To briefly return to *When I Lived in Bohemia*, and its unsympathetic papa:

Not only did I daily write verse, but I published such sins against sense in the local paper; and there, in bad type, they were seen by my father, flaunting their boldness in the faces of his genteel friends, who considered verse-writing as heinous a sin as Sabbath-breaking.[70]

If a small explosion took place at Ashburn Hall upon the reading of the Saturday paper, it was only what Fergus Hume had expected. The poem was a signed statement of intent, a gauntlet thrown down for the benefit of his father and the Dunedin literati:

Richard Wagner

> Hail to the courage which gave
> Voice to its creed, e'er the creed
> Won consecration from time.
>
> [MATTHEW] ARNOLD

O thou whose dauntless spirits ne'er knew fear,
And joined beneath the magic of thy hand
Three Muses in one strong undying band,
To stand alone without a single peer.
Lo! Europe casts her laurels on thy bier;
And through the breadth of that harmonious land
Which, by thy massive genius, long was spann'd
Each cheek is wet with the regretful tear.
Wagner! though stilled the hand which once could bring
Aeschylean music from the throbbing lyre—
Though we shall see no more thy spirit wing
To those proud heights to which it did aspire—
Yet will thy name through coming ages ring,
And be to every heart a beacon-fire.

> F. W. Hume
> 16th February, 1883.

The poem was the work of a pretentious twenty-two-year-old—'throbbing lyre', indeed! The 'Civis' column, in the *Otago*

Witness, promptly critiqued and sent it up, most amusingly, if rather bruisingly for Hume.[71] Perhaps for this reason, Hume's next publication, a review that appeared in the *Oddity* a month later, returned to anonymity, though there was nothing to embarrass a budding author here. It was a long, thorough but glowing discussion of Robert Buchanan's *The Martyrdom of Madeline*, in a colonial edition by Melbourne publisher George Robertson.[72]

Buchanan (1841–1901) was then a well-known writer of Scots background. He was what Hume hoped to be, a successful author in London. It had not been easy—Buchanan did not really strike gold until he took to adapting English literary classics for the Victorian stage. One of these adaptations was *Sophia*, based on *Tom Jones*. It was a play that would prove fateful for Hume, and for the actor cast in Australia as Fielding's villain, Blifil.

The review shows much of Hume's thought, but also displays him as a young writer of much polish, almost flawless in terms of the heavy Victoriana style, well read and erudite. He namedrops works by French and English major writers, displaying his knowledge as if auditioning. Though geographically distant, he shows familiarity with the London literary and theatrical scene. He states that 'anyone who knows journalistic London can have but little doubt as to who is meant' in Buchanan's roman à clef—but Hume knows it only from afar. He can recognise Labouchère, the literary man, journalist and Radical MP, yet to add his famous amendment to English law criminalising homosexual acts. Here appears also the amendment's victim, Oscar Wilde, barely disguised as 'Omar Milde'—whom Hume also recognises. Some of Hume's preoccupations are evident even at this early stage: Henry Irving, doyen of British theatre; and Bohemia, something wonderfully attractive to a young man from a city where public probity was the rule, and everyone knew what his father did for a living.

He approvingly cites Buchanan's critical distaste for 'The Fleshly

School of Poetry', produced by the Pre-Raphaelites and Swinburne, which Hume describes as 'diseased and morbid', adding 'every healthy-minded man will agree with his estimate of it'. Buchanan had charged his fellow poets with immorality and a frankness about sex he found disturbing. Hume continues with an attack on Swinburne: 'the splendid wealth of words and rhyme therein contained are used only to clothe vile things, to wrap, as it were, cloth of gold around the loathsome bones of a skeleton.' Strong words, even if Hume was unaware that Swinburne was a homosexual masochist and fond of caning. He reads as prim, protesting too much.

When Hume addresses Madeline's martyrdom, he shows a quick sympathy: 'against a fallen woman the self-righteous world harshly closes its doors.' He knew the consequences: women mentally damaged by prostitution and drink were inmates of the Dunedin asylum. Hume finishes by approvingly quoting Buchanan: 'until a man's life is as pure as he would have the life of the woman he loves, he has no right to throw one stone at the most fallen women in the world.' In context it indicates a young man who was high-minded, idealistic and probably virginal.

In this precocious work, Hume positions himself as one well suited to join the ranks of London literati. He had gained his law degree, his nights were free from study, and he could scribble as much as he liked. Ashburn Hall was a success, and now the Hume family awaited Mary and Bessie, returning from Glasgow as saloon (first-class) passengers on the *Waihora*.

It should have been a triumphal reunion, the family celebrating Fergus's law degree and the daughters' overseas music honours. But when the ship arrived on 1 April, the Humes got an unpleasant surprise. The voyage back had suffered heavy storms, in which Bessie had fallen and injured her spine. Later that month a homecoming concert was given, at which both sisters sang, with Morli in atten-dance. Bessie was able to perform, though giving encores reluctantly, with no critics noticing anything wrong. But the injury left her an invalid, physically constrained and emotionally shattered.

Bessie would be confined to bed for three years, recovering from paralysis and gradually managing to walk again. In time she would work successfully as a music teacher, as did her sisters. She had gained an overseas qualification in 'voice cultivation' (a type of elocution).[73] Although she made a life for herself, she never achieved the professional career her voice deserved. The girl who wore orange silk and roses to a ball, as a Spanish opera heroine, was never the same.

Bessie's injury might have been viewed as an act of God, against hubris and the folly of venturing into the dubious, alluring Arts. The most praised and talented Hume sibling had been devastatingly struck down. It left Mary as the only aspiring singer in the family. A safe if uneventful life awaited her in Dunedin. To escape with no possibility of returning a failure, to succeed at the life of Art, to be a vicarious justification for Bessie—it had to be possible. And so Mary waited, planning, saving and performing, when not teaching with Sara and caring for Bessie. The impetus now would come from Fergus. He had fulfilled his part of the bargain with his father and had the freedom to follow his artistic muse. All he needed was the opportunity.

5

ACROSS THE FOOTLIGHTS

Dunedin, to 1885

The boy—he was just one-and-twenty—rather effeminate and wholly romantic, had greatly desired to go on the stage also. But Beryl, three years older than he was and five times as practical, had insisted that he should become a solicitor. She knew, none better, how weak was Willy's character, and hoped that a solid profession, such as the law was, would steady him. As an actor, the society of Bohemia would have ruined his nature, while the calm, logical surroundings of the law kept him within bounds.

ACROSS THE FOOTLIGHTS[74]

Ngaio Marsh and Fergus Hume are New Zealand crime writers with international reputations. He came to fame in the nineteenth century; she was a Queen of the Golden Age, a rival of Agatha Christie. Thus, within fifty years, two major detective authors emerged from the South Island of New Zealand. Marsh was born in Christchurch in 1895, nine years after *Hansom Cab*'s publication, and she began her first book in 1931, the year before Hume died. He would have been much in colonial memory as she grew up, an inspiration, a local boy made good in London.

But the pair have more similarities than place and their

crime-writing profession: they had madhouse keepers in the family. Marsh's grandfather was Edward Seager, Superintendent of Sunnyside asylum in Christchurch. He lost his job at the same time as James Hume, and never recovered his social position. While he was as able and kind as Hume, he was less tough and enterprising.

James Hume was merely a spectator at moral-management entertainments, but Seager participated, a performing artiste. He put on magic shows, levitating his daughters. Asylum theatrics influenced three generations of his family. His daughter Rose became a noted amateur actress, marrying Henry Marsh, another skilled amateur—and their daughter Ngaio, besides her writing, was a superb theatre director, especially of Shakespeare. Indeed, her OBE was more for services to the theatre than for her novels.[75] She discovered actors James Laurenson, who played Arthur Upfield's Bony for television, and Sam Neill.

Fergus too caught the theatre bug from moral management, but his yen was to be a playwright. Although he might live in the madhouse, he was well situated for the latest dramatic fare: on nights when the Luna and Sheridans were not playing, he was only a short walk from the theatres of central Dunedin. Theatre in Otago had followed hard upon the goldrush, beginning in 1862 with a horse bazaar mucked out and converted for the evenings to a theatre. The players who strutted the Dunedin stage were professionals on the antipodean circuit. They would gain dedicated theatres and the attentions of the great colonial theatre entrepreneurs: George Coppin, and the J. C. Williamson firm, who licensed Gilbert and Sullivan operas. Very quickly homegrown playwriting appeared, with an 1863 dramatisation of Mary Braddon's Sensational *Lady Audley's Secret* by young Julius Vogel, later Premier of New Zealand but then editor and part-owner of the *Oddity*. His play originated in Dunedin and toured Australia successfully.[76]

Theatricals were major celebrities in Victorian culture. Touring kept them almost constantly in motion, across the globe. Pages of nineteenth-century magazines are devoted to their now forgotten faces and names: Maggie Moore, Gustavus Brooke, Joseph Jefferson. They captivated Fergus Hume. He not only attended the theatre, but would assiduously court the visiting companies, trying to place his playscripts. It is possible he wrote for or performed with the Sheridans, although his name is never mentioned in their newspaper coverage. His sisters accompanied on piano and—Marcus apart— that seems to be the extent of the Hume family's performances at the asylum under the gaze of pater James.

Theatre was, like the opera, viewed with suspicion by the respectable. Actresses were popularly regarded as little better than whores: they put themselves on public display, even if they did not become the mistresses of powerful men, like Lillie Langtry with the Prince of Wales and former actress Mary Braddon with her publisher, John Maxwell. Actresses playing pantomime became women in tights, taking the part of Principal Boy, or similarly transvestite 'trouser' roles, which showed off their rounded, shapely legs. Their counterparts were men in drag, the Pantomime Dame. The theatre was somewhere the rigid Victorian rules of class, race and gender could be suspended, onstage: a centre for display, not always heterosexual. In *Across the Footlights*, Hume describes two theatrically minded siblings: 'Nature had made a mistake by giving the masculine nature to the girl and the feminine nature to the boy…' The ambiguity of the stage made it a locus for those of same-sex inclinations.[77]

Consider Cecil Riverton, who appeared in Dunedin with Cary's Opera Company when Fergus Hume was a law student. Gilbert and Sullivan's *HMS Pinafore* and *The Pirates of Penzance* were performed with an unusual twist: the contralto roles of Little Buttercup and Ruth were performed by Riverton. The *Oddity* reviewer found the performance credible, while demurring that Riverton had indulged onstage in a 'furious flirtation' with Pinafore's bosun—something definitely not in the libretto.[78]

Riverton was in real life Robert Gant (b. London 1854). For most of his life he was a North Island chemist, but from 1879 to the early 1880s he toured the colony with amateur and semi-professional dramatic companies, playing blackface and opera. Gant was short and slight, and onstage performed femininity convincingly, though the audience knew from the programme he was male. Fergus Hume, as a great fan of opera in general and Gilbert and Sullivan in particular,[79] would have attended the Cary performances—he may even have reviewed them.

Hume was only an aspiring writer, but given his dramatic aspirations, which meant networking determinedly with theatrical professionals, he almost certainly met Gant backstage in Dunedin. They would have got on famously. Gant was also a masher, a charming and popular man. He knew how to hide, like Poe's purloined letter, in plain view. Onstage, Gant negotiated sexual roles with ease. Offstage, his sexual identity was equally complex. The surface innocence of the Victorians, with the sexual unmentionable, meant nobody raised an eyebrow at the town chemist organising amateur theatrics in which he and his male friends assumed drag. Gant's photo albums, collected by Chris Brickell under the title *Manly Affections*, are palpably homoerotic: a photo labelled 'Good-bye!' shows Gant kissing another man. He walked a fine line, successfully, and in the process left a rich legacy to queer studies.

However convivial Hume found Gant, his main purpose was to persuade the visiting theatricals to perform his scripts. In 1883, with his father busy and relatively distant at Ashburn Hall, Fergus achieved his theatrical debut. In October, the Princess Theatre hosted the Merry Thoughts and Happy Moments company, more usually known by the names of its leaders, D'Arcy Stanfield and Fred Dark. The troupe were a temporary alliance of young, knockabout Australians, whose members moved between colonies and companies, providing comedy, skits and songs. They played two short pieces by

Hume, a farce called *Once Bitten, Twice Shy*, described as being written specially for the company, and the burlesque *Dynamite, or the Crown Jewels*. The theatre was 'tolerably well-filled', the curious, family and friends attending—with the exception of the invalid Bessie, James and Aunt Fergusson, who were occupied at Ashburn Hall.[80]

The farce concerns a woman-hating old general, who consents to the marriage of his nephew only after a comic blackmail by the young man's intended—a strong role that allowed Mrs D'Arcy Stanfield to play both a young woman and (disguised) her aunt. Hume wrote roles for actresses which gave them space and prominence. It seems strategic, a professional courting of older, talented, artistic women, a type he knew and liked well, from Bessie and Mary onwards.

The *Oddity* thought this apprentice piece 'amusing', but with no 'special merit'. It was followed by *Dynamite*, less rehearsed. The reviewer found its puns of variable quality. It featured characters such as a King Noodlehead, suffering from DTs, and his son, Prince Folly, described in the programme as:

A modern *swell*—a dasher; as *well* a masher,

Who saves his father's kingdom from a *smasher*.

Actress Amy Horton took this trouser role, making the character 'as dashing as possible'—plainly enjoying herself. Hume made an impression with her and she would not forget him, which was precisely what he had intended.[81]

The *Oddity* declared that 'there is little reason to expect the piece would become in any way popular.' Here the reviewer was wrong. The troupe took it to regional towns and to Wellington city, where both critic and audience found it 'very mirth-provoking'. The two pieces would be repeatedly performed during the eighteen months Fergus Hume remained in New Zealand—and D'Arcy Stanfield would reprise the farce in Australia as *The General*.[82] Fergus Hume is also reported as directing a play in late 1884, called *Tried and True*, probably his own.[83] More significantly, Hume made his first sale outside New Zealand, the poem 'A Ballad of Arcadie', published in the October number of the *Theatre*. Its editor was the influential critic Clement Scott, who would write:

> I do not know Mr Fergus W. Hume, save that I read some charming verses of his sent me some time ago, that I thought them remarkably clever, that I printed them and begged for more even so far away as Australia, for perfect rhyme and faultless rhythm are rare gifts in the eyes of one who has scribbled verses since boyhood.[84]

Hume had made a theatrical start with farce and low comedy, but he essayed more serious drama. Now he managed a coup with the leader of a visiting English troupe, the noted actress Marie de Grey (1852?–1897), making her first Australian tour. De Grey's range extended from Shakespeare to the popular crime melodrama *East Lynne*; but she was also a successful manager, who would not have taken on an unknown talent lightly. In Dunedin Fergus presented her with his play *A Woman Scorned*, a cynical comedy of married manners, which she debuted in Christchurch in March 1885. Though performed towards the end of a long touring season, the piece had been rehearsed with care, and was acted impeccably. Again, Hume had written a strong role for a leading lady.

On the night, de Grey followed Hume's play with classic fare, the trial scene from *The Merchant of Venice*, where she played Portia. The contrast did not show Hume up as a rank amateur. The public received the play warmly, and reviews were largely appreciative. There was some nitpicking: the denouement needed more development, and the dialogue tended towards the 'vapid commonplace'. More serious was the charge that while Hume's attempt 'to found a school of Colonial dramatists' was commendable, the piece flirted with the immoral. Yet he was described as having genius, if intermittently displayed.[85]

Hume had been cautious, waiting until he had made a name for himself in local theatre before casting his net wider. Now the relative success of *A Woman Scorned*, another poem accepted by Scott and the connection with de Grey gave him the impetus he needed to book his passage out of New Zealand.[86] Sister Mary, now nearing old-maid territory, accompanied him, perhaps partly to look after her youngest brother, or with the hope of a second try at a professional singing career. They were not the only Humes to depart Dunedin that year, for Marcus would immigrate to New South Wales. He had musical schemes, and would join his father-in-law, Walter Bell, in business. Both he and Mary were farewelled in benefit concerts, Marcus's a blackface extravaganza.[87]

In early May 1885 the siblings went down to Port Chalmers, waved farewell to family and friends, and boarded the steamship *Te Anau*. Fergus was twenty-five, Mary nearly thirty. She would return for performances and family visits; Fergus did not, except briefly in his imagination. Only his 1893 ghost short story, 'A Colonial Banshee', makes major use of New Zealand as a setting. It is witty and blackly comic, set in Queenstown, where a banshee follows the doomed scions of an Irish family to the colonies. Here Fergus shows what he could do with the sublime scenery of the South Island. The narrator climbs to the top of Ben Lomond: 'There I was accustomed to sit for hours among the ice and snow watching the Earnslaw glacier flashing like a mirror in the sunlight, and the snowy range of the Southern Alps standing like fairy lace-work against the clear blue sky.'[88]

Bittersweet it is to appreciate a landscape while knowing to live there will not fulfil your artistic ambitions. New Zealand would for decades remember Fergus Hume, his name reappearing in the colony's newspapers, mostly with serialisations of his popular novels. He never forgot his home: in his preface to *Hansom Cab* he stated he 'belonged to New Zealand'. It had been his artistic cradle, but Australia would make him famous.

6

WHEN I LIVED IN BOHEMIA

Melbourne, 1885

'…I have been in Melbourne.'
'Ah, that's too much like London.'
'Say rather San Francisco. Melbourne is wonderfully like 'Frisco.'
THE FEVER OF LIFE[89]

When Fergus and Mary Hume arrived in Australia in May 1885, they found a city much like Dunedin: built on gold money, grown fast. Melbourne was a bustling, go-ahead metropolis, the wealthy commercial capital of the country. Sydney in comparison was then staid, conservative and in the economic doldrums. From its humble village origins beside the Yarra only decades earlier, Melbourne now approached half a million in population, the largest urban centre in Australasia. Only three cities in England—the capital, Manchester and Liverpool—were bigger. 'The London of the South', crowed its citizens.[90]

They had reason: the city was at its most architecturally beautiful, with even suburban town halls ornate and grandiose. Small wonder in early 1885 the English journalist George Augustus Sala coined the term 'Marvellous Melbourne'. Local cynics, who lived with the polluted Yarra, full of abattoir, industrial and human waste, including unwanted babies, a sad consequence of the rigid morality and lack of contraception, responded wryly: 'Marvellous Smellbourne'.

Melburnians were cosmopolitan in their tastes, stylish, flashy and fun-loving, as well as enthusiastic consumers of sport and liquor. The biggest game in town was money-making, through stocks and land speculation. The radical English writer Francis Adams visited Australia in the 1880s, seeking copy and health, and found Melbourne's inhabitants 'lean and high-strung, with the alternations of languor and activity which the terrible changefulness of their climate gives them, they wear themselves out in all they do, mistaking the exercise of nervous energy for pleasure'.[91]

Some extraordinary talents were developing in the boom-town city, young people with great futures—like Fergus Hume. Nellie Melba, then Mrs Armstrong, had in 1884 debuted as a professional singer, frequently heard in the city's concert halls. Alfred Deakin was a rising politician and lawyer. Artist Tom Roberts had just returned from studies in Europe; the following year he, Frederick McCubbin and Arthur Streeton, the nucleus of the Heidelberg Impressionists, would hold painting camps at rural Box Hill. Ettie Richardson, later a famous novelist under the pseudonym Henry Handel, was a teenage schoolgirl at Presbyterian Ladies' College.

The city also figured at the forefront of social change. The eight-hour day had been inaugurated in 1856, and was now commemorated with a public holiday. Australia was not, as its reputation proclaimed, 'a workingman's paradise', but it was progressive. A few select women attended Melbourne University, and in 1884 Henrietta Dugdale and others formed the Victorian Women's Suffrage Society. Dugdale had published a feminist utopia, *A Few Hours in a Far-Off Age* (1883); another utopian dreamer was Joseph Fraser, a phrenologist whose *Melbourne and Mars: My Mysterious Life on Two Planets* (1889) would feature gender equality and no personal wealth, with fountains of electricity supplying free power.

Melbourne was also an entertainment capital. To take one week alone, the last in July 1885, when *Hansom Cab*'s narrative begins, the choice included: lectures, whether improving, freethinking or on the poetry of Adam Lindsay Gordon; balls; concerts; opera; minstrel shows; annual socials of groups such as the Acorn Lodge; canary and pigeon shows at the Town Hall; church bazaars; and drama, from the grand theatres of the city centre to amateur players presenting *The Bohemians* at the most un-Bohemian Temperance Hall.[92] Only on Sundays, the day of rest for Christian Melbourne, did the amusements fall silent, to be replaced by church bells. Even the libraries and galleries were closed.

Mary and Fergus, arm in arm, flâneur and flâneuse, wandered like autumn leaves, exploring the city and revelling in the sights. In his Melbourne Trilogy, Fergus leaves a record of the boom-town city that is nigh unsurpassed. We see Collins Street and the Block, where the wealthy and fashionable strolled and shopped. The Fitzroy Gardens, a respite of greenery and statuary. St Kilda's mansions and its pier. And above all, Bourke Street, with its theatres and Saturday-night crowds, only a short walk away from the city's central hell: the slums, with their opium dens and brothels. In *Miss Mephistopheles* Hume even includes perhaps the first description of a Chinese restaurant in Australian literature, complete with wonton making and soy sauce.[93]

All these locations were easily accessible, by cab, train or foot, from East Melbourne, where the Humes settled. Their only known address is 103 George Street, 1886–7.[94] The actual house has been demolished and replaced by serviced apartments, but enough of the boom-time terraces survive for an ambience of pleasant, ornate gentility. Pleasant also, should Hume haunt his former street, is the East Melbourne Public Library, diagonally across the road. It stocks several of his books.

The listing at George Street suggests Hume had the funds to rent a house, sharing the costs with Mary and at least two others: his brother James, who would follow from Dunedin, and an English actor, Philip Beck. Mary 'kept house for the lot',[95] hard work unless a maid was hired for the dirtier tasks. But the thrifty choice for the young Humes, just arrived and with limited funds, was lodgings of the sort described in the final book in the Melbourne Trilogy and the most autobiographical, *Miss Mephistopheles*:

> The apartment…was furnished comfortably, but the furniture had a somewhat dingy look. The carpet was threadbare, except under the table, where there could be traced some vestiges of its original pattern. A cottage [small upright] piano was pushed into a corner slanting ways, and beside it was a great untidy pile of music. At one end of the room, a desk covered with papers, and immediately above it a shelf containing a small array of well-worn books. Near the desk stood an aggravatingly bright sideboard, whereon were some glasses, a jug of water, and a half-empty bottle of whisky. Four or five lounging chairs of wicker-work were scattered about, covered with rugs of wallaby fur, whilst the walls and mantelpiece were almost covered with photographs, mostly of women, but here and there a male face, showing the well-known features of Beethoven, Chopin, and other famous musicians.[96]

In the novel those sharing the digs are not siblings, but musician Ezra Lazarus and the hero, author Keith Stewart. The pair collaborate artistically on a light opera, such as Hume did write in Melbourne: *His Excellency*, a three-act comedy libretto with music by Alfred Plumpton (1848–1902). Although unperformed, it was described as charming and sparkling, Hume's libretto being 'full of wit and fun'.[97]

Plumpton was a man after Hume's sartorial heart, one of Melbourne's most stylish dressers. Professionally he was a composer ranging from popular song to sacred masses. In London he had collaborated with W. S. Gilbert—something to delight the fannish Hume—and in Melbourne novelist Marcus Clarke (1846–1881), author of *His Natural Life*. When Hume knew Plumpton he wrote musical criticism for the *Leader* and the *Age* while also directing the choirs at two Catholic churches: St Francis and St Patrick's Cathedral. His favours extended to another Christian sect, he being musical director at Presbyterian Ladies' College.

Plumpton's personal life was equally complex. Though married to pianist Madame Carlotta Tasca, he romanced Caroline Hodgson, alias Madame Brussels, keeper of an exclusive brothel in Lonsdale Street. She was separated from her husband, a policeman: the rumour was that Plumpton had fathered her daughter. Plumpton is also alleged to have pimped for the brothel, with a regular allowance of sovereigns from Hodgson to 'shout' prospective punters. Like many outwardly respectable males in Melbourne, such as Justice Redmond Barry—on the bench by day, with his mistress by night—Plumpton kept his lives separate, if within walking distance.

Men could move between the worlds of vice and virtue; women, particularly those above the working class, could not without penalty. Both Humes would have known Plumpton, but Mary risked moral censure if she ever met Madame Brussels. Female employment depended on a reputation for virtue. Hume in contrast had the masculine freedom to experience Melbourne at its best and worst, researching for his writing projects. He gives lines to *Miss Mephistopheles'* Stewart that rail against the double standard: 'I'm sick of hearing the incessant railing against women—good heavens! are we men so pure ourselves, that we can afford to cast stones against the sex to which our mothers and sisters belong?' Hume knew about Plumpton's double life, for he worked with the musician even after it was exposed. If he visited Madame Brussels' establishment, it is unlikely he went as a client, even with a 'shout' from his musical friend and collaborator.[98]

Madame Brussels' haunt is long gone, but much of Hume's Melbourne remains. It is possible to follow his route from East

Melbourne to the city centre: an easy stroll across Fitzroy Gardens, past the houses of Parliament, then covered in scaffolding for the classical colonnade and portico. This walk recurs in the Melbourne Trilogy. In *Hansom Cab* Detective Gorby trails suspect Brian Fitzgerald to his lodgings, a house in Powlett Street, East Melbourne, near Cairns Memorial Church, a massive Presbyterian edifice. Almost certainly this church reappears in the opening sequence of *Miss Mephistopheles*, where on a wet winter evening the flatmates lounge deliciously snug and warm, watching the holy make their umbrella'd way to the church opposite. Mary Hume could not laze, let alone be Sabbatarian, for she had a job as principal soprano of a church choir (quite probably one directed by Plumpton).[99] *Hansom Cab*'s hero and its author thus apparently have the same address—a private joke, another poke at Presbyterianism. Hume would also claim in his preface to have drawn his landladies from life, along with Calton and Mother Guttersnipe.

The city centre was where the Humes had designs, Fergus on the theatre and Mary on the musical scene. Already they had encountered major personalities passing through New Zealand: playwright George Darrell had leased Dunedin's Princess Theatre briefly in the 1870s and had toured with Signor Morli, Mary's singing teacher, in the Simonsen Opera Troupe.

Of the Hume siblings, Mary achieved exposure first, and quickly: several weeks after arriving she appeared at Melbourne's Town Hall in a 'Grand Patriotic Concert'. The publicity 'puffed' her as a 'Prima Donna Soprano…Just arrived from Europe, where she created a perfect furore, under the tuition of the celebrated Signor Alberto Randegger'.[100] It was not strictly true: Mary and Bessie Hume had travelled to Europe to study music, but in 1882–3. The notice also implied she was European rather than what she was: colonial-bred and hence inferior, per the terms of the cultural cringe.

Nellie Melba had made her first major public performance at the Town Hall a year before, to great acclaim. Her name appears alongside Mary Hume's in Melbourne music advertisements until March 1886, when Melba left for Europe; she would apply to Signor Randegger, but be refused because he was taking on 'no new pupils'.[101] In Melbourne the two sopranos competed: Mary had overseas study credentials, but Melba was a local lass, received rapturously. The Melbourne papers chart Mary's appearances and the critical response: on the whole good, but Mary fell short of Melba's diva quality. Her technique was flawed, and she did not make as many appearances as Melba, nor as much money—let alone a splash. By August she advertised her services as a singing teacher and in early 1886 achieved a permanent position at Park Place Ladies' School in South Yarra.[102]

Mary had escaped Dunedin before, but for the first time in his life Fergus was free from both his father and the scrutiny of the 'unco guid', the respectably rigid Scots satirised by Burns. Fergus aspired to Bohemianism, a relatively new concept derived from Parisian journalist Henry Murger's 1851 *La Vie de Bohème*. In Hume's Buchanan review he had described Bohemians as 'those brilliant spirits who create and sustain the literary, musical and artistic character of the age'. The colonies might be distant and regarded as uncivilised, but in their urban centres the artistic-minded formed their little enclaves. Fergus would write of Bohemian Melbourne and London in similar terms: of garrets, witty fellowship and suppers in the wee hours. In *Madame Midas* and *Miss Mephistopheles* he clearly describes the Yorick Club, of which Plumpton was a member: 'It was a Bohemian club, and among its members were stock-brokers, musicians, journalists and actors, so that, whatever the moral tone of the place, the conversation was generally brilliant, albeit rather malicious.'[103]

The use of the word 'moral' betrays a certain anxiety. Fergus and Mary were far from pious Dunedin, but equally physically and spiritually removed from Murger's dissolutes, or the absinthe-drinkers drawn by Degas and Lautrec. They might be living in a free-wheeling subculture, but their intent was success—achieved by hard work and avoiding temptation. The whisky bottle in the opening scenes of *Miss Mephistopheles* was not their vice. They were sensible Scots, though Fergus was never as canny as his father.

When Fergus wrote the novel *When I Lived in Bohemia* (1892) he began with 'An Introductory Drama' summoning the ghost of Murger. The shade upbraided him for omitting the demimondaine— the kept women of Parisian Bohemia, the Melbourne equivalent being Madame Brussels and her ilk. Such matter was permissible in the French novel, but 'England is bounded on all sides by morality'.[104]

Two of Fergus Hume's great Melbourne predecessors were genuine Bohemians: Marcus Clarke and Mary Fortune (c. 1833–c.1909), a crime author who would be described as 'probably the only truly Bohemian lady writer who has ever earned a living by her pen in Australia'.[105] Clarke married an actress, something in *Hansom Cab* regarded as unforgivable by parents of the 'rigid Presbyterian' persuasion. Both Clarke and Fortune fell foul of conventional Melbourne, the brilliant Clarke dying too young and in poverty. Fortune lived into old age, but as an alcoholic with criminal associates.

Fergus himself would observe in *Miss Mephistopheles* that 'Bohemianism is charming in novels, but in real life it is generally a hunt after what Murger calls that voracious animal, the half-crown.'[106] If he were to establish himself as a man of letters in Melbourne he needed a means of support. He did not intend to be a lawyer first and a part-time scribbler second. Wilkie Collins' legal training informed his crime novels, though he had been left money in his father's will and thus could support two mistressses and write without penury. Hume did not have that luxury.

His first tilt at literary Melbourne was journalism. A new weekly magazine, *Table Talk*, had advertised for contributors. Its proprietor was Maurice Brodzky (1847–1919), an outsider with an eye for talent and a tendency for trouble. Brodzky came to Australia in the wake of the Franco-Prussian war, making a suitably dramatic if damp entry by being shipwrecked. He became Australian correspondent for the London *Daily Telegraph*, as well as writing for local papers like the *Herald*. But his history of Melbourne Jewry proved defamatory and he was bankrupted. Only his relationship by marriage with the entrepreneurial Fink family freed him: they included lawyer and arts patron Theodore Fink, reputed backer for *Table Talk*.

The opening number of *Table Talk* stated its intent:

> Colonial society has attained such a definite stage of devel-
> opment, has become crystallised into such a concrete and
> enduring form, that it merits more systematic and compre-
> hensive treatment than it has hitherto received at the hands
> of journalists…Society…has begun to assert its influence
> in these colonies in no uncertain or ambiguous manner.[107]

By that Brodzky meant high society, the wealthy colonial elite. *Table Talk* was to be 'devoted exclusively' to its interests—although Brodzky's statement that it would not involve gossip, spite or slander was soon forgotten. In time he would turn into a brilliant muckraker, publishing stories no one else in Melbourne dared touch.

What Brodzky thought society was interested in largely comprised: theatre, politics, fashion, finance and fashionable balls or weddings. For the latter he employed young women aspiring to the new career of journalism, such as the Irish Agnes Murphy, who had been stranded in Melbourne due to a reversal in family fortune and nearly starved. Now she gained space in his Women's Pages.

Fergus Hume placed signed articles in *Table Talk* on theatre and his beloved Gilbert and Sullivan, and the poem 'My Lady Disdain', dated June 1885. Thereafter his name vanishes from the paper until the release of *Hansom Cab*. It could mean he wrote pseudonymously—wise if he wrote drama criticism while aspiring to be a playwright. Or did the connection cease as an act of brotherly loyalty? On 17 July 1885, in a review of the Melbourne Liedertafel's Handel Bicentenary concert, *Table Talk*'s music critic wrote: 'Miss Mary Hume attempted "From Mighty Kings" but failed utterly'. It was the worst review she had ever received.[108]

Brodzky could be spiteful, heaping acerbic comments on Agnes Murphy for years after she left *Table Talk*. But he never commented adversely on Hume, and indeed provided the first press notice for *Hansom Cab*. Otherwise Hume seems not to have contributed to the Melbourne papers. In *Miss Mephistopheles* Stewart complains, 'I have seen editors, and have been told there was no room on the press.'[109] Hume lacked Uncle Marcus's Dunedin press connections and competition was fierce. He did make friends with *Argus* contributor James Hingston, who wrote travel articles. Hingston (b. 1830), a bachelor who lived surrounded by books and papers in the George Hotel, St Kilda, was a notary public and literary man—exactly the type for Hume to like and cultivate.[110]

Around this time Hume tried to sell *Professor Brankel* again, most likely as a newspaper serial. *Brankel* is clearly the 'psychological story' (its subtitle) he hawked around on his arrival, but 'was universally refused'.[111] The failure clearly rankled. Hume would write his debut out of his personal bibliography, claiming in the preface: 'Up to that time I had written only one or two short stories, and the "Cab" was not only the first book I ever published, but the first book I ever wrote.' The novella was wild and woolly, but by no means deplorable. Yet it failed to find publication in Melbourne, at least in 1885.

Various accounts survive of how Hume earned a living in Australia. A bank clerk, says one source—alarming if true, for in Hume's Melbourne fictions young bank clerks tend to defraud their employers.[112] More authoritative is the testimony of a contemporary, the Melbourne correspondent of the *Colac Herald*:

> Whilst in Melbourne he was one of the most diabolically
> busy men I knew. He was always at some kind of writing,
> and had a novel, a play, a burlesque, poetry, and comic opera

all at hand at the same time. He use to work with fever-ish energy, and all the time had employment in a lawyer's office.[113]

This lawyer was Sydney Raphael, a Melbourne solicitor, for whose practice Hume worked as managing clerk. Quite probably the job came about through Brodzky. In *Miss Mephistopheles* Ezra Lazarus finds work for Stewart at his father's pawnbroking business—in reality, Hume's employment was more upmarket. Clerking for Raphael was less time-sapping than trying to establish himself at the Melbourne bar, had he so wished. It functioned as a day job, leaving Hume time for writing, observing and acquainting himself with the local dramatic scene.[114]

Hume wanted to be a writer, but above all a dramatist. It was something with which he had already had some success in New Zealand. Surely Melbourne would welcome his work.

7

ACROSS THE FOOTLIGHTS II

To me there is something grand in this restless crowd of people, all instinct with life and ambition—the gas lamps jar upon your dream, but they are evidences of civilisation, and the hoarse murmur of the mob is like the mutterings of a distant storm, or white waves breaking on a lonely coast. No, my friend, leave the enchanted cities to dreamland, and live the busy life of the nineteenth century.

MISS MEPHISTOPHELES[115]

For a colonial intending a career in drama, who was ambitious but too cautious to travel to London immediately, Melbourne was the obvious destination. It was the busy theatrical capital of Australia, with a dedicated What's On in the daily publication *Lorgnette*, and an assortment of venues. Traces of their glory survive the wreckers' ball in the Princess and Her Majesty's Theatres, but there were other venues, now lost: the Opera House, the Theatre Royal and smaller venues, such as the Bijou, which Hume alters slightly for *Miss Mephistopheles* (1890):

> The 'Bon-Bon' was the smallest, prettiest, and most luxurious theatre in Melbourne, and was exclusively devoted to farcical comedy, burlesque, and opera-bouffe [comic operetta in the Offenbach style] the latter class of entertainment

being now the attraction. There was no pit, the circle and boxes being raised but little above the level of the stalls. The decorations were pink, white, and gold, the seats being covered with pale, rose-coloured plush, with curtains and hangings to match, while the electric lights, shining through pink globes, gave quite a warm glow to the theatre. The dome was decorated with allegorical figures representing Momus, the God of laughter, and Apollo, the God of music, while all around the walls were exquisitely painted medallions of scenes from celebrated operas and burlesques. The proscenium was a broad frame of dullish gold, the curtain of roseate plush, and on either side of the stage were life-sized statues of Offenbach and Planché in white marble. Altogether, a charming theatre more like a cosy drawing-room than a place of public entertainment.[116]

A delectable destination, but it was not for Hume. In *Miss Mephistopheles* the hero Stewart gets his play performed and it is a smash success—a wish-fulfilment for Hume. He might have been a local hero in Dunedin, but in Melbourne he was a nobody in a new city. 'Of course,' comments Victorianist Sue Martin, 'he might not have been very good.' But he believed he was: a reasonable expectation, given his New Zealand reception.

Melbourne's theatre was already rigidly controlled by a small group of entrepreneurs, actors and writers. The opening number of *Table Talk* commented: 'Melbourne boasts of three distinct and wealthy theatrical managements—Messrs. Williamson, Garner and Musgrove (the Royal and Princess); Messrs Rignold and Allison (Her Majesty's Opera House); Messrs Majeroni and Wilson (Bijou); and it would be difficult to discriminate as to which is the most distinguished for doing the least to popularise the drama.' By that, serious drama was meant, as opposed to light comedy and pantomimes, with their ready audience. Hume's farces and burlesques would have fitted the bill in Melbourne, but the competition was stiff and unfriendly to the newcomer.[117]

J. C. Williamson & Co., referred to as the Triumvirate, dominated, with two theatres in Melbourne, and in 1885 in the process of acquiring rights to two others in Sydney and Adelaide. The partnership of James Allison and George Rignold, an English Shakespearean actor specialising in melodramas, had two venues, in Melbourne and Sydney. The 'Bon-Bon'/Bijou was run until October 1886 (when the Triumvirate took over the lease, increasing their market) by Eduardo Majeroni, a former Garibaldi red shirt, and W. J. Wilson. They had their own New Zealander in William Luscombe Searelle, a writer of comic operas described by *Table Talk* as 'a veritable musical genius, in his own estimation'. If Hume wrote these words, he was wisely anonymous, since they also applied to him.[118]

Also powerful were the actor-playwright-managers such as George Darrell, who wrote melodramas about new chums' adventures in the Antipodes. His *The Sunny South* (1883) travelled successfully to London the following year. Further down this hierarchy came the dramatists, like Garnet Walch, who specialised in pantomimes and comedies, rich in local colour and dire puns. The pond in which Hume hoped to make a splash was already crowded.

Another factor was the cultural cringe. Overwhelmingly the colonial theatre managers preferred imported overseas works. *Table Talk* writer 'Paul Prompter' voiced a common complaint:

> I note that Messrs Williamson, Garner and Musgrove announce that their theatres are open 'for the production of all the English and continental successes'. Therefore I suppose the managers, who certainly know their own business remarkably well, have decided that there is not much chance of anything like an Australian success. So Australians must do with their pieces as wine merchants used to do with Madeira. Send them around the world that

they may be better appreciated when they come back here.[119]

In *Miss Mephistopheles* Hume fictionalises his struggles to become a dramatist in Melbourne. He includes this exchange between manager Ted Mortimer and Stewart:

'I can write home to London and get successful plays with big reputations already made.'

'Yes, and pay big prices for them.'

'That may be,' replied the manager imperturbably; 'but if I give a good price I get a good article that is sure to recoup me for my outlay. I don't say that "Faust Upset" isn't good, but at the same time it's an experiment. Australians don't like their own raw material.'

'They never get a chance of seeing it,' said Keith bitterly, 'you of course look at it from a business point of view, as is only proper, but seeing that you draw all your money from Colonial pockets, why not give Colonial brains a chance?'

'Because Colonial brains don't pay, Colonial pockets do.'[120]

The only way Keith Stewart can have his work performed is by rescuing the child of star actress Caprice (Kitty Marchurst) from a road accident. He writes her a play, and she uses her influence to get the work performed, on favourable financial terms.

A glance at what played in Melbourne in 1885 shows how difficult it would have been to break in as a new talent with colonial material. The year began with Amy Horton, Hume's Prince Masher in Dunedin, performing in the pantomime *Sinbad* at the Opera House, with another pantomime, *Cinderella*, at the Theatre Royal. In May J. C. Williamson's Theatre Royal staged the first Australian performance of Gilbert and Sullivan's *Iolanthe* (it had already played Dunedin). Popular English novels were also dramatised at the Opera House, with Rignold starring in *Called Back* (1883) by Hugh Conway, a now forgotten mystery-romance bestseller. A rather more literary dramatisation at the same theatre was George Eliot's *Adam Bede*. In July the famous playwright Dion Boucicault brought an imported English troupe to the Theatre Royal, presenting his own work.[121]

The Bijou played the light continental, Offenbach or Sardou. Besides Searelle they presented a play by Robert Whitworth, an established dramatist in Melbourne. In June George Darrell's new play, *Squatter*, debuted at the Opera House. Walch had *Spoons*, a new play performed at the minor theatre St George's Hall, unsuccessfully. He only scored big at the end of the year, in pantomime. And so the year went on, with imports of various quality and far less local content, the year ending with Amy Horton returned from touring, in Walch's pantomime *Sleeping Beauty*, complete with Prince Austral, and Rignold chewing the scenery in *Faust*.

Hume would comment in his 1892 preface to *Hansom Cab*: 'I was bent on becoming a dramatist, but, being quite unknown, I found it impossible to induce the managers of the Melbourne Theatres to accept, or even to read a play.' He could have returned to the amateurs in their drawing rooms, or rehearsing *The Bohemians* in the Temperance Hall. But he was impatient, a young man in a hurry.

Since he was blocked in one direction, might he go sideways? Write a successful novel, perhaps, which would make him impossible to ignore? In Dunedin he had displayed his talents in different literary fields before succeeding in getting his work onstage. For Melbourne all he needed were the publications, and the resultant publicity. He would recollect in his preface: 'At length it occurred to me I might further my purpose by writing a novel. I should at all events secure a certain amount of local attention.'

And, since he really did want to be a successful dramatist, he name-checked, even brown-nosed, the biggest theatrical manager in the city. In chapter twelve of *Hansom Cab*, as the excitement of the murder case has reached a fever, Hume sends up theatrical hopefuls, such as himself:

…one young man of literary tendencies had been so struck by the dramatic capabilities of the affair that he thought of writing a five-act drama on it—with a sensation scene of the hanging of Fitzgerald—and of offering it to Williamson, for production at the Theatre Royal. But that astute manager refused to entertain the idea, with the dry remark that as the fifth act had not been played out in real life, he could not see how the dramatist could end it successfully.

If Hume's life was a play, the Melbourne scenes had so far failed to come to a satisfactory conclusion. In the new act he would introduce new matter, new themes for his writing. It was going to be a success, he was sure of it, and make him a sought-after dramatist.

8

A CENTENNIAL SONG
Hume's Crime Forerunners

Aye! a hundred years are ended, vanished in the gulf of Time
  Let them go and carry with them all their load of guilt
and crime

'A CENTENNIAL SONG', BY PHILIP BECK AND FERGUS HUME

Fergus Hume related in his preface that *Hansom Cab* came from market research:

> I enquired of a leading Melbourne bookseller what style of book he sold most of. He replied that the detective stories of Gaboriau had a large sale; and as, at this time, I had never even heard of this author, I bought all his works—eleven or thereabouts—and read them carefully.

Who was this Gaboriau, and why was he so popular in 1880s Melbourne? To answer it is necessary to consider the history of crime fiction, particularly in Australia.[122] Crime content can be found in Australian writing from the beginnings of European settlement, precisely because of the national origins as a penal colony—something noted in 'A Centennial Song' with the mention of 'guilt and crime'. Those transported were the subject matter of what we would now term true crime: murder ballads and broadsheets, the legal theatre of trials and public hangings, and a bestselling compilation of villains, *The Newgate Calendar*.

Crime fiction has a creation myth: that it began with Poe, an immaculate genre conception with his 1841 short story 'The Murders in the Rue Morgue'. Mythic indeed: crime fiction's origins in the late eighteenth and early nineteenth century were more polygenetic, with DNA coming from various sources, from legal reform to the development of policing and forensics. It arose from a stew of genres, where different forms of writing met and mingled promiscuously. Theatre melodrama was one ingredient, along with the Gothic novels of Ann Radcliffe, with their use of prolonged suspense—the word 'mystery' derives from the Gothic. Radcliffe's 1794 *The Mysteries of Udolpho* is ancestral, not least in title, to *The Mystery of a Hansom Cab*.

For crime fiction, true crime was the major ingredient, a content in search of form. In the early 1800s newspapers became mass market, with daily production and a cheaper price. So was enabled a continuous coverage of crime, true-life serialisation reporting on developments in an investigation, the stars the detective police, reconstructing the stories behind criminal events. A narrative construction thus gained familiarity: the story of a crime, beginning with a murder and gradually revealed through an ongoing police investigation, concluded with the mystery solved.

This fragmented temporal structure was new to the novel form, with its straight linear progression from birth to romance to death. Using crime as subject matter was also fraught with moral anxieties: would crime publicised, even in fiction, create more crime? So the pulpits thundered, but the public thought otherwise: 'Murder-Mania' was a ubiquitous obsession. Celebrated cases created a multimedia storm, featuring in everything from pulpits to puppet shows and porcelain figurines.

Numerous writers contributed to this developing genre. William

Godwin, the father of Mary Shelley, wrote *Caleb Williams* (1794), regarded as the first fictional representation of an amateur detective. Sir Edward Bulwer-Lytton and the celebrated spiritualist Catherine Crowe both published bestselling crime novels in January 1841, four months before Poe's 'Rue Morgue'. Crowe's *Adventures of Susan Hopley; or, Circumstantial Evidence* featured three female detectives. But these works tended to be isolated, without a label, let alone a sense of genre. By the 1860s more of a school arose with the popular Sensation novels, full of murder and bigamy, although not all of their writers married matter to the emergent crime narrative form.

An author who did was the young French editor and writer, Émile Gaboriau. Beginning in 1865 he created the *roman policier*, the original police procedural novels, with a series detective, M. Lecoq. Gaboriau's career was short, for he died in 1873, but he was enormously popular in France. His fandom would cross borders, with the German statesman Bismarck an admirer, despite his low opinion of the French. Yet it was not until the early 1880s that the publisher Henry Vizetelly brought Gaboriau to the English audience. Vizetelly realised the potential of European novels in translation: good writing, and not subject to English copyright, with the consequent pesky need to pay the author.

Vizetelly began with 'only the very best samples of modern French fiction of a perfectly unobjectionable character…issued in well printed shilling volumes'. Sales proving low, Vizetelly turned to objectionable French novels: 'Finding that works of a high literary character did not take, we bethought ourselves of the favourite novelist of the Parisian *concierge*, namely, Gaboriau.' Here he struck gold: Gaboriau and his followers, who reprised the young master's characters after his death, resulted in sales of 'considerably more than a million' for Vizetelly over 1881–8.

When labelling his product, Vizetelly initially termed it 'Gaboriau's Sensation Fiction'.[123] The anglophone market provided its own label:

'Detective Fiction' is found in the press from late 1881. Vizetelly is best remembered for publishing Zola's *Nana*, which saw him jailed for obscenity. But he had a major effect on the development of detective fiction in bringing Gaboriau to a wider audience.

The London correspondent for the Melbourne *Argus* commented on Gaboriau:

> His style is common-place, his writings are destitute of poetry and humour, but he is the first amateur detective of his age. Even Edgar Allan Poe is his inferior. Gaboriau is more life like, and unites the most attractive story-telling with the exactness of a police report. His works are being rendered monthly into English, and I predict for them an immense circulation in this country.

Presciently, the writer added: 'In these days of mutilation and literary pillage, I wonder it has not struck some "conveyancer" to adapt these tales in their details to English soil.' Here he refers to the common practice of taking an existing text and changing the setting to suit the audience: French into English, or British into American, as happened to the first American detective novel, *The Dead Letter* (1866) by Seeley Regester (Metta Victor), which was pirated and altered by the English *Cassell's Magazine*. It would not be English soil that best naturalised Gaboriau, but American and Australian, with *Hansom Cab* an imaginative response rather than an adaptation.[124]

Hume was not the first to adapt crime fiction to Australia. Immigrants had arrived with an established taste for reading crime, true and fictional, and set to naturalising it, just as they did with foxes, sparrows and rabbits. But it was a slow process, only coalescing generically in the mid-1800s, when interest from gold-seeking immigrants created a market for Australian tales, including crime. The authors who responded to this challenge were contemporaries of Dickens, Mary Braddon and Wilkie Collins. They were even more colourful: bigamists, drunks, (literary) thieves and general reprobates.

Consider Sydneysider John Lang (1816–1864), the first Australian-born author. He was a lawyer, descended from a First Fleet convict. Genes, temperament and environment created a ratbag—Lang caused trouble everywhere. He was even jailed for libelling the East India Company. As a novelist he created the first Australian detective in his 1855 *The Forger's Wife*: one George Flower, based on Sydney identity Israel Chapman (1794?–1868), like Lang's grandfather a Jewish convict turned policeman. In form, however, it was rather more of a picaresque romance than a detective mystery, Flower being less deductive than violent.

Lang did not have direct literary followers until 1865, with a burst of creativity in the colony of Victoria. In January the *Hamilton Spectator* published the short story 'Wonderful! When You Come to Think of It!', a sprightly parody name-checking Poe, with a detective-fiction fan as amateur sleuth. The author was one 'M. C.', almost undoubtedly the teenage Marcus Clarke. In September, a popular fiction magazine debuted in Melbourne: the *Australian Journal*. From its first issue the magazine featured crime.

George Walstab, its editor, had personal experience of the subject. He had been a policeman, the result of an 1850s drive in the colony to recruit young gentlemen as mounted police cadets. The goldrushes had increased both the population and crime, and the official response was to try to create an elite force, officer material. Though the cadet system foundered, it did offer good material for crime writers. In England, the notion of a detective-hero was fraught by class issues, with most actual police coming from the lower class, while most fictional protagonists were middle–upper class. For crime writers in Victoria, the cadet system rendered the police as unproblematic heroes.

The *Australian Journal* opened with the serial *Force and Fraud*, the first Australian murder-mystery novel, by Ellen Davitt (1812–79), a sister-in-law of Anthony Trollope. She had been the most powerful woman in Victoria's secular education system. Jobless and widowed by the 1860s, she turned to journalism. Like Lang she had a family connection with crime: her father, Edward Heseltine, had embezzled thousands of pounds from the Yorkshire bank he managed. In *Force and Fraud*, she intertwines a romance with a tight mystery plot. The novel does not feature a police detective, rather a series of keen amateur sleuths—a common model of the time. But the mystery structure dominates the narrative, it being an assured whodunnit.

Also in the first issue was 'The Shepherd's Hut; Or 'Tis Thirteen Years Since', described as the memoirs of an 'Australian Police Officer'. It begins on Melbourne's mean streets, in the goldrush 1850s:

> its rows of wooden huts, with their tin or shingle roofs, interspersed with tents, mud hovels, drinking booths, and here and there a row of stone houses lifting their heads above their humbler brethren; streets that might be better termed rivers of mud, with tree stumps yet uncleared away in their midst; carts drawn by oxen or horses, struggling through the mire, and often hopelessly stuck in some deep rut; drivers swearing and cracking whips, diggers and adventurers, often drunk and disorderly, reeling or trudging through the mud slough, for fragments of paving only existed here and there…

The story appeared anonymously, but was the work of James Skipp Borlase (1839–1902?), a former lawyer. He had immigrated to Victoria in 1864, and soon after deserted his wife, Rosanna. Borlase was ignominiously arrested in Tasmania and returned to Melbourne. The couple reconciled, but Borlase had effectively destroyed his legal career. He took up writing, though with a tendency for plagiarism. The passage above is quite possibly not his work.

'The Shepherd's Hut' elicited a reader's response, a story called 'The Stolen Specimens', written from the viewpoint of a cadet policeman on the goldfields. The author was Mary Fortune, who seems to have taken her infant son and run away from her Canadian husband, arriving in Australia in 1855. Three years later she briefly and bigamously married Percy Brett, like Walstab a cadet police-man. Thus she had inside knowledge of the police force, and could write convincingly in the detective persona. Within a short time, the *Australian Journal* had both Borlase and Fortune writing the first Australian detective serials.

Few of these pioneering Melbourne writers would stick with crime. Walstab is said to have translated Gaboriau; Clarke became editor of the *Australian Journal* in 1870, and wrote *For the Term of His Natural Life* as a serial there. This original version had a murder-mystery structure, but it was something Clarke did not pursue further. Ellen Davitt eventually returned to teaching, but it destroyed her health. She died, in poverty, of cancer and exhaustion in 1879. Sisters in Crime have named their Davitt award after her. James Skipp Borlase was sacked by the *Australian Journal* for plagiarising Sir Walter Scott. He published his stories—and one of Mary Fortune's, unattributed—in London as *The Night Fossickers and Other Australian Tales of Peril and Adventure* (1867). Finding colonial literary life too ill-paid and difficult, he returned to England and a minor career as an adventure-story writer, for adults and children.

Only Mary Fortune made a career of crime, writing the longest known early crime series, 'The Detective's Album', comprising over five hundred stories, serialised from 1868–1908. Her 1871 collection of the same title is one of the rarest items in crime bibliography, the first book of detective stories published in Australia. She wrote as Waif Wander (a self-description) and W. W., her identity being concealed from her readers: besides her bigamy she had an illegitimate child, and was known to police. She drank and consorted with criminals, including her son George, who would spend most of his life in jail. In 1874 she was even wanted by the police as a reluctant witness in a case of rape.

Fortune was the most prolific and important Australian precursor of Hume, and although of his local antecedents Hume cites only Marcus Clarke in *Hansom Cab*, in his search for publication he must have investigated the *Australian Journal* and found 'The Detective's Album', with Fortune's sleuth Mark Sinclair appearing monthly.

Table Talk's Brodzky certainly knew who she was. In 1878–9 the *Australian Journal* had begun serialising Brodzky's autobiographical serial *Ben-Israel*, only to pull the plug halfway through. When the opportunity came, he took an icy revenge on the *Australian Journal*'s star crime writer, and by extension the magazine itself. Fortune's life and work intersected unpleasantly in mid-1885, with her son being jailed for robbery under arms. Brodzky publicised the connection between mother and son, most pruriently:

> Social philosophers have a pet theory that the publication of the lives of notorious criminals tends to create successors in the line. It is however seldom that a parent errs in this respect and writes works of fiction which tend to foster crime, but it appears that the literary efforts of the mother of the young man Fortune one of the National Bank robbers induced him to start his criminal career. He is the son of a lady who wrote a series of 'Detective Stories' in a Melbourne publication...under the name of 'Waif Wander'. It is a bitter reflection for this unhappy lady to think that some of the stories which she wrote in all innocence may have tended to mould the character of her child to such an extent as to render him a felon with a spirit as venturesome and daring as any of the criminal heroes which she pourtrayed.[125]

Mary Fortune apart, *Hansom Cab* is an open book as regards Hume's influences, his reading, theatre and music tastes. He makes Felix Rolleston a crime buff, citing Gaboriau (and his followers), Mary Braddon and also *The Leavenworth Case* (1878) by Anna Katharine Green, Gaboriau's major American disciple. Green was a serious woman, staunch in her Presbyterian faith. She would not have been impressed that Felix's reading was termed 'of the lightest description'.[126]

Crime historian Stephen Knight opines that these references seem more market placement than actual source matter. Gaboriau might have been cited as inspiration, but there is little in *Hansom Cab* to suggest that Hume actually read him slavishly—or as Gaboriau's followers did, continue Lecoq's adventures. What was important was that Hume appealed to readers with the same tastes as Felix. Crime fiction, as Vizetelly and other publishers were realising, had appeal across class, the emerging mass-market audience. Of the authors Hume cited and hoped to emulate, all had a devoted readership. But what Hume was about to do would equal or surpass them.

THE SPIDER
Spinning the plot

> But if you write a detective novel, you state a hard and fast crimi-
> nal case, and in order to carry it out to a logical conclusion you are
> as bound by that case as though it actually happened. Then you
> must have all police-court business at your fingers' ends, be well
> up in legal matters, know something about the medical profession,
> and be careful about every statement you make. You must conceal
> the real criminal, lay the blame on all the other characters in the
> book; yet, when the end comes, you have to prove that it is quite
> natural the real criminal should have committed the crime.
>
> WHEN I LIVED IN BOHEMIA[127]

How did Hume write his novel? Crime fiction was so new that there
were no writerly guides, beyond what could be gleaned from close
reading of his precursors. Certainly his legal experience gave him an
advantage with the criminal subject matter. Apart from that, he learned
as he went, on the job, spinning his fictional web. In later years it would
be stated that 'Nowadays he selects his title first'—leading to such
eye-catchers as *The Crimson Cryptogram* or *The Scarlet Bat*. But using
the title as starting point could have been his practice from the first.[128]

The Mystery of a Hansom Cab seems to be a natural if calculated extrapolation from a novel by Gaboriau follower Fortuné du Boisgobey, *Le Crime de l'Omnibus* (1881). Its translations had various titles, one American edition being *The Mystery of an Omnibus* (New York: Munro, c. 1882). The novel is mentioned in *Hansom Cab*'s first chapter. That a hansom cab was a vehicle perfectly suited for murder is not an obvious thought, but it is a brilliant one. In today's taxicabs, the driver and passengers share the same space. With the hansom the driver is outside, sitting high and behind the passengers. He cannot see into the cabin, and communicates with the passengers through a trapdoor in the roof. On a rough road, the rattle of wheels on stones meant that it was impossible to hear anything from inside the cabin. Late at night, the cabin of a hansom cab offered both anonymity and privacy, a moveable crime scene.

Hume said in his preface that the notion occurred to him during an actual hansom-cab ride: 'The central idea i.e. the murder in a cab—came to me while driving at a late hour to St. Kilda, a suburb of Melbourne.' The light of a hansom cab is outside the cabin, for the driver's rather than the passenger's convenience. Inside would have been dim, but just light enough for scribbling down his idea—if he carried a notebook. If not, his starched white shirt cuff would have sufficed, a detail appearing in various late nineteenth-century novels, and surely a bane to the laundress. Or did he use the flyleaf and endpapers of his current reading, perhaps the du Boisgobey book itself? In London, a few years later and a successful author, he would claim always to carry a volume of poetry by Herrick in his pocket. In Melbourne, an unknown, his reading was probably much less elevated.[129]

Hume, his idea duly noted, could then have gazed up and around at his surroundings. As he mentally set his opening scenes, tracing the route down the great boulevard, did he observe what he could make use of, for verisimilitude? Like the belvedere tower of Government House, which would later figure in the background of the novel's first cover? And Melbourne Grammar, where the murderer alights?

That Hume was travelling to St Kilda late at night probably meant he was off to a swell party, such as he describes in the book, and in evening dress himself. Did he spend some hours socialising and networking before returning home to East Melbourne in another hansom, alone with his thoughts for the novel? He had the scene of the crime, and a victim, with the cabman up and behind, all unaware. But how might the killer get away without the cabman able to describe him later? Perhaps the killer could wear a hat with a wide-enough brim to conceal his face. What about the wide-awake? It turned up at the side but with the back and front of the brim down. All that might be seen of the face from above was the mouth and heavy moustache.

Did Hume then look down at his evening dress and laugh, as he realised the solution? That night in the ballroom the women had been distinctive and bright as parrots in their frocks—emerald brocade, cerulean satin, vieux rose mousseline de soie—the bread-and-butter for the social journalists jotting down dress details in their notebooks. In contrast the men were uniformly black and white in their penguin suits. He had witnessed cross-examinations where a uniform obliterated all other identifiers, the clothing more memorable than its wearer: 'A policeman came to the door…what? No, I don't recall anything else, he was just a policeman.' If the victim were similarly in evening dress, he also gained anonymity, creating suspense as to just who he was, as well as why and how he was murdered.

Hume never wrote anything like a how-to book of crime-writing. However, a letter he later sent from Italy to his publishers gives a rare insight into his methods:

> Dear Sir,
>
> I enclose a synopsis of The Fever of Life—that is as much synopsis as I can give at present. During the writing of a novel I often change the plot so I can say nothing about it

at present. New ideas, new characters constantly suggest themselves and I am guided as a rule by the natural filling out of the words throughout.

Under these circumstances the enclosed is all I can send but I think you will see from it that the tale will be strong & pathetic. Regarding this I think you can safely trust me as plots are my strong point. I have given you a sub-title but I hope it will not be used as I do not like sub-titles—they smack of the Minerva Press[130] & the belles lettres. If enclosed is not enough please write me and I will forward the plot—but I hope that you will find this sufficient.
Yours truly
Fergus Hume[131]

Having got his idea, Hume set about putting it on the page. How to begin could have been as simple as opening the morning paper the next day and observing the latest crime reportage. Good, he could start with Hingston's employer the *Argus*, a paper surely to be impressed at the mention, and by imitating the form of the crime report. Then would follow the inquest, Q and A, again as reported in the press, and next the reward offered, a very short chapter three. Only then does the action proper of the novel begin, with Hume's detective Gorby making his preliminary investigations. These introductory chapters are marked by strong narrative, sharp dialogue and a sense of the visual that suggests the theatre, as when Gorby addresses his reflection in the mirror. Their effect is to ensnare the reader, to keep them reading as Hume spins out the narrative, setting up his clues and red herrings.

When did Hume write? Most likely in the evenings and weekends, when not socialising with his boho mates or at the theatre. The specific date of the murder, the early morning of 27 July, might well be the date of Hume's original idea for the novel, given its self-referential games. From there he plotted a detailed 'skeleton' of his narrative—something very necessary with the whodunnit structure, where information is released gradually, in clues. He would claim in the preface that the outline took him two months of painstaking planning work.

He made some deliberate narrative choices. One obvious difference from Fortune and Gaboriau is that *Hansom Cab* does not have a single detective, with the investigating shared by policemen Gorby and Kilsip, lawyer Calton, and Brian the hero. Here Hume follows an old model of the crime novel, used by Sensation authors such as Braddon. It was slowly being superseded by the notion of a single detective as hero, as used by Poe with his Chevalier Dupin, by Fortune and Gaboriau, and later to gain dominance with Doyle's Sherlock Holmes.

If Hume had followed Gaboriau closely *Hansom Cab* might have been a police procedural. But the English novel, with its middle-class audience, privileged the gentleman hero. This 'snobbery with violence' worked against the reality of the working-class police detective. As a New Zealander Hume did not know about the Victorian police cadets, although one of their number, Hussey Malone Chomley, had risen to be Police Commissioner. He has his detectives lower-class and poorly educated: in the Fitzroy Gardens, the authorial voice of Hume knows the significance of the marble statuary, but Gorby is ignorant of classical mythology. Thus a young man only raised into the middle class by emigration claims superiority and denies his class origins.

The structure of his novel plotted, Hume then completed a first draft only to find, as he noted in the preface, he had 'not sufficiently well concealed the mystery upon which the whole interest of the book depended'. A perfectionist's eye was at work here. The novel went through at least another draft, which added an additional villain, for Hume's original murderer was too obvious a culprit. Hume also strove for credibility in his setting, conducting extensive research into seamy Melbourne.

At some point he shared his plot with pals. The *Bulletin* correspondent 'Boheme' recalled:

> One night, at a supper, Hume announced to a band of friends that he was writing a book. The announcement was received with good-natured derision, but Fergus, nothing abashed, proceeded to give a brief outline of the plot of the 'Hansom Cab' yarn. 'And,' he wound up, with his characteristic lisp, 'I'm going to put on the local colour with a spade.'
> He did too.

Hume's lisp is not mentioned elsewhere. It may have been merely a masher affectation.[132]

The reference to local colour shows Hume understood the importance of place to detective fiction, how the setting influenced the crime and in turn could make a narrative distinctive. Melbourne as he depicted it was a European city in the Antipodes, familiar yet exotic to overseas readers. For locals it was a self-validation, something important in the settler culture, with its perpetual sense of inferiority at the far end of Empire. He also noted a coming market trend in the book trade, away from the three-deckers, multi-volume novels of high Victoriana, to shorter narratives, more portable and cheaper in price.

Two different accounts by Hume state that he was ill and penniless while writing the novel, on which he blamed 'some very slippery writing'.[133] But after much time and effort, most likely by the end of 1885, the novel was finished to his satisfaction: he knew he had a good product. *Hansom Cab* had transcended Hume's initial impulse to write a commercial success. He had poured all his skill into the book, from his knowledge of the law to writing dramatic dialogue, and it showed. All he had to find was a publisher—surely a much easier task than getting his work on the Melbourne stage.

10

NOT WANTED
Booksellers, Readers & Publishers

Melbourne, 1886

'Do you ever read?' asked Miss Jaffray [...].
'Oh yes; society newspapers and French novels.'
'But they are so improper.'
'Nothing amusing is improper to my mind,' said Lady Jim,
calmly; 'and I really did skim through a page or two of Dickens.
Horribly dull, I thought him.'
'Oh!' Miss Jaffray gasped again. 'He did so much good.'
'Perhaps that is why his books are dull.'

LADY JIM OF CURZON STREET[134]

In the summer of 1885–6 the artist Tom Roberts, then young and unknown, stood on the balcony of Buckley and Nunn's Drapery and painted the streetscape to the west. In his *Bourke Street*, the light is white, intense; the street below a dusty, bustling vista of *Hansom Cab's* Melbourne. No trams yet, but horsepower aplenty. Drays deliver ice; shoppers sport parasols, postmen their red uniforms. *Allegro con brio*, Roberts originally called the painting, a musical term meaning to play briskly, with vitality—a good description both for boom-town Melbourne and *Hansom Cab*.

In *Bourke Street* a particularly relevant detail is the sign: BOOKSELLERS DUNN COLLINS. A 'leading Melbourne bookseller' recommended Gaboriau, but Hume does not state who it was. Two men could claim that title. The first was George Robertson (1825–1898), a canny but conventional Glaswegian resembling a bluff sea-captain. He was apprenticed to the book trade at the age of twelve, but saw opportunity in goldrush Victoria. Almost as soon as he disembarked in Melbourne he made money, opening a case of books on the wharfside and selling the lot. From that beginning he prospered, dominating the colonial book trade for more than thirty years.

The other leading bookseller's premises would have figured in Roberts' painting, had the easel been tilted differently. Opposite, in Bourke Street, was a major attraction of boom-town Melbourne: Cole's Book Arcade, with a bright rainbow painted on its facade. Edward Cole (1832–1918), an unsuccessful gold miner, began with a market bookstall and ended with an emporium. Though Cole was in appearance a typical Victorian patriarch, with a long grey beard like coarse clematis, he was in many ways Robertson's opposite: eccentric and freethinking, with innovative marketing nous. He even used his quest for a wife as publicity—which worked! Cole was a perfect example of successful (self-) advertising, a new dark art in the nineteenth century.

Arcades, those covered thoroughfares lined with small shops, were often found in cities of the nineteenth century. The Book Arcade differed in that it was devoted to one business, an entertainment centre—with the Coles living above it in an apartment, raising their family (six children to Robertson's fourteen) and conducting seances. This three-storey temple of the book eventually sprawled from Bourke to Collins Street, with the intervening Howey Place glassed-in, a fernery. The stock, new and second-hand, Cole claimed amounted to a million books. The Arcade also included refreshments, a band, bric-a-brac and even a menagerie. Customers were encouraged to stay and read for as long as they liked.

Cole and Robertson were at the top of their profession in Melbourne, competing in a very busy market. The 1885–6 Sands & McDougall's *Melbourne Directory* lists under Booksellers & Stationers 140 businesses. Some specialised: of the three women booksellers listed, two ran religious bookshops. Others diversified: Samuel Mullen (1828–1890) sold books in the Block, but his establishment operated primarily as a high-class lending library, at a guinea's annual membership. Mullen's Library is mentioned in *Hansom Cab*, although Hume is not exactly complimentary about the romance his heroine Madge Frettlby borrows. He did not expect his book to become part of Mullen's library stock, for they loaned only durable hardbacks and *Hansom Cab* was a paperback. Nonetheless Mullen's staff knew Hume, first as a customer, and then as an author.[135]

These suppliers met a great demand as for the first time a mass book market existed, due to compulsory education. The majority of the population had at least primary schooling: the 1881 census for Victoria showed the adult literacy rate was close to ninety per cent.[136] The printed word dominated, news coming from the papers, and information from the book. Reading was a virtuous activity, with the Bible or religious texts the most prestigious forms, followed by poetry. To read was edifying, as with children's primers or self-help manuals. It was linked to advancement, particularly in the socially mobile colonies. 'We was coming to better ourselves,' wrote immigrant Sarah Davenport, in a memoir with much gusto but little awareness of spelling or grammar.[137]

An engraving published in Melbourne *Punch*'s Almanac for 1887 shows scenes at the Public Library (now the State Library of Victoria). A boy reads travel and adventure, a bald man with glasses a volume of science. Another man in a top hat glares up theatrically from a book of drama, and a pale aesthete resembling Robert Louis Stevenson broods over poetry. The only woman pictured, young and demure, has the caption Fiction, a word often spoken scornfully.[138]

Reading for pleasure was regarded with some suspicion. Family fare, like Dickens, was permissible, a shared pleasure if read aloud around the hearth. William Pyke (1859–1933), Cole's first employee, recorded in his diary for 1882: 'Read a chapter of The Red Eric aloud to the family'—a popular novel by R. M. Ballantyne, best known for *The Coral Island*. Otherwise objections to novels ranged from their frivolity to their possible depravity. French novels in particular were morally dubious, because they were less prudish than their English counterparts. In *Hansom Cab* the victim's bookshelf includes Zola, of whom Detective Gorby comments: '…if his novels are as bad as his reputation I shouldn't care to read them.'[139]

Yet despite these anxieties, fiction was as huge as the crinoline skirt, with magazines such as the *Australian Journal* dedicated to it. Novels appeared in journals and newspapers in instalments, as they were written, prior to book publication. The era produced literary and popular classics: works by Dickens, George Eliot and the Brontës, but also *Dr Jekyll*, *Sweeney Todd* and *Dracula*. Once released, books found eager audiences across the globe. Reading matter travelled, and reading in transit became a habit, on ships and on the railways, which led to bookstalls at stations like W. H. Smith's in England. The Melbourne equivalent was W. M. Baird, at Spencer and Flinders Streets. The least Australasian railway station, whether city or country, had a kiosk selling supplies for the journey, including newspapers and cheap paperbound books. A term came into use: railway novels, similar to today's airport novels. Poet Andrew Lang wrote, in his 1884 'Ballade of Railway Novels': 'These twain have shortened many a mile, / Miss Braddon and Gaboriau.' He also mentions du Boisgobey. When Hume also cited these three authors in *Hansom Cab*, he was aiming at the railway novel market.

In the colonies book consumption differed from Britain, where the price of quality new novels—the hardbacks—was inflated, affordable only by the wealthy or the subscription libraries. From the 1860s publishers recognised that a smaller but very keen book market existed in the Empire, particularly in the seven Austral colonies. Thus the colonial edition was created, which provided the latest novels at a reduced rate to these distant booksellers, with the proviso that they had to buy in bulk. Australasia took one third of the colonial editions, far more than anywhere else. Its readers were by far the largest consumers of exported British books.[140]

In Hume's Melbourne, the ingredients existed to create a block-buster: a highly literate, book-loving population with disposable income, living in the centre of the Australasian book trade. Even in the 1860s it was reported that the local consumption of books was 'vast',[141] something only greater two decades on, with the increasing population.

But first Hume had to get his novel into print. In Dunedin, thanks to Uncle Marcus and his press connections, *Brankel* had been published as a serial. In Melbourne, nobody would look at it. Likely he had gained a reputation as a pushy pest, a nobody from Māori Land with pretensions to greatness. Still, with its Melbourne setting, he could be hopeful of serialisation for *Hansom Cab*.

A healthy market existed for fiction in Australian newspapers and periodicals. Much was imported, overseas reprints, as in the Melbourne *Once a Week* (from the publishers of the *Argus* and *Australasian*), which syndicated US pulp fiction, often crime, for threepence. Yet local writers including Rolf Boldrewood and Ada Cambridge gained a market. The *Australian Journal* had declared in 1871 that it would only publish original fiction with colonial settings and colonial interests. Proving their point, that year they serialised Marcus Clarke's *For the Term of His Natural Life*, though nothing subsequently had been so successful. However, the only response known to a *Hansom Cab* serialisation is that the editor of the *Australasian*, David Watterston, rejected the manuscript with 'scorn'.[142]

94

Much about Hume and his publishing history is about bypassing obstructions, like a game of career chess. No theatre exposure? Try writing a novel. No newspaper serialisation for *Brankel*, or subsequently for *Hansom Cab*? Then try the book publishers. That meant returning to the booksellers, because in Melbourne they were frequently the same, with publishing a smaller but not unprofitable sideline to their book and stationery trade. All that was needed was a printing press, portable information technology able to be loaded onto a cart and transported—to any new settlement or goldfield that could support newspaper advertising, or even on major steamships like the *Great Britain*, which produced its own ship's newspaper with contributions from the passengers.

Some 120 Printers & Publishers are listed in Sands & McDougall, mostly printers, handling everything from wedding invitations to auction listings. The category also included newspapers and magazines: the *Herald*, the *Argus* and the *Age* (all referred to in the Melbourne Trilogy), but also numerous local papers and magazines, from *Lorgnette* to the *Turf Register*. On this list were two British book publishers, colonial postings at the lucrative edge of Empire: Cassell and Ward Lock. Familiar names, to a keen young reader from Dunedin with his own manuscripts to sell. Fergus Hume would have jotted down the addresses and gone visiting.

However, his first call was undoubtedly on George Robertson, who has been termed the father of Australian publishing. Certainly Robertson was the first large-scale, systematic Australian publisher, setting up important links with the overseas trade, primarily importing, but also, on a smaller scale, selling colonial books back to the centre of Empire, where he maintained a London office. It has been claimed that the colonial edition was his idea. The Austral book trade felt the effect of his decisions, good and bad. Mullen had been Robertson's friend and employee; after they fell out Mullen established his own successful rival business. They were not on speaking terms, eschewing Christian forgiveness even when co-publishing a book of sermons.[143]

Robertson was similarly responsible for Cole. Here again he created a competitor, by rejecting his manuscript *The Real Place in History of Jesus and Paul*—a work of theology so unorthodox that Cole had to publish and sell it himself. Thereafter Cole maintained a small but heavily promoted list, mostly his own compilations such the famous *Cole's Funny Picture Book* for children.

Robertson's first publication came in 1855, three years after his arrival in Melbourne: a sermon preached at the Presbyterian synod in Geelong, by Reverend Macintosh Mackay, published at the synod's expense. From these humble beginnings Robertson would publish some six hundred works over a forty-year period: poetry, the first book publication of Clarke's *His Natural Life*, schoolbooks, textbooks, children's books, works on natural history, Australiana, editions of overseas bestsellers. Importing books was the major part of his business. He could thus wear the occasional publishing mishap, as when he lost £90, then a large amount, on poet Henry Kendall.

Publishing could be risky for authors—or even deadly. Clarson and Massina, the firm behind the *Australian Journal*, published Adam Lindsay Gordon's poetry. When he received their bill for his *Bush Ballads* (1870), he saw no prospect of paying it, and shot himself on Brighton beach. That fact was widely known, as Gordon's posthumous star rose higher, and became a source of embarrassment for these practical men of business. Their bill for Mary Fortune's one book the following year likely contributed to her homelessness. She found refuge in the Melbourne Immigrants' Home for the destitute and disreputable. The tragedy worsened when her teenage son George was arrested and committed to the Industrial (Reform) School, which sent him on a downwards path of crime.

Printing and publishing books in the colonies was difficult: production costs were high and there was the perennial problem of obtaining good quality paper (still an issue for Australian book publishers today). Douglas Sladen, a popular author and promoter of Australian writing, recollected in *My Long Life* (1939):

> It was almost impossible for an author to sell a book to a publisher. He had to bring it out at its own expense, in a cheap and ugly form, whatever the selling price was, and when it was published, if it had not a public waiting for it from a personal interest in the author, it never found a public.[144]

Here he referred to his personal experience with Robertson, publisher of his poetry collection *Australian Lyrics* (1883).

Author Ben Farjeon had typeset his own serialisations for the *Otago Daily Times*, but Hume lacked that useful ability. He began walking the streets like the hero of *When I Lived in Bohemia*, with his manuscript baby under his arm, going from publisher to publisher. *Brankel* had been written as a commercial proposition, sensational and popular. *Hansom Cab* was even more calculated to appeal to local tastes. But according to Hume's preface:

> Having completed the book, I tried to get it published, but every one to whom I offered it refused even to look at the manuscript on the ground that no Colonial could write anything worth reading. They gave no reason for this extraordinary opinion, but it was sufficient for them, and they laughed to scorn the idea that any good could come out of Nazareth—i.e., the Colonies.

This last remark was actually a cliché. The *Australian Journal* had commented in 1868 that it was 'until recently a received axiom, potent and undisputed'.[145] Certainly it represented the colonial cringe writ large. But if by 1868 it was questioned, by 1885 it was quite untrue. Writers living in and writing about Australia got published, earning critical and commercial approval. Clarke's *His Natural Life*, with its vivid convict-era setting, had been a successful book for Robertson in

Australia in 1875, and in London with the major publisher George
Bentley, three years later. The pair brought out a new joint edition
of the book in 1885 to accompany its dramatisation.

If Clarke was not sufficient example, consider the success of Ada
Cambridge and Rosa Praed. Cambridge lived in Victoria with her
vicar husband, contributing serials regularly to Australian papers, and
publishing two novels with Bentley in 1879 and 1882. Like Clarke,
she was English born, bred and educated, arriving in Australia as an
adult. Colonial origins, like Hume's, might have seemed a handicap,
but it did not affect Praed, who published her fifth and sixth novels
in 1885. She had lived in Queensland until she was twenty-five, then
migrated to England. Though living in London, she did not eschew
Australian settings in her work.

More detail on the initial publisher response to *Hansom Cab* is
provided at second hand. Hume had:

> offered it to all the Melbourne publishers without success;
> then to the New South Wales publishers, and they all refused
> it contemptuously. He personally appealed to the managing
> director of the biggest publishing company in the Australian
> colonies, who told him that even if he took the financial risk
> and published the work himself, his firm would not put
> their name to it…[146]

This managing director can only be Robertson, here refusing to
publish *Hansom Cab* even on commission, something that would now
be considered akin to vanity publishing. The author paid for initial
printing costs and the advertisements. If the book was a success, any
profits would be shared with the publisher. Jane Austen's first novel,
Sense and Sensibility, was published in this fashion. The alternative
model had the publisher buy the copyright, taking the risk, but also,
if the book sold well, all the profits. Such was the publishing fate of
Pride and Prejudice and Arthur Conan Doyle's *A Study in Scarlet*.

Robertson had views on what he wanted to publish. He was no fan of crime fiction, with not even the lucrative 'true crime' on his publishing list. When *His Natural Life* had been rewritten and condensed down to book version, its more Sensation genre aspects—the mystery structure of the serialisation—disappeared, at Robertson's request. Quite probably Robertson sent *Hansom Cab* to an influential figure he employed as reader: *Age* co-editor David Blair, who wrote for *Table Talk* and probably knew Hume. Blair was politically progressive but an orthodox Presbyterian; he might not have appreciated the rival *Argus* appearing in the opening sentence. In any case Robertson had the final say, rejecting the book on moral grounds: it is recorded that he objected to its 'coarse language' (no worse than 'God' and 'damn') and 'scenes of low life'. So might well have James Hume, also a clever but conventional businessman, with the same Glaswegian accent. The similarities between father and publisher were probably a little too close for Fergus's comfort.[147]

The account cited above continues, apparently with the same speaker: 'that it was no use offering a book to the Australian public that had not previously been submitted to the judgment of the English trade; that it was a colonial work written by a colonial and therefore was not worth putting a penny into.' These words were not those of Robertson, who had successfully sold *His Natural Life* to the British market. He was, in his limited, respectable fashion, committed to colonial writing. In 1854 he had written to the *Argus* that: 'Although a man of trade, I take a deep interest in the literary and social progress of this colony.' If he had helped to make 'good books more plentiful and cheaper', then he had done good 'and put money into my purse'. Commerce and virtue here met: a common attitude in Hume's Melbourne. And it was Robertson who considered himself arbiter of what was good.[148]

The account would therefore appear to be a conflation, in its first part quoting Robertson, but in the second the condescending tones of the overseas publishers' representatives in Melbourne, Ward Lock or

Cassell. At this time their major focus was on importing their colonial editions, authors like Praed whose commercial worth had been tried and proved in the home market. The firm Collins also had an office, in Sydney, but their response would have been similar. To read the English readers' reports on Australian manuscripts of the time is to see colonial cringe being imposed from above. Rudeness is one of the few perks of the job, but what is said shows that colonial manuscripts were regarded as inferior, along the lines of expressions like 'colonial manners' (that is, no manners).

On Henry Lawson's *In the Days When the World Was Wide*:

> Mr Lawson is a third-rate Mr Paterson, and Mr Paterson was not quite a first-rate poet. The latter did occasionally show some faint perception of the proper business of poetry, Mr Lawson never shows any. His ideas have been the common property of all Australian writers since Gordon; his execution is a bad imitation of Kipling at his slangiest and vulgarest roots. This sort of stuff is no great thing at its very best; and in Mr Lawson you have it, I should say, at its very worst. These rhyming kangaroos are becoming a nuisance.[149]

A third source on this dispiriting period of Hume's life cites colonial book economics for the rejection: 'A Melbourne firm of first rank declared that if Mr. Hume published it at his own risk, which he might do, they would not be able to dispose of 500 copies in twelve months.'[150] Here again Robertson is the likely speaker, with sound business sense—which in the event proved overly pessimistic.

Hume's weary travels from publisher to publisher lasted, he claimed, six months.[151] That length of time indicates that, despite his words in the preface, the manuscript was being read, not rejected unseen. He undoubtedly approached Cole, who might have been sympathetic, but up to that time had published no original fiction. The *Australian Journal* did publish crime-fiction books, but they had passed on *His Natural Life* (Clarke being too much of a handful) and their edition of Fortune's stories had not been successful. Small firm W. S. Inglis, primarily a bookseller and printer, produced a magazine, *Once a Month*, with serials by local and imported authors, as well as visitors like the fiery Francis Adams. His book *Australian Essays* they published in May 1886—but shortly afterwards the magazine folded due to lack of subscriptions, and the publishing part of the firm went into receivership.

Did Hume try overseas publication, as he had with his poems? A tantalising hint is provided in the dedication to the first edition of *Hansom Cab*, to: 'James Payne, novelist—his kind encouragement of the author.' James Payn was an influential man, a Sensation novelist and editor of the prestigious *Cornhill Magazine* from 1883–1896. Payn is also cited in the opening chapter, along with Gaboreau (Gaboriau). Both names were misspelt.

In the annals of detective fiction, Payn is famous for publishing Arthur Conan Doyle's early fictions. To have gained such a dedication he must have seen Hume's writing, in the context of rejecting it gently. At this stage of their early careers, Doyle and Hume were competing for the same English markets, with mixed success. Did Payn see and reject *Brankel*, which seems most likely? Did Payn also have time to be sent *Hansom Cab*, then read and reject it before its eventual publication in late October 1886? If *Hansom Cab* was completed by late 1885, or early 1886, it certainly seems possible, given the speed of the mail steamers. If so, then Payn passed on the two hottest properties in contemporary crime fiction, for he also rejected Doyle's first Sherlock Holmes tale, *A Study in Scarlet*.

The major reason for Doyle's rejection—as far as could be ascertained, for Payn's handwriting was nigh illegible—was length. As a novelette the text was too long for a single issue but too short for serialisation. Payn also used the words 'shilling dreadful', which could indicate he felt the crime subject matter was not suitable for the

Cornhill. But otherwise Payn encouraged Doyle's writing, as he did Hume's. If he saw *Brankel*, it was likely refused for the same reasons as the debut Holmes, for it too was short—eighty-seven pages in book form. If he also thought *Hansom Cab* was better suited to the shilling-shocker format, then he would be proved spectacularly correct.[152]

Hume can be pictured collecting his manuscript yet again, trudging the Melbourne streets disconsolately back to his rented home, his siblings and his Bohemian friends. He was now in his second year in Melbourne, with no headway either in the theatre or the press, the novel he had intended to remedy this situation repeatedly rejected by publishers. Did he turn his head at the common sound of a printing press at work with a sudden wild surmise: that he could do it himself? In his preface he wrote: 'The story thus being boycotted on all hands, I determined to publish it myself.'

Unfortunately, that part of the tale was quite untrue.

11

ACROSS THE FOOTLIGHTS III

Autumn—Winter, 1886

One night they would play farcical comedy; then Hamlet,
reduced to four acts by Mr Wopples, would follow on the
second night; the next night burlesque would reign supreme;
and when the curtain arose on the fourth night Mr Wopples
and the star artistes would be acting melodrama, and throw
one another off bridges and do strong starvation business with
ragged clothes amid paper snowstorms.

MADAME MIDAS[153]

In 1886 Hume's fortunes began to improve. A clairvoyant predicted it, reading his cards:

> A great change is shortly going to take place in your life. You
> will suddenly become famous in Australia. Why, I cannot
> exactly tell you, but it will be through something you do in
> art and literature. Then you will go to England, and you will
> find not only England, but all the world talking about you.

The prophecy amused Hume, a wry smile under his moustache, for just then his fame looked 'particularly unattainable'.[154] He could not even sell *Hansom Cab*, the vehicle intended to attract interest for his playwriting. Yet unexpectedly in the autumn his busy theatre networking started to pay off. Hume achieved a small but significant entree into the Australian drama scene. A friend from Dunedin days, the actress Amy Horton (Prince Masher in his *Dynamite*), had formed her own burlesque company, and offered him work.

Hume omitted Horton from his 1892 preface to *Hansom Cab*, in which he claimed Australian theatre had scorned him. It did not suit his narrative. For her he wrote localisations, in which an imported play would have topical references added to the place of performance. It was hack work, but required skill and wit, and was a source of income for colonial playwrights.

How did it work? Consider a modern localisation of, say, W. S. Gilbert's 1873 burlesque *Happy Land*, in which three politicians find themselves in Fairyland. In England, the trio would be versions of David Cameron, Nick Clegg and Boris Johnson. Not all the jokes would be intelligible to an Australian audience, so the localisation would substitute the original characters with Tony Abbott, Clive Palmer and Bill Shorten. In 1880 *Happy Land* was localised in Melbourne by Marcus Clarke, as part of his perennial search for literary income. He did it with too much enthusiasm and the Victorian government, facing an election, considered themselves libelled. They banned the play.

Localisations were usually innocent good fun and Hume—who, unlike Clarke, was a spiritual thinker rather than merry trouble-maker—was in no danger of legal proceedings. For *Hansom Cab* Hume had studied Melbourne intently, and knew the local colour. His two localisations were *Little Don Giovanni: or, the Maid, the Masher and the Marble Man*, by English playwright Henry James Byron (who contributed Widow Twankey and Buttons to pantomime), and Ben Farjeon's burlesque *Dr Faustus*, rendered as *Faust, MD* in *Madame Midas* and *Faust Upset* in *Miss Mephistopheles*. Again, Hume emphasised the leading lady, with Amy Horton playing the title trouser roles. Both plays debuted in April-May at St George's Hall, in Bourke

Street, a venue that might be 'small cheese', with its eight hundred seats, 'but important'.[155]

April was also the month when Hume made another theatrical coup, in befriending influential British actor Philip Beck. Like Hume, Beck (b. 1855) can be found in the 1861 census, at St Leonards-on-Sea, Sussex. His origins were similarly humble: his widowed mother ran the family baking business. From the age of eighteen he worked as a professional actor, first in the provinces, then London and internationally, touring and playing with stars like Ellen Terry.

Beck was physically slight, but of great dramatic presence. He was strikingly handsome and charismatic, with a thick moustache and a smouldering gaze. He also had a beautifully modulated voice, 'in the very front rank of modern elocutionists' and a prodigious memory, with the ability to recite chapters of Dickens or whole plays by heart.[156] Although versatile, leading-man material, his real forte was the melodramatic villain. The baker's son had a dark side, expressed on and, as Hume would discover, off stage. His life seemed charmed: in 1879 he toured North America, surviving two railway accidents and a fatal fire in Toronto. He was universally liked, an entrepreneurial man with sporting and literary interests. But he also suffered from ill health, which brought to an end his management of the Olympic Theatre in London.[157] Underneath the attractive, suave facade, Beck lived with chronic pain, neuralgia.

Medical advice to seek a warmer climate seems to be the reason Beck travelled to Australia, but he was already intrigued by its emergent literature. At an 1884 dinner held at London's Bohemian Savage Club for the touring Australian cricket team, Beck recited Australian poetry. The *Age*'s cricket writer responded with Adam Lindsay Gordon's horsy ballad 'How We Beat the Favourite'. Beck learned that poem too. The following year, he attended another evening of Australian readings, complete with eucalyptus saplings.[158]

Beck arrived in Melbourne at the beginning of April 1886, intending to perform Shakespeare in one-man shows. His advent was heralded in the colonial newspapers—he was handsome, accomplished, a rising star. Hume, as he had in Dunedin, would have sought Beck out, hopeful of selling his plays and earning that elusive overseas cachet. But J. C. Williamson, whom Hume had so far failed to impress, got there first. The Triumvirate made Beck an unrefusable offer, signing him up for interstate productions starting with the plum role of the Demon in *The Crimes of Paris*. Work for Williamson would keep Beck out of Melbourne for most of the remaining theatrical year.[159] Hume had only a few days before the actor took the Sydney train, but it was enough to establish—at the least—a friendship that would blossom into a literary collaboration. It would also have a profound, though murky, influence upon *Hansom Cab*.

Beck's precise relationship to the book depends on the dating of an anecdote that was related to an English journalist and saw print only in the next century. It mutated in transmission and is clearly unreliable—although most intriguing. The title under which it appeared was 'The Romance of Fergus Hume', which did not necessarily refer to a love affair: the story was a melodrama in reality complete with victim and moustache-twirling villain.[160]

It began:

> In a poor room in Melbourne, alone, and without a shilling in the world, lay Fergus Hume, journalist for the time being and author to be, fighting a raging fever, and getting considerably the worst of the encounter. For many months previous to this the young fellow had been working night and day at a melodramatic story of multitudinous chapters, so that when illness overtook him delirium very soon followed, and became an unpleasant competitor to reckon with. And thus he lay, unconscious at one moment and conscious at another, but never, when conscious, less troubled of mind, because in this state he could realise the weight of the debt

which his illness was packing on his shoulders, and knew the anxiety of owing a none too lenient landlord three or four weeks' rent.

This opening paragraph contains definitely two factual errors. The first is that Hume was hardly alone in Melbourne—Mary and later James Hume Jr lived with him. An exaggeration here, to emphasise his dire straits? If Hume's siblings were at work, however, then he could have been alone in bed when a visitor was shown in by the equivalent of *Hansom Cab*'s Mrs Hableton or Mrs Sampson. Secondly, Hume was a solicitor's clerk, not a journalist, apart from his small work for *Table Talk*. But certainly, by his own account, during the writing of *Hansom Cab* he was not only short of money but also unwell.[161] At the worst he might have been sacked, because of his illness, and for being too busy with the theatre and his novel. Unemployment benefits were then a futuristic fancy—he could easily have been in debt and in fear of eviction.

The account continues:

It was during one of these painful intervals of consciousness that a friend called to see him—an actor from the Bohemia in which the young writer had spent many nights, much money, and, perhaps, not a little health. Seeing how badly it went with him, and hearing how badly it went with his pocket, the actor generously (as it seemed at the time) offered to see Fergus Hume through his trouble so far as were concerned the settlement of immediate debts and the supply of so much a week until the sufferer should feel strong enough to resume work. A delirium of incoherent but unmistakable gratitude broke from Fergus Hume's lips—a delirium checked on the part of his companion by a cold recital of 'conditions'.

The good Samaritan demanded a price. Hume had something he wanted. In this narrative it was *Hansom Cab*, 'loaded with the possibility of fortunes' even when unfinished. The deal was that Hume complete *Hansom Cab* and share its profits. Furthermore: 'the actor was to go half shares—in profits, not in work—in all books and plays written subsequently to the novel in question—was, in fact, to be half owner until death on either side should cancel the matter of the author's brains.' If Fergus Hume happened to die, then the unfinished novel became the property of the actor, to 'deal with it as he liked'.

A contract was allegedly signed between the pair—incredible given that Hume was a qualified lawyer, however poor and delirious at the time. And after 'some weeks Fergus Hume—thanks, it will be admitted, to the careful attention of the actor—pulled round; and in course of time—and not a very long time either—the novel was finished, published, and circulated'.

Was the story true? Mistakes can be found in it, as noted, but when it appeared in print readers were able to recognise the actor as Philip Beck, though described as Australian rather than English. Significantly Hume is not known to have denied the story: there is something to it, even if it is not wholly accurate. But the major problem is that Beck's arrival in Australia in early April 1886 meant he had only six months to befriend Hume and play a sinister role in the birth of *Hansom Cab*. For almost all of that time he was acting in Sydney (April and July to September) or Adelaide (May to June).

Beck would not make his first appearance on the Melbourne stage until 18 September. It was hardly enough time for Hume to recover from illness and finish the book before it went to the press in the next month.[162] In any case, other accounts have *Hansom Cab* completed and going from publisher to publisher for months, suggesting completion well before Beck's arrival on the scene.

The likely scenario is that Hume, selling himself and his work to Beck, gave the actor a favourable description of the book on their first meeting in Melbourne. Beck was already interested in Australian writing and only a few months later would play the leading role of Rufus Dawes in the first Sydney dramatisation of *His Natural Life*, strutting the boards in chains and the broad arrow.[163]

It is likely that Hume visited Beck interstate, witnessing his triumphs as well as trying to sell *Hansom Cab* to Sydney publishers. Otherwise they only met when Beck passed through Melbourne on the way to his Adelaide and Sydney commitments. Apart from that, they no doubt corresponded, with Hume able to report information sure to heighten Beck's interest: that in June Amy Horton had reprised his adaptations in Brisbane, again with good reviews, and that he was writing a play for the tragedian George Rignold, also to be produced in Brisbane.[164] Rignold at the time was touring New Zealand, where Hume's name would have cropped up repeatedly, particularly in the South. Did Rignold wonder if he had underestimated the pushy young man with his scripts? If Hume had a following in Māori Land, then why not ask him to write something, see what he could do?

In this context the sickbed contract can be reinterpreted. Most likely it happened in the Melbourne winter, just as Hume's theatrical stars were rising, but also a season for major illness. Hume, if not actually delirious, was certainly very sick. Beck may not have mopped Hume's fevered brow with his monogrammed handkerchief, but he certainly overwhelmed the sick man with kindness and his dangerous charm. He was at the height of his profession, and working for Williamson's, Hume's theatrical desideratum. Small wonder that under that magnetic gaze a starstruck, physically weakened Hume was persuaded into artistic idiocy.

While nothing sexual occurred—at least on this occasion—a seduction took place. What passed between the two would be described as Hume selling 'himself to the Devil', a Faustian bargain, or at least to a stage villain.[165] Beck helped Hume, paying his debts and providing a per diem until he recovered, but being a man of sharp theatrical business he demanded his price. *Hansom Cab* would work well on the stage, that was obvious, but it was not quite what Beck wanted.[166] The best parts for him were melodramatic villains, centre-stage roles that suited his dark edge. As the Demon he was 'so thorough-paced a villain that a large section of the audience called him before the curtain to hoot at him'.[167]

Beck would have wanted a dedicated playwright all to himself, not one shared with the far more powerful Rignold, with his own companies and theatre leases. Rignold's interest in Hume seems a catalyst for the extraordinary deal, Beck responding jealously and opportunistically. Beck played real-life cad with Hume. Clearly something on paper was signed. A newspaper report stated that Beck: 'had at one time a remarkably advantageous partnership with Hume, who had, indeed, ultimately to pay a stiffish sum to get out of it'. They certainly collaborated on plays and one published poem, 'A Centennial Song'. Nothing suggests that Beck and Hume wrote novels together, though Beck most likely had first refusal on Hume's theatrical dramatisations.[168]

Beck enjoyed success, but in a notoriously uncertain profession. He was in funds from the Williamson work so could have supported Hume, paying off the landlady and other debtors, while Hume recovered. However, the evidence would suggest that *Hansom Cab* was completed well before the sickbed contract. Thus Beck could not have financed the book's last stages of writing. But did the account, garbled in transmission, actually refer to him financing something else?

Like the publication of *Hansom Cab*?

12

THE MASTERMIND
Frederick Trischler

'If ye ken the Screepture ye'll see God helps those wha help
themselves.'
  'That means you do all the work and give God the credit,'
retorted Gaston, with a sneer; 'I know all about that.'

MADAME MIDAS[169]

Philip Beck rescued Hume at a low point in his fortunes. But the
publisher who saved *Hansom Cab* from oblivion was another player
entirely, a young man named Frederick Alfred Sheppard Trischler.
He was irrepressible, in even more of a hurry than Hume. Freddie,
or 'Little Trischler', as he was called, inspired affection. A photograph
of the time shows him handsome, with fair curling hair parted in the
centre, a fashionable drooping moustache and a polka-dot tie. His eyes
are small and pale, deep set, his gaze singularly direct. There is a sense
of suppressed energy, a dynamo at rest. One newspaper described him
as Hume's 'good angel'. Another source called him an 'energetic little
devil'. Angel and devil—to Hume he would be both.[170]

Trischler's story is complex, incomplete and not helped by him
being an even more unreliable witness than Hume. Variously he
would claim to be a 'Melbourne man', an 'Old Australian' and to

have been a friend, even schoolfriend, of Hume in Dunedin. These claims are quite wilful, for Trischler was, if anything, a Londoner. In disowning his history he gained the freedom of a colonial: to be go-ahead, pushy, unconventional, and even unmannerly in the production and promotion of his books.[171]

Like Hume and Beck, Trischler appears as a small boy (b. 1856) in the 1861 English census. His mother, Anne Ellen Trischler, was the widow of a commercial traveller and 'gentleman'. The name Trischler is German, but the family were English. Anne is said to have been presented at the court of Queen Victoria, but in the census she lived in a Regent's Park apartment, with lower-middle-class artisans as neighbours.[172] Anne and her three children lived off 'interest of money and MS copying'.

If Frederick Trischler sought adventure and travel he found it in the Merchant Marine, qualifying as a second mate in 1875. Crossing the Atlantic to New York he took a guided tour around the house of the millionaire Vanderbilts. He was impressed and inspired—he too could be a venturesome capitalist![173] He left the sea for business, choosing Christchurch, New Zealand as his landfall. His mother and sister Nora followed in 1878, with elder brother Walter working his passage as a deckhand. A family story recalls that en route the Trischler women refused to acknowledge Walter, being touchy about their status.

In Christchurch in 1879, Frederick married (Sophia) Lucy Dunsford, of a military family from New South Wales. His occupation was given as accountant. The celebrant was Henry Crocker Marriott Watson, who that year would publish a utopia, *Erchomenon*, with a London publisher. Trischler distinguished himself in the Canterbury Rowing Club and became a grain broker before going bankrupt, owing about £1000. Most likely Hume never knew this aspect of Trischler's past.[174]

Trischler flitted between Melbourne and New Zealand, seeking opportunity. In 1881 Nora Trischler also married, to George Henry Merton, Headmaster of Cathedral Grammar, an elite private primary school. Frederick, a witness, was described as a commercial broker, of Melbourne. His eldest son (Frederick) John was born late that year, in Christchurch. By October Trischler had found work as a commercial traveller in cigars. The next month he and his wife visited Dunedin, which may be where they first met Hume.[175]

Such was not the typical background for a publisher, but it showed flexibility, enterprise and a fondness for risk—which often landed Frederick in the mire, but just as often not. Trischler and his young family sailed in 1882 for Melbourne again, where another son was born in late 1883: Henry Inglis Rosslyn Trischler. The second name comes from W. S. Inglis & Co, the Melbourne publisher, who were Trischler's employers. In 1885 the firm had seventy employees, a printing plant and lithography works, and was publishing a small but select list, including the magazine *Once a Month*. Though a small operation, Inglis had a partnership with a London publisher. Trischler worked as their advertising canvasser.[176]

Due to his merchant seaman's card, Trischler was highly mobile. His next move was across the Pacific, where he would claim American experience with Bancroft's, based in San Francisco, which he described as 'the biggest publishing firm on the Pacific slope'.[177] Their specialty was legal and reference works, but in America Trischler would have been exposed to dime novels, a hugely successful publishing model— small, cheaply produced books with huge print runs. Dime novels had begun with anything that would sell: self-help books, cookery, action-melodramas and anti-slavery novels. In the 1880s dime fiction became dominated by crime, with popular series detectives such as Old Sleuth. If Vizetelly's shilling editions of Gaboriau were one model for *Hansom Cab*, the dime novels were another.

Trischler also had some literary or journalistic aspirations. An 'F. T.' published travel articles in *Once a Month*, between February and

May 1886. Trischler seems the most likely writer, given the subjects included San Francisco and, ominously, its fire brigades. In April Bancroft's premises burnt down, with losses of half a million dollars. The catastrophe sent Trischler back across the Pacific, to Melbourne again.

Trischler would claim his American experience had been followed by managing in Australia 'a large business for the Californian firm with which I was connected. But the business could not be made to pay.'[178] No evidence exists that Bancroft's operated in Australia. The business that could not be made to pay—and which it is unlikely that Trischler managed—was Inglis. Overestimating the Australian market they found themselves in serious financial trouble by mid-1886 and became insolvent, their assets sold.

Trischler found himself unemployed again, at a loose end until he saw the possibilities in *Hansom Cab*.[179] Stories of how he discovered the manuscript vary: either by accident; via a mutual friend; or through encountering his 'old chum' Hume, unpublished and despondent. The friend could have been Inglis author James Hingston; certainly Inglis would have been among the publishers who saw and rejected *Hansom Cab*. In Hume's own words, to an interviewer: 'Mr. Trischler, who was connected with a publishing firm in Melbourne, took a fancy to the story and undertook to arrange for its publication.'[180] In using the word 'connected', as Trischler also did, Hume was being deliberately vague, for an advertising canvasser was hardly an acquisitions editor.

Trischler said himself that he had a notion of starting his own publishing business, something for which he needed commercial manuscripts. He knew he had struck gold immediately with *Hansom Cab*: 'I commenced that MS. about eight o'clock one evening, and could not put it down until I had finished it about seven the next morning. I decided there and then to publish it.'[181]

Trischler would have seen a precedent. Hugh Conway's mystery novella *Called Back*, which had been rejected by the major English publishers, became a runaway bestseller when published by the small Bristol press Arrowsmith for the Christmas market, in 1883. Despite its unpromising premise—the hero is temporarily blind, the heroine temporarily amnesiac—it achieved sales totalling 300,000. Trischler's operation would be tiny, probably little more than him and Hume, but he could see his way to becoming an antipodean Arrowsmith.

If the business ideal was Arrowsmith, then the model for publishing the book could be found in the success of the Old Sleuth dime novels, Vizetelly's Gaboriau series and most recently Robert Louis Stevenson's *Dr Jekyll and Mr Hyde*, published in January 1886 in America and Britain. These were all small, paperbound books, cheaply sold: the Gaboriau books and *Dr Jekyll* had a recommended retail price of one shilling, five dollars in today's money. The 'shilling shocker' was an established market niche, the penny dreadful with inflation.

What was the deal between Trischler and Hume? A friend would report that Hume had been 'disgusted with all the worry and trouble he had had' over *Hansom Cab* and glad of anything that would get the book out.[182] The most likely model for their business arrangement was a hybrid commission form, with the pair agreeing to split profits, should the book sell any copies at all. The copyright did not at that stage figure as significant to either man, so speculative was the venture. Trischler would later be asked directly by a journalist whether he bought copyrights or published on commission. He did not answer directly, but responded by trumpeting his use of royalties:

> Every author whose work we publish shares in our success,
> and is paid a royalty on every copy of the book that we sell.
> I learned my business in America, where we are not in the
> habit of grinding people down for the sake of making a lot
> of money out of their literary abilities; and I don't propose

to do it here. Every author shares *pro rata* in our success.[183] Bob Sessions, former publisher with Penguin Australia, opines that Trischler probably paid a ten per cent royalty, a good rate for the time. But as regards *Hansom Cab* in Australia, nothing is known for certain.

Hume and Trischler chose the printing firm of Kemp & Boyce, who had never done anything remotely like a crime novel before, but were willing to try.

At Inglis, Trischler had solicited advertisements. He could by such means raise revenue for *Hansom Cab*, but not all that they needed. None of those involved had much capital. How Trischler supported his small family after the failure of Inglis is unknown, but he must have had some form of employment, not well remunerated. His mother died in England in January 1886 and it is possible he had a legacy. However, a family story has it that the Trischler brothers had an inheritance, which Frederick invested in South African diamond mines and lost the lot.

Hume had been bailed out by Beck not long before. His family would have been of little financial help. And money was badly needed, a large sum, since Trischler proposed an ambitious and expensive print run unprecedented for a novel, let alone a first novel, in Australia.

13

MADAME MIDAS

*All at once matters changed; she made a lucky speculation on
the share market and the Pactoclus claim began to pay.*

MADAME MIDAS[184]

If there is one issue about *Hansom Cab* divisive for experts on the
Australian book trade and its history it is the size of the novel's first
print run. Hume claimed in his preface that 'an edition of, I think, some
five thousand copies was brought out at my own cost'. That his account
is dubious is indicated by the telling phrase 'I think', for a self-publisher
would surely recall how much he printed. In contrast Trischler had no
doubts about the figure, putting it definitely at five thousand copies.

Even now, with a bigger population but far more competition for
readers' attention, an initial print run of five thousand copies is large
for an Australian novel. For 1886 the size seems improbable, huge and
daring. John Loder, collector and bibliographer of Australian crime
fiction, regards the figure as vastly inflated: 'Just seems nonsense.'
Jeff Prentice, formerly with Angus & Robertson publishing and a
researcher of Australian book history, agrees: 'I don't believe a word
of it.'

The publisher that told Hume they would not be able to dispose of five hundred copies in twelve months was only being realistic, especially with a new, unknown novelist. Trischler himself noted that most colonial editions were of five hundred to one thousand books, two thousand being considered a very large number. Prentice considers the local print runs to have been much smaller, around a hundred copies, of which only a small proportion would have been bound. The majority would have been warehoused as unbound sheets, to be bound should the need arise, an early version of print on demand. Even in the 1920s, the average impression of an Angus & Robertson book was one thousand copies.[185]

Others, usually publishers, see no problem with the figure of five thousand copies. Henry Rosenbloom of Scribe, a highly efficient Melbourne small publisher, comments: 'I'm sure it was true.' Rosenbloom cites his 2003 publication of *Shantaram* by Gregory David Roberts, which had an initial hardback print run of twenty thousand and sold out in a week. It would eventually sell around forty thousand hardbacks and then over ninety thousand paperbacks before the author took the rights back.

Everyone agrees that certain lucky books take off like rockets. 'When you get a phenomenon,' says Bob Sessions, 'it runs and runs and runs.' *Shantaram* is one example; another, close to Hume's time and certainly in recent publishing memory, was *Cole's Funny Picture Book*. It appeared in 1878, a scissors-and-paste compilation of verses, puzzles, games and pictures. Cole had aimed for the highest production values for a retail cost of one shilling: the same price and principle as Vizetelly. Extraordinary sales figures were claimed by Cole for the book with as many as 600,000 copies said to have been printed, though this figure is disputed by Jeff Prentice and others.

If the print run for the first edition of *Hansom Cab* were truly five thousand copies, and not simply an example of braggadocio, what sort of costs would have been involved? Unfortunately Kemp & Boyce's records have not survived, nor have those for Inglis and George

Robertson. Neither has the English equivalent, Vizetelly—and in any case the economics of publishing were different, production being more expensive in the colonies.

Some information survives about the economics of nineteenth-century Australian publishing. In 1870, when Adam Lindsay Gordon shot himself, he owed between £50 and £70 for the printing costs of his two books of poetry.[186] The most detailed records start in the 1890s, from Sydney's Angus & Robertson (also a George, but no relation to the Robertson of Melbourne). Examining A&R's ledgers shows their first editions tended to have smaller print runs than *Hansom Cab*, and sold at a higher price. Banjo Paterson's *The Man from Snowy River, and Other Verses* (1895) had a print run of 1250 copies, which proved overcautious: two thousand more copies had to be printed, which sold rapidly despite a retail price of 5/-. In 1896 the print run for Henry Lawson's first book of stories, *While the Billy Boils*, was three thousand copies, also at 5/-, of which nineteen hundred sold in the first fortnight. One month after publication two thousand more copies were printed.[187]

Nothing in A&R's early records parallels a five thousand copy print run to be sold at 1/-. The closest is Louise Mack's *Teens* (1897), which did have a print run of five thousand, though with higher price and production values. A&R's first attempt at the burgeoning young-reader market, *Teens* was aimed at girls, with bound covers and illustrations by George Lambert. The A&R ledgers show production costs were over £600.[188] *Hansom Cab*'s printing would not have cost as much, but a three-figure sum can be posited. Hundreds of pounds, in contemporary money, was more like our thousands. *Hansom Cab* was not of the same quality as *Teens*, but it was not a cheap publication, either, with production values above the pulp.

Just who paid for the printing? Trischler, when 'booming' himself as a publishing entrepreneur several years later, would claim to have published at his own financial risk.[189] In the preface, Hume said *he* did, but that was after he had quarrelled with Trischler and wrote him, like much else, out of his personal history. If five thousand copies really were printed, then that was a huge gamble, and something that neither Hume nor Trischler could have afforded. Philip Beck was in work and could have contributed, but acting was a notoriously unreliable profession.

Hume did know another 'good angel', one of the most extra-ordinary women of the era. Alice Cornwell (b. 1852) had consoled herself after a marital breakdown by gaining a practical knowledge of geology. She preferred to be an independent woman of business, prospecting for gold in Ballarat, than an unhappy wife. Her self-confidence is shown by the name of her enterprise: the Midas Company. Hume was her 'sincere friend', describing her as 'the first Victorian lady miner'.[190] A photograph from around the time the two knew each other shows a young woman apparently conventional and feminine from the chin down, tightly corseted in a dark gown trimmed with fine lace, wearing on her high collar a brooch in the form of a dog. But her hair is short, almost mannish, and she wears no earrings. The chin is determined, and she gazes into the camera as if staring it down. Hume knew women who were tough, like his mother and Aunt Janet, matrons of the madhouse, and talented, like his sisters and actress friends. Alice Cornwell combined both, in a formidable package.

Like the Hume family, the Cornwells had found social mobility through immigration to Dunedin. Father George left his work as a railway guard behind and reinvented himself as a prominent builder and entrepreneur. Alice was of similar age to Mary and Bessie Hume, and also highly musical—she thought it her major talent. The link between Alice Cornwell and Fergus Hume thus likely began with music, and in Dunedin.[191]

The Cornwells moved to Melbourne for building projects from the railways to Parliament House. Alice married young, in 1875, to John

Whiteman, more than thirty years her senior, a Melbourne publican and politician with a blacksmithing background. He also had a predilection for poetry: George Robertson published his *Sparks and Sounds from a Colonial Anvil* in 1873. A son was born, but the couple stormily separated, Alice reverting to her maiden name. In an incident of 1882 Whiteman harassed his wife, invading her father's hotel and refusing to leave without her—George Cornwell called the police, and charged his son-in-law with trespass and assault.[192]

Alice Cornwell liked men of letters—besides her two husbands and Hume, it is claimed that she wanted to be a patron to the young Henry Lawson.[193] She would certainly have looked favourably on the publication of a novel by a friend, but probably not to the extent of paying for a print run of five thousand copies. Although she was confident of her Ballarat mine, great riches had yet to eventuate. But there were other forms of assistance. As the *Bulletin* correspondent 'Cobbler' noted: 'Thanks, however, to fortunate share specs. on advice received from Miss Cornwell (the woman financier—Madame Midas of his novel) he was enabled to publish the work.'

Hume would tell an interviewer his Melbourne days were spent 'between Literature, the law, and the Stock Market'. He possibly made an allusion there, for the journalist to whom he spoke worked for the *Sunday Times* (a paper that Alice Cornwell had bought). Otherwise Hume is not known to have speculated. Trischler did, and later became a stockbroker. The opening chapters of the novel Hume wrote about Cornwell, *Madame Midas*, certainly show the heroine playing the stock market successfully—and earning her nickname. Given her mining knowledge, she could have told Hume which shares to buy. One good investment would have been the Broken Hill Proprietary Company Limited, that new company being floated successfully in 1885, the same year as Cornwell's Midas mining venture.[194]

Later in *Madame Midas* villain Gaston Vandeloup makes a share killing after eavesdropping on two stockbrokers. They have a scam, depicted knowledgeably: inside information on a goldmine withheld, until the shares have been bought up cheaply. Once the riches are revealed the share price rises, with a rush on the shares—which are then sold at a high profit by the insider-traders. The auctorial voice otherwise expresses disapproval of the share market, with the Great Humbug Gold Mining Company, 'which influential men are floating in a kind of semi-philanthropic manner to benefit mankind at large, and themselves in particular'.[195] It does not suggest a successful share trader, rather the reverse. But was Hume simply desperate to get *Hansom Cab* into print, enough to forget his scruples?

Trischler had the most business experience and was by nature a risk-taker. He would have been the one most likely to have actually dealt with the share market, buying low and selling high. As these profits were specifically intended for *Hansom Cab*, Hume could claim with some justification in the preface that the book had been brought out 'at my own cost'. Trischler then took the financial risk of printing, distributing and publicising the book. Thus they both, in their different ways, told the truth.

Hume and Trischler had their manuscript and their capital, so were free to publish. But the inexperienced pair made mistakes. The proof-reading had faults, hardly surprising if it occurred under conditions in the Trischler household, with its small children. A rare account of contemporary proofing survives in William Pyke's diary. Late one winter night, Pyke found himself with his attention divided between proofs, a pot of milk heating over the fire, and little Bubbles, his baby daughter:

> June 18th 1888:
> 10.10…I am now rocking her to sleep with my right foot. Wife in bed worn out with days work. I have been correcting proofs for Coles Family Advisor for the last two hours.

As soon as milk boils I will take my supper and go to bed…
It's getting cold. I must draw the blanket around my legs.
The draught blows in under the door so…It's now 10.30 the
milk has boiled over into the fire so I think I had better get
my supper and retire to rest.[196]

Some extraordinary mistakes in *Hansom Cab* did not get corrected
at proof stage. Acland Street was rendered as Ackland, laughable
for Melburnians, but both Hume and Trischler were immigrants.
The name Gaboriau was misspelt, the author being dead and in no
position to protest. But James Payn was very much alive and not likely
to be impressed with his name being rendered as Payne both in the
dedication and the first chapter—a spectacular instance of brown-
nosing gone wrong. It meant Hume would not be able to mail the
dedicatee a copy of the book.

A more significant mistake involved copyright. During the
nineteenth century the English-speaking book market was split
between the Empire and the American publishers, neither recognising
the other's copyright. Pirated editions of English books in America,
and of American books in England, were common: American Metta
Victor's *The Dead Letter* was pirated by *Cassells' Magazine*, with all
the details changed so that the book read as if originating in England.

George Robertson felt strongly about the issue, protesting the
pirated US editions of popular English authors entering his domain.
As a businessman he objected to his prices being undercut, but he
also realised that American piracy affected Australian authors,
as happened with *His Natural Life*. The fledgling book trade had
received protection, along with other colonial productions from
paintings to patents, by an act of Parliament in Victoria in 1869. The
law required that two copies of every book published in the colony
be taken to the Public Library for legal deposit, with the copyright
entered in a register. Failure to do so would incur a fine.

Hume, as a New Zealander with only serial publications to his name, might not have been aware of the Victorian law, and Trischler was similarly inexperienced. Kemp & Boyce, as printers, certainly should have known the law. But Hume did not register the copyright of *Hansom Cab* for nearly six months, until 20 April 1887. This failure could have been disastrous had some other publisher realised the opportunity—an assumption of copyright protection was made when one did not exist.[197]

The evidence suggests that Hume had other things on his mind as his book neared publication. He had come to Melbourne to be a dramatist and this ambition preoccupied him still. He kept busy writing his plays and networking with theatricals, such as the new Brough-Boucicault company. When a telegram from J. C. Williamson to Beck was delayed, Brough-Boucicault snapped up the actor. Now temporarily based in Melbourne, Beck moved in with the Humes, presenting a major, if fun, distraction. From their association as friends and co-dramatists Hume expected much—not least the chance of placing his plays. At least now *Hansom Cab* had its release, and he was confident his strategy to gain attention from the novel would finally work.

From the printing presses of Kemp & Boyce the copies of *Hansom Cab* emerged, ready for the waiting market of readers. Hume's fellow colonials had failed to recognise his talent—it was English actors and managers, and the ex-Londoner, Trischler, who tended to see his potential. But nobody, except perhaps Trischler, could foresee what was coming with *Hansom Cab*.

14

THE UNEXPECTED
Publication

*'Ah,' said Fanks with a smile, 'you have a touch of detective
fever. I suffer from it myself notwithstanding my experience.
The unravelling of these criminal problems is like gambling;
a never-failing source of excitement; and, like gambling, chance
enters largely into their solution.'*

TRACKED BY A TATTOO[198]

The first edition of *The Mystery of a Hansom Cab* is an unimpressive
object. It is small, in octavo format—a term from the early days of
printing, indicating that a large sheet of paper has been folded eight
times after being impressed with the type. The cover is paper, as leather
binding was too expensive for a small publisher with a limited budget.
Paper covers were used for the cheapest books. It took Allen Lane's
Penguin Books imprint of 1935, which presented quality reprints in
an inexpensive format, to make paperbound books fully respectable.
In today's terms, *Hansom Cab* was a trade paperback.

Cheap Victorian fiction was also colour coded bright yellow,
leading to the term 'yellowbacks'. In *Madame Midas* the religious
Mark Marchurst finds a yellowback in his daughter Kitty's room,
'which he handled with the utmost loathing'.[199] *Hansom Cab*'s cover

differed in being of a light blue-grey colour. It was not held together with glue or staples, as was usual with yellowbacks, but carefully stitched, as was typical of more expensive, upmarket books. 'Quite a good job,' comments John Loder, who also notes that the paper is 'nice'. Perhaps Trischler obtained some stock from Inglis after its bankruptcy. The book does not easily fall apart, nor does the paper readily disintegrate. The soft cover does tear—which could lead to it being discarded when damaged.

The spine does not, as is usual in library and publishing practice, give the author's name and book title. It reads CHIPPERFIELD in block capitals, a firm of ironmongers in Elizabeth Street. On the verso of the title page is more advertising for Chipperfield: a line engraving of its premises, with the tag 'It will pay you to take a Hansom Cab and go to the above street and buy your ironmongery'. The copywriter had clearly not read the book nor seen the cover, else he might have suggested a Chipperfield poker as defensive weaponry.

The preliminaries and endpages of the book contain advertisements, as if Trischler or Hume walked around Melbourne, from small business to small business, seeking funds. In some instances advertisers who liked fiction were targeted: Chipperfield and Kruse, makers of insecticide and indigestion cure (possibly an interchangeable product), bought space in *Once a Week*. Others included Warner's 'Safe' Rheumatic cure and the American Carriage Company, the 'largest manufacturer of light vehicles in Australia'—another example of literal-minded canvassing.

The cover of the book lists various descriptors, the first being 'sensational', an existing publishing category, promising such thrilling matter as murder and bigamy (as indeed could be found in *Hansom Cab*). Secondly, it is proudly identified as a Melbourne novel, somebody having noted that—as with the localisations—Melburnians liked reading about themselves. The third catchword is 'mystery'. Detection did not need to be mentioned, as these three bases of appeal covered the market. There was no subtitle: Hume said he disliked them.[200] In smaller type comes the author's name, which had yet to gain selling power. What dominates the cover is a cheap but highly effective engraving, in which the dramatic moment of murder is shown, but with the victim's and killer's faces obscured.

There was no blurb, for that would not be invented until the new century. Recent editions of the novel have lost its dedication to James Payn and also an introductory quote, apparently by Hume himself: 'As marine plants floating on the surface of waves appear distinct growths yet spring unseen from a common centre, so individuals apparently strangers to each other are indissolubly connected by many invisible bonds and sympathies which are known only to themselves.' It may have disappeared for hinting too much at the plot denouement, but anyone who has lived in a small city will be familiar with the concept therein. In his short time in Melbourne, Hume had met old Dunedinites, the music scene, theatricals, journalists, the Yorick Club, lawyers and the denizens of Lilly Lon. He would call on all these human resources as he sought an audience for his book.

Now they had their product, they had to sell it. But how? The more advanced publishers knew the value of advertising: Vizetelly spent £1000 on publicising his literary translations.[201] An important local precedent had been set by *Cole's Funny Picture Book* (1878). Cole had a plan beyond immediate profit. He intended to benefit from the 'increased goodwill' and custom the book would bring his Arcade. It would be the only place it would be available for sale, neatly saving him the costs of distribution. But first he had to make consumers aware of the book.

Cole began advertising in the Melbourne *Herald*, his favourite medium for publicity, in early October 1878. The notices appeared weekly for six weeks, then bi-weekly, and on Christmas Eve a final full-column advertisement announced the book's publication that day.

Parents in the 1800s had large families and the idea of 'the cheapest child's Picture book ever published in the world' appealed. Review copies were also sent 'to absolutely every newspaper in the colony'. On Christmas Eve the Arcade opened with the book prominently displayed in the window. It may have had only a few hundred copies, but by the time the Arcade closed that day all had sold.[202]

Trischler and Hume did not have Cole's publicity budget. What they could do was create a buzz, 'that swirl of word of mouth'.[203] It is something that publishers in the Australian market know can be crucial. I had the following exchange with Nick Hudson, former CEO of Heinemann Australia.

> **LJS:** You mentioned word of mouth: can that be deliberately and effectively created for a book? I think something of the sort was used for *Hansom Cab*.
>
> **NH:** The answer to your simple question is simple: yes and no. Yes, it is called publicity. And no, it doesn't always work. Nobody buys books they have never heard of by unknown authors, so the aim of the publicity is to increase awareness of the existence of a book. A really stunning review or, better still, a relevant news story can get the process going...
>
> If you have a good book, every sale will generate a new round of chatter, and hence further sales. If it is a mediocre book, even a good review or news story will get nowhere, because although a few people may buy it as a result of the review or story, they will be disappointed and it will go no further...The tighter the market the easier it is to locate the chatterers and get the chatter going. Any good book has a market. However, the more diffused that market is the harder it gets to generate audible chatter. I have never really managed it with fiction, where the market is totally diffused...
>
> I'd say that the principles were the same [in Melbourne in

1886]. They did not have the social media we have, but there were still reviews, dinner tables and garden fences, to say nothing of pubs and clubs. I suspect that gossip got around almost as quickly and just as widely then as it does now. But there was less of it—less news and fewer new books, so the chances of any given item or book getting on the grapevine were probably greater.

I would not consider it impossible that fifty per cent of book readers in Melbourne would have heard of *Hansom Cab* and twenty-five per cent would have read it within months of first publication. Today, simply because of the amount of chatter, a similar book would have been heard of by ten per cent and read by two per cent.

Someone who did manage to create word-of-mouth with fiction was Henry Rosenbloom, with *Shantaram*. John Hunter, now a publisher himself but then involved with the production, calls it a 'crazy freak' success, with the publisher's sales representatives wording up the booksellers over a series of months.

Hudson, Sessions and Rosenbloom had sales representatives, but *Hansom Cab* would have had initially little to rely on other than the efforts of Hume and Trischler—and their friends. As theatre review-er Clement Scott noted, talking about drama critics: '…they never decide the fate of the play. The public voice does that. The advertising is done by a contented and delighted audience. Each one goes home and tells a dozen friends, each friend tells a dozen more…'[204]

If Trischler and Hume were to be believed, in the case of *Hansom Cab*, those dozens turned into thousands, and a phenomenal amount of copies sold.

15

ANSWERED

Yes, after years of weary waiting, after money had been swallowed up in apparently useless work, after skeptics had sneered and friends laughed, Madame Midas obtained her reward.

MADAME MIDAS[205]

The evidence suggests that the release date of *Hansom Cab* was planned very carefully. Cole aimed for the Christmas market, then and now the busiest season in the book-buying year, with his *Funny Picture Book*. Trischler released his book so that it was distributed and readily available for another busy period: Melbourne Cup week.

Cole first spotted the business opportunity of the crowds travelling in and out of the city to attend the famous race. While the Cup was being run central Melbourne was effectively dead, with businesses closed for the Tuesday public holiday. William Pyke recorded the 1878 Cup in his diary: 'In the afternoon the town was almost deserted.' When the crowds returned to the city, by train, omnibus and hansom from the races, Cole realised the benefit of being open: Pyke wrote that evening he worked till ten-thirty.[206]

Indeed, when opening the Bourke Street Arcade Cole deliberately chose Cup Day 1883 and heavily advertised the event. The appeal of a bookstore that was effectively an entertainment centre—including refreshments and a band—proved so overwhelming that he had to improvise crowd control.[207] The consequence? A short-lived but significant link was made in the public mind between book-buying and the public holiday.

Saturday 23 October was the release date for *Hansom Cab*, which meant Hume had a day off work to spruik his wares.[208] It suited Cup week well. A novel with a horse on the cover—what better time for it to be released, with the city race-mad? The cover art could also have been used for posters and postcards, cheaply printed en masse by Kemp & Boyce. They would have been displayed on walls throughout the city and distributed to interested businesses across the Austral colonies.

Although Robertson would not initially have taken orders for something he had disapprovingly rejected, Melbourne had many other book outlets. For two of them—Cole and Mullen—the interest was personal. Cole had published his own book successfully, despite the knockback from Robertson. A man of quick and unconventional sympathy, he gave space to books not many would stock, such as *The Answer* (1911) by eccentric sex reformer William Chidley, which argued sex should only occur in spring, between true lovers and without an erection. The Arcade had space and resources to promote *Hansom Cab*, with the staff worded up to recommend it to customers.

Mullen had his own history with Robertson, and knew Hume as a customer; he had even earned a mention in *Hansom Cab*. From one of Mullen's staff we get the sole description of Hume on publication day. In all his sixty-three years of bookselling, Leonard Slade never forgot the arrival of *Hansom Cab*. Hume made a personal delivery of his stock, left 'in a hansom cab and dashed all over the suburbs as an advertisement'.[209] The visual effect would probably have included a banner (as seen in the newsreel for the 1925 *Hansom Cab* film).

Hume or Trischler probably got the idea of moveable advertising from J. C. Williamson, who that June publicised *His Natural Life* by sending out six men in convict dress, chained together, with guards in police uniforms. They drew crowds, and the real police arrested them for being an unauthorised procession. Such blatant advertising was a novelty, and Trischler could see how effective it was. One cab would not form an illegal procession, so Hume could avoid arrest. Though it was tempting, publicity-wise, a lawyer would be understandably nervous about getting on the wrong side of the watch-house bars.[210]

Review copies were sent out prior to the official publication, both in Melbourne and across the Tasman. A good review could make a book, as with *Called Back*. In that instance the champion was Henry Labouchère, who had been recommended it by a friend. He bought a copy as he passed through Waterloo station, the stall clerk admitting that the book was not selling well. It being too foggy to read in the train, Labouchère kept *Called Back* for bedtime—and was kept up until 4.30 a.m. In his society weekly, *Truth*, he penned a rave review. Two months later the book had sold thirty thousand copies, a number that, thanks to a dramatic version, increased ten-fold over the next few years.[211] *Dr Jekyll and Mr Hyde* met similar success after a favourable review in *The Times*.

The first notice for *Hansom Cab* appeared in *Table Talk* of 22 October, one day before the official publication. The short notice appeared in the prime news position of the second page. However, it tended to the cautious and descriptive: 'Mr. Hume has evidently seen a great deal of Melbourne life, as many of the scenes described by him are very realistic.' The conclusion was that the book was 'well worth one shilling'. It may not have been Brodzky's favourite read, but he clearly felt his protégé deserved some favour.

Another review came six days later, in Melbourne *Punch*, then a compilation of humour and society gossip. Here the reviewer was no fan, complaining the book bore 'a strong resemblance to the shilling horrors with which we are now deluged, and it is no compliment to say that this Melbourne production holds its own amongst those thousand and one volumes of crime and mystery'.[212]

No compliment—but those with a taste for shilling shockers now knew about this new product, intriguingly from Melbourne and, even more intriguingly, said to be equal to the considerable competition. On the day before the Cup another review appeared in the Melbourne *Daily Telegraph*, short, but favourable—a stimulus for demand.[213] People would have started asking for the book all over the city.

For Cup Day sales, the best place was the Arcade, with business brisk as an early morning gallop. And if Cole sold out, it was only a hansom-cab trip to Kemp & Boyce or Hume's lodgings in East Melbourne for more copies. The sight of the books coming in and out of the shops, Bob Sessions observes, would have been more publicity, indicating that a rush was happening on the product. Again, a banner could have been prominently displayed on the cab.

Not only in publicity did Trischler innovate. In England he boasted that he opened accounts with new suppliers ignored by the conservative book trade. Here he sounds like a twentieth-century publisher, seeking to sell books in Target or Woolworths. Clearly he sought out every outlet possible. As a former commercial traveller in cigars, Trischler knew a key point of sale were the transport nodes. On Cup Day the railway stations of Melbourne opened and with them kiosks, stocking newspapers, cigars and cheap reading matter— railway novels such as *Hansom Cab*. The two busiest stations, Flinders and Spencer Street, had W. M. Baird's railway bookstores. In addition copies could have been sold at the racecourse itself, at a designated stall or using colporteurs, itinerant booksellers, as Trischler would later use to hawk his books on the streets of London.[214]

Melbourne's population was approaching half a million, but on 2 November 1886 it swelled with visitors from the country, inter- state and even from overseas: more customers for *Hansom Cab*. The weather was perfect: 'a warm, soft, fragrant day'. Newspapers estimated 150,000 people went to the Cup. 'Well, dear, the crush was tremendous,' wrote *Punch*'s 'Gladys' in her 'Lady's Letter'. Arsenal won 'by the grace of a neck' at odds of twenty-five to one—similar odds to a small-press book, from the corner of the British Empire, becoming a major success.[215]

The following weekend, Hume's product placement of the *Argus* in the opening line of his novel paid off: a *Hansom Cab* review appeared in the *Australasian* Supplement for 6 November, a weekly from the same firm. Despite the editor having previously rejected the book for serialisation, it was becoming impossible to ignore. Whoever wrote the review did not know Hume, for it assumed he was a Dunedin resident and therefore unable to check his proofs![216] Though the notice was short and not exactly a rave—'quite as good as the average of such [Sensation] productions, and better than a great many'—it let the book speak for itself by quoting a long, attractive passage from chapter ten, describing a Melbourne institution, the Block. Furthermore, somebody did Hume a huge favour by placing the review beside a popular columnist, whose readers were *Hansom Cab*'s target audience. The Vagabond (Julian Thomas), was another Robertson author, a specialist in vivid journalism of colonial life. His fans could very easily transfer their affection to *Hansom Cab*, which depicts Melbourne with a journalist's eye. That review alone made the book's Melbourne reputation.[217]

By that stage *Hansom Cab* was becoming that rare thing, a genuine publishing phenomenon. How fast it sold out was variously stated by Hume to be eleven days (in his 1888 interview with the *Sunday Times*) and three weeks in his 1892 preface. Trischler stated that by 11 November (after Cup week and the *Australasian* review) he had 'not a single copy left'—which could simply mean he had sent all five thousand out.[218]

The most extraordinary claim came from Auckland, just as the first New Zealand reviews appeared. On 20 November the *New Zealand*

Herald quoted figures to give anyone involved with the Austral book trade, then and now, envious pause: 'Some 2200 copies of the book were sold within three days of its publication.'[219] In comparison, Rider Haggard's thriller *She*, first serialised then released as a book in early 1887, sold a thousand copies in a week—in the much larger English market.[220]

Rowan Gibbs, bibliographer of Hume, considers: '2200 in 3 days is credible—assuming it is largely bulk sales to the trade.'[221] If true, Hume, Trischler and their associates must have been dancing in the Melbourne streets, their prayers answered. Against enormous odds, Hume had not only brought out his novel, but achieved an incredible success.

The first edition of *Hansom Cab* rapidly sold out. In that it joins a select tradition, the bestsellers and sometimes classics of Australian literature: *The Man from Snowy River*, Lawson's *While the Billy Boils*, *The Songs of a Sentimental Bloke* (also rejected by the Melbourne Robertson's firm[222]), *Monkey Grip*, *Shantaram*.

But that was not all the book would do. Selling out the first edition was only the beginning of its stratospheric rise.

16

THREE READERS
Maudie, Edith and Minnie

Madge was seated in one of these comfortable chairs and divided
her attention between the glowing beauty of the world outside,
which she could see through a narrow slit in the blind, and a new
novel from Mullen's, lying open on her knee.

HANSOM CAB[223]

Reviews of *Hansom Cab* survive, but what was the reaction of the ordinary readers, not journalists nor literary folk, who read it simply for pleasure? What sort of people were they? Did they give the book as presents, lend it to their friends, read it aloud to the family circle?

We know the names of three early readers, two of them young women on opposite sides of the Tasman, entirely different in background and circumstances. The first was a Melbourne girl who bought or was given a copy of *Hansom Cab*, from the October 1886 printing. She proudly inked her name and address on the title page: G. Maudie Manton, Tenilla, South Yarra. Ten months later she married and her name changed.

Tenilla was in Domain Street, South Yarra, then and now a good address. Maudie, born in Sydney in 1865 and christened Grace Maude, came from the enterprising colonial upper class. Although the family had a famous English ancestor, gunsmith Joseph Manton, they were multilingual and multicultural, with a French-Mauritian grandmother, and were also great travellers. Maudie's father, Frederick Julien Manton, was a former New South Wales parliamentarian who had already gone bankrupt in two different colonies. In Melbourne he lived in high style, but to safeguard the family assets, Tenilla was in the name of Maudie's mother, Caroline Manton, and left in her will to her seven children.

Frederick Manton was entirely the sort of person to figure in Hume's Melbourne Trilogy: an extravagant speculator, of whom melodramatic secrets might be suspected. Maudie was similarly a Madge Frettlby, a society miss. Like Madge she was also a reader. That she wrote her name in the book indicates that after her large family had finished reading it, she lent it out to her greater acquaintance—and wanted it back. Was one of these readers a man employed at the other end of the street, who like her retraced *Hansom Cab*'s murder route every time he travelled down to central Melbourne? The book's release does coincide with their courtship.

Joseph Tompson (b. 1855) had studied at London University before immigrating to the colonies, for employment, but likely also his health. By 1886 he was Science Master at Melbourne Grammar, in his thirties and a childless widower. Joseph and Maudie married in July 1887. He was ten years her senior, a serious man—did he appreciate the literary frisson of a murder being discovered just outside his workplace? For the Mantons the match would have been respectable rather than brilliant, less for money than love, but with five daughters (like the Bennets of *Pride and Prejudice*) it was welcome.[224]

That a copy of *Hansom Cab* was owned by a woman living so close to the novel's opening scenes indicates how it resonated with Melburnians, fictionalising their familiar surroundings with the added thrill of crime. A later reader, Norman K. Harvey, the first bibliographer of *Hansom Cab*, wrote: 'I am attracted to the subject for the simple reason that I was born and lived until I was over thirty years of age, within half a mile of the scene of many of the incidents of the story. Indeed for twenty years my home was in Powlett Street, East Melbourne, about 150 yards from where Fitzgerald lodged.'[225] And, indeed, not far from where Hume lived himself. A further sensation would have been the scenes of low life, which men like Frederick Manton would have known about, but of which respectable womenfolk were supposed to be ignorant.

Another copy of the first edition, held in the Mitchell Library, indicates the appeal *Hansom Cab* had for women readers. On the flyleaf is a name, but written in pencil, half-erased. 'Edith' can be read, but the surname is illegible. Even an ultraviolet-light scan does not reveal it. Between pages six and seven is a single long, fine, dark hair, perhaps from the mysterious Edith, who liked the book enough to add her name to it. Other than that the book shows no great signs of being read.

The final reader in this select sample, whose copy has not survived, was Trischler's sister-in-law Mary, known as Minnie, a teenager born in Ireland. If the Mertons were the most upwardly mobile of the New Zealand Trischlers, then Walter, Frederick's elder brother, represented the opposite. When in 1885 he married Minnie (Mary) Hogan, aged sixteen, at the Catholic Presbytery in Blenheim, he was thirty-four and a labourer.

Walter was a cheerful, colourful man who liked a drink but lacked Frederick's moneymaking drive. A family story has Walter sailing off to collect an inheritance, returning to Minnie dressed to the nines but penniless. Possibly the inheritance was from Anne Trischler, who died in early 1886, something which would date these events close to *Hansom Cab*'s publication.

If so, the bad news could only have been communicated to Minnie in person, for Walter had married an illiterate. The family recalled her musing, 'What on earth made him, with so much education, marry me with no learning whatever?' Walter was not a teacher, like his brother-in-law Merton, but he taught his wife to read and write. Despite the hardships of their early married life, living in a tent in the bush, with Walter working as a clerk or on the railways—not to mention ten babies in seventeen years—Minnie became a devoted reader. When she finally had a solid roof over her head she filled the annexe off her bedroom, usually a dressing room, not with clothes but books, shelved on three sides, floor to ceiling, her personal library. Proudly she boasted that she had read every one of them.

On Minnie's shelves would have been *Hansom Cab*, sent across the Tasman, perhaps as a peace offering. If Minnie had been unimpressed with the story of the lost inheritance, she could not have resisted a good story. A year after her marriage, she might not have been able to read a novel by herself, but Walter could have read it aloud to her, part of her continuing education.

Minnie Trischler seems the perfect example of the Victorian aspirational reader. Books became for her an enduring source of pleasure, and she would be an education martinet for her nine surviving children, seven of them daughters, but all of whom went to high school. *Hansom Cab* had significance in her journey towards literacy, even without the family connection. To her it meant more than her brother-in-law's publishing enterprise, for she told her grandson that Frederick had written *Hansom Cab*, being adamant on the issue.

It is easy to see how the misapprehension might have arisen: a parcel sent across the Tasman containing a first edition of *Hansom Cab*, 'a little sample of my work'. Frederick did have some literary or journalistic aspirations, with his contributions to *Once a Month*, and he would have edited (and proofread, poorly) the novel. Yet authorship was something that Frederick did not apparently claim himself—although he claimed much that was on the dubious side. Someone else, even more dubious, would also claim authorship of the novel; and others, decidedly up to no good, would claim to be Fergus Hume himself.

That money was to be made from even a pretended association with *Hansom Cab* is a further indication of its popularity. Minnie, Edith and Maudie—more women with those names would read the book, worldwide.

17

THE YEAR OF MIRACLE

'In real life,' cried Diana, 'more incredible things take place than can be conceived by the most fantastic imagination of an author.'
THE SILENT HOUSE IN PIMLICO[226]

As 1886 closed, demand was increasing for *Hansom Cab*. The little book was being passed from hand to hand, among Maudie Manton's circle, among the many keen readers of Melbourne and beyond. Yet nobody, not even Trischler, had expected it would go so fast. Kemp & Boyce had not kept the type standing, ready for re-use, but had distributed it. The thousands of words in *Hansom Cab* had been separated into their component metal letters and filed away in alphabetical boxes, upper and lower case. Now the typesetters had to go to work again and reset, an expensive process and not to be achieved immediately. At least money was not a major problem anymore. Trischler had revenue from the books sold and would have ploughed his profits into the new printings.

Hume stated that the second edition of the book took two months to be published. Trischler spoke of a more rapid turnover, with increasing figures: that he followed the first edition of *Hansom Cab* with another edition of five thousand, then another five thousand, followed by an edition of ten thousand. That would have made a total of twenty-five thousand copies within a few months. Bibliographer Rowan Gibbs: 'All I can say is that I've found nothing to disprove this.'[227]

Bob Sessions comments that Trischler's figures are consistent with the book becoming a phenomenon, sales small at first, then increasing exponentially. 'Everybody did everything right,' he notes: from the author who researched his market and plotted his whodunnit carefully, to the publisher who packaged an attractive product and marketed it with real brilliance. As a result, *Hansom Cab* became a fad, the book that everybody had to read, commodity capitalism at work.

Yet if Trischler did print a second edition of *Hansom Cab* in 1886, it was not reported in the papers—as far as is known. No copy identified as belonging to this edition survives. The only reports known of the second edition are from early 1887: the *Wanganui Herald* said that it was 'going off rapidly' in February, and Melbourne *Punch* reported a second edition of 5000 copies in May.[228] These reports would suggest that Trischler's reported two 1886 editions of five thousand each, following the first successful printing, were a furphy.

If the second edition is problematic, so too the third. Labelling it as the third edition was a misnomer. A new edition means resetting the type. Most likely it was the second edition's type kept and pressed into service again, or stereotype (in the original sense of the word) a mould taken from the type and cast in metal. That makes the book in bibliographic terms an impression rather than a new edition. Trischler may not have known the difference, or else merrily ignored it, for a new edition sounded more impressive in publicity. One copy is known to have survived of this 'third' edition.

The possibility exists that exaggeration could have been a clever strategy of Trischler's, to make sales a publicity point for *Hansom Cab* from the very start: the book became a bestseller because it was claimed to be a bestseller. 'Publishers always exaggerate,' says Nick

Walker of Australian Scholarly Publishing. Brodzky, when re-printing Trischler's claims, dryly and discreetly implied he didn't believe a word. 'I hope the public has not been deceived by the quantity of news that has been published on the subject,' he wrote.[229]

One piece of evidence, recorded many years later, suggests Trischler's sales figures were pure puffery. In 1922 Scottish business-man James Glass (b. 1848) published a memoir, *Chats Over a Pipe*. In it Glass recalls that he travelled to Australia for his health. He saw the opportunities in Marvellous Melbourne:

> When unpacking my baggage I fortunately discovered a few sample boxes of the new steel pens, which I had named—'Ball-Pointed.' It seemed a pity that in a fine business city, such as Melbourne, I should remain idle. I got a few business cards printed, and then I called upon the leading stationers in the city to try to sell my pens. But there was nothing doing. I was told by every one, 'There are too many varieties of pens already on the market and we don't want any more.' 'All right,' I told them, 'you'll want them before I leave the city', and they did.
>
> I then called on the two leading newspapers—the *Argus* and the *Age*, and engaged in each for three days a prominent space, at a total cost of £24. I wrote out an advertisement that no one could read immoved, and then interviewed the editors, inducing them to insert a short notice.
>
> While waiting a couple of days for the advertisements to soak in, I had a narrow escape of becoming a millionaire. To fill in my time I bought at a bookstall, a book published locally, 'The Mystery of a Hansom-Cab.' After dinner that night I began reading it, and couldn't put it down till I had finished it, long after midnight.
>
> The following morning I went to the bookstall, and asked the address of the author, with an idea of buying

the copyright. I was informed that the author, Mr. Fergus Hume, was a clerk in a suburban branch bank, and would be glad to take £5 or £10 for the copyright—the sale of the book being so small.

While waiting outside a stationer's shop for a car to take me to Mr. Hume's address, the stationer came out and said —'Excuse me, but are you the gentleman who called here the other day with 'Ball-Pointed Pens?' 'Yes, that's so, but you didn't want any.' 'Well, I want them now. The shop is full of people all wanting these pens. Have you stock with you?' 'No,' I replied, 'but I have samples in my pocket.' 'Then,' said he, 'as you know more about them than I do you can send me £50 worth assorted.'

That morning I had a triumphal progress through Melbourne—every stationer wanted the pens, and before lunch I had sold £250 worth.

'The Mystery of a Hansom-Cab' was forgotten, and my chance of becoming a millionaire was lost. On my return home I found that the copyright had been bought by someone else. The book was published in London, and had an enormous sale. The profits on the book, together with the stage rights, must have realised a big fortune. It was a narrow squeak!

Glass's ball-pointed pen advertisements can be found in the Melbourne papers of mid-February 1887, at a time when *Hansom Cab* was otherwise supposed to have sold an immense number of copies. Whatever else this anecdote provides, it is evidence of the power of advertising in the late 1800s—and the attractive proposition that *Hansom Cab* presented to enterprising businessfolk.[230]

Now the name Fergus Hume spelled success the public wanted more of his brand: shilling shockers. Hume did not have any new product ready, but he did have *Professor Brankel*, short but sufficiently sensational to satisfy the market. It might previously have been roundly rejected by the trade, but station bookseller W. H. Baird had witnessed firsthand how *Hansom Cab* sold. He put his name and money behind a print run by Kemp & Boyce.

This edition does show a change not only in Hume's status, but also in his philosophy. In Dunedin, he had been intrigued by metempsychosis; now he moved from ancient arcana to new esoterica in the form of theosophy. Although this marriage of Western and Eastern mysticism had yet to be formally established in Melbourne, its philosophy would have been readily available at shops advertising 'Advanced Books', which included topics like cremation, psychopathy (psychology) and anti-vaccination.[231] To *Brankel* Hume now added an opening quotation from *The Occult World* (1881), by theosophist Alfred Percy Sinnett: 'The body is the prison of the soul for ordinary mortals but the adept has found the key of his prison and can emerge from it at pleasure.'

Like the signed poem to Wagner, Hume was making a statement of his beliefs. It expressed a disaffect with the body that reappears in his works, particularly in terms of gender. Did he find his body a prison? Or felt himself no ordinary mortal? Certainly as a writer that was true. Pious Dunedin would have termed such talk heathen, and yet Hume's philosophical journey was no stranger than that of Arthur Conan Doyle, who abandoned Catholicism as a young man and whose search for meaning led to him to spiritualism, and also fairies.

Kemp & Boyce also went through their own metamorphosis. They moved to better premises, advertising themselves as Printers, Engravers, Lithographers, Publishers and Manufacturing Stationers. Their annual wayzgoose (printers' outing) became newsworthy, with more than one hundred people attending.[232] Sticking with sure success, in between printing yet more copies of *Hansom Cab* they branched out into shilling crime shockers by other writers. Since their star author did not have another novel ready, a gap in the market existed for similar hopefuls—and it helped to be a young theatrical with Māori Land connections. Actor and playwright Henry Hoyte (Henry Harbord McDonald) contributed a novella, *The Tramway Tragedy*, published in mid-1887, which again borrowed from a Boisgobey title, *The Railway Tragedy*.[233] Thus was the theme of murderous transport continued.

Even the radical writer Francis Adams turned sensational with *The Murder of Madeline Brown*, allegedly written in three days.[234] All that is known of Kemp & Boyce's business dealings are Adams' terms: he was paid £10, and his novel had a reputed royalty of 2d per copy (a rate of sixteen per cent, very high for the time). Was it a similar deal to *Hansom Cab*, or did success make Kemp & Boyce generous? Although *Madeline Brown* would not rival *Hansom Cab*, it sold an estimated seven thousand to ten thousand copies. Adams is said to have earned £45 from it; Kemp & Boyce would have done even better.[235]

In June 1887 Alice Cornwell also struck gold—literally. Being as much of a networker and self-publicist as Hume, she invited the visiting travel-writer Baroness Brassey to pan for gold at her mine. Several days later a nugget of 167 ounces was discovered and, as was the custom with large lumps of gold, given a name: Lady Brassey. The find emboldened Cornwell, and she and her maid took passage to England in early August, intending to float her company internation-ally. Reaching Colombo by September, she was met by a telegram: another nugget had been found at the mine, a monster the size of a long, uneven loaf of bread, weighing 617 ounces. The nugget got the name of another titled lady: Lady Loch, wife of the Colonial Governor. Madame Midas was now turning everything she touched to gold.[236]

Hume had not yet written a follow-up to *Hansom Cab*. A dramatic tale of golden treasure—with a heroine he knew and admired—was a story simply too good not to use. Alice Cornwell had helped him with *Hansom Cab*. Now there was an opportunity to recompense her, as Hume best could, with another book.

In this light *Madame Midas* can be read as a very long thank-you letter from Hume to Cornwell. It also had a not-so-hidden agenda: denigrating Cornwell's ex-husband Whiteman, who had, as was legal and conventional for the time, sole custody of the couple's son, to whom she had no access. The novel can be read as a cold revenge: biographer Fiona Gruber describes it as a 'massive collusion' between Hume and Cornwell. It carefully avoids libel, thanks to Hume's lawyerly training—the Mr Midas of the novel has been carefully written so as not to resemble Mr Whiteman. He could only take legal action against the consequent theatre productions, and even then unsuccessfully.

But *Madame Midas* seems more than a favour returned, or Hume being chivalrous to a wronged woman. It also suited Cornwell's purposes in England, the novel being handy publicity for an unknown mining magnate from the Antipodes and, even worse, a woman. Public relations were an emerging dark art of the late 1800s, a factor of increasing importance in public life. Cornwell would show herself adept at it, working the surprise factor of her gender as much as possible.

If *Madame Midas* was written for its titular character, then the meaty villain's part was written for Beck. But though Hume and Beck would cooperate on the poem 'A Centennial Song', the actor was not involved in the novel's writing. He was busy at work, and although Melbourne was his base, often toured interstate.[237]

Someone who did assist with the novel was a trusted reader: a woman who wrote to the *Sydney Stock and Station Journal* in 1913 about Hume. She was identified only as 'J. M.', 'a socialist, a thinker and a worker', affluent enough to later visit Hume in England. Radical, intelligent, well-off and a reader of the *Sydney Stock and Station Journal*: who was this mysterious woman? Most likely 'J. M.'

was Janet Michie (b. 1848), best known as an activist, speaker and writer—including letters to the press—for the Victorian votes for women campaign. She also worked as a real-estate agent, one of the first women to enter that profession in Victoria.[238]

Michie could have met Hume through her menfolk in Melbourne law: she was the daughter of QC Archibald Michie, and sister-in-law of Justice Thomas A'Beckett. There was also a press connection: her father wrote for the *Herald* and *Punch*, and was additionally the Victorian correspondent for *The Times*. The family had a mansion in St Kilda, a destination for Hume in his *Hansom Cab*. Michie fits a type of women with whom Hume associated: clever, professional, older and independent. They liked Hume and would assist him in his career. Most frequently these women were actresses, like Amy Horton and the American Carrie Swain, famous for trouser roles, who bent gender on stage and maintained careers beyond the marital.

'J. M.' wrote: 'Crediting me with some critical judgment, Fergus used to bring each chapter of this novel to me and read it [presumably aloud]. Then we discussed it and made alterations as we thought necessary.' She recalled Hume as 'nervy' and meticulous, consulting a medical expert about poisons, lest critics accuse him of inaccuracy. He also went to Ballarat and conducted extensive research into the mines.

Why did Hume feel he needed a second reader? He could have been anxious with second-novel syndrome. Moreover, his inspiration and source, Alice Cornwell, was in England. Cornwell was a trailblazer, as was Michie, but they were part of a greater trend. The world was changing: women were entering offices and universities, even cycling. They were claiming new rights, something that would lead directly to suffrage, achieved relatively quickly and easily in the colonies, but a bitter, drawn-out and bloody process in England. Writers were beginning to write heroines unprecedented in fiction, which would in the 1890s become known as the 'new woman' novel, as with Miles Franklin's *My Brilliant Career*. Hume here anticipated a literary trend, especially in combining his new woman story with crime. The turn of the century saw a rise of female detectives, and real-life female PIs, even in Melbourne.[239]

While neither Madam Midas nor her model were exactly what we would term feminists, for the time she was certainly transgressive. The business fraternity muttered that Cornwell was Bohemian, 'too candid and unconventional', with the cutting comment: 'women oughtn't to meddle with business.'[240] While women had been active in commerce throughout the nineteenth century, the scale of Cornwell's operations was genuinely challenging. In London she bought the *Sunday Times* and invested in other large business ventures.

But while Hume was busy drafting his second novel, planning was underway to make his first a successful business venture in London. A genuine third edition of *Hansom Cab*, with the text revised slightly, would appear in late 1887. The year since the book had been published in October 1886 had been miraculous for Hume, his printers, his publishers and his friend Alice Cornwell. But the miracle was not over yet, for the London publication of *Hansom Cab* would transform it from colonial phenomenon to international sensation.

18

THE PICCADILLY PUZZLE

How *Hansom Cab* Became an International Success

It is all rubbish, what the newspapers say about fortunes being made out of novel-writing. No one ever made a fortune, at least, what the world would call a fortune in this age of millionaires—by his pen yet.

WHEN I LIVED IN BOHEMIA[241]

Trischler gave several accounts of how *Hansom Cab* travelled to England and international success. Interviewed by the *Pall Mall Gazette*, he claimed:

> The success was so marked that I naturally thought of England…I thought I would send a couple of 'feelers' first. I communicated with a couple of well-known London publishers, whose names I give you in confidence. Certain terms were submitted to me, which however I did not accept. If Messrs. So and So can afford to offer me so much for the English copyright (argued I), why shouldn't I do equally well, if not better, by coming over to England and exploiting the book myself?[242]

The other account, a letter to the press, differs. Here copies of *Hansom Cab* reached London independently, and provoked a response:

" Discovered this El Dorado of Literature."

The boy reader from *When I Lived in Bohemia*, illustrated by Cyril R. Hallward.

James Hume, attributed to John Irvine.
Collection of Toitū Otago Settlers Museum.

Mary Hume, attributed to John Irvine.
Collection of Toitū Otago Settlers Museum.

Above: Park House by John Irvine.
Presented to the Misses Hume
on New Year's Day, 1876.
Collection of Toitū Otago Settlers Museum.

Inset: The young Fergus Hume?

Left: Frederick Trischler.
Photograph courtesy of David Green.

Teenage Alice Cornwell, by Ballarat
photographer William Bardwell, shortly
after her marriage to John Whiteman.
Photograph from the collection of Tony Rackstraw.

Philip Beck in *The Crimes of Paris*,
Melbourne *Punch*, 23 September 1886.

Caricature of Fergus Hume from New
Zealand magazine *Land and Sea*, 1888.

Minnie (Mary) Trischler with her daughters Norah and baby May.
Photograph courtesy of David Green.

Beck, from an obituary
in Melbourne *Punch*,
16 January 1890.

The author and Phancie,
from Hume's *The Chronicles
of Fairy Land*, illustrated
by Maria L. Kirk.

"YES, IT IS FAERYLAND," PIPED A SHRILL VOICE

A London publishing house instructed their agent by cable to offer me certain terms for the international copyright. At this time I had no intention of publishing in England, but this offer opened my eyes. The agent receded somewhat in his terms, and I broke off negotiations and offered the copyright to another publishing house of high repute, making the terms, as I thought, prohibitory. Within four days of the receipt of my letter they wrote back offering me seventy-five per cent of what I asked. I refused it...[243]

Cable was expensive, reserved for special announcements (such as the death of Wagner). The London publisher clearly took *Hansom Cab* very seriously. William Pyke, who was in some position to know, said that Routledge offered £100. He wondered if Hume 'would have done better eventually if he had accepted the offer'. His own non-fiction compilation of quotations, *Conduct and Duty*, published the same year as *Hansom Cab*, had also been published in England, with six thousand copies sold. Pyke ruefully noted that he should have got £100 for his copyright, instead of £25—showing what he considered a fair return.[244]

Hume can never have known about the Routledge offer, for he would surely never have sold the international rights for half that amount. Fifty pounds was still a considerable payment for the time, and he called it a 'good sum'. Although the novel's success and the overseas interest had caused him belatedly to register his copyright, on 20 April 1887, Hume simply did not believe it would be a success in England. In this opinion he was a victim of the cultural cringe, for he was fatally wrong. Had he but known, he told the *Sunday Times*, he would never have sold his copyright. But he did, to a Mrs Jessie Pearson Dove Taylor on 24 August 1887. She was the wife of George Nicholson Taylor, Manager of the Land Credit Bank. Shortly afterwards Jessie Taylor and Trischler, the business partners in *Hansom Cab*'s overseas push, both left for England.[245]

Hume's luck deserted him here. Trischler was not a publisher like Arrowsmith, who had paid Conway £80 for *Called Back*'s copyright. When the book proved a bestseller, Arrowsmith offered Conway a royalty deal for the next six years—the major sales period anticipated for the book. In the event, it was Arrowsmith who had the most luck, for Conway died the following year.[246] What, given sales of approximately half a million, should Hume have been paid? Years later in London, George Sims, himself a writer of crime with the pioneering *Dorcas Dene, Detective* (1897–8), told Hume over lunch that *Hansom Cab* ought to have made him £10,000—a figure which would have set him up for the rest of his life.[247]

What Trischler was proposing to do in England would require, if not thousands of pounds, then a sum far greater than the amount spent on the audacious edition of five thousand. He sought help, joining forces with 'a few Melbourne capitalists'—in Stephen Knight's words, 'politely called entrepreneurs'.[248] Jessie Taylor was the only one named in official documents, but her husband surely had involvement. Trischler arrived in London mid-October 1887, in his luggage another production of Hume's, a dramatised version of *Hansom Cab*. If his gamble pulled off again, then there was extra revenue to be made in theatrical productions of successful books, the Hollywood blockbusters of the Victorian era. Hume did not sell the copyright in this work, showing he had more hope for it than the novel.

Alice Cornwell, now a mining magnate, was also in London. While no evidence survives to show her involvement with the overseas publication of *Hansom Cab*, she was a clever businesswoman. Did Trischler approach her for advice? She had her own major projects, opening an office in Victoria Street and exhibiting the monster Lady Loch nugget. Trischler's own office, 'a little pig-stye' in Ludgate Hill, was only a short walk away.[249]

On 28 October 1887 *Hansom Cab* was entered in the English Register of Copyrights. Trischler would claim he sent to Victoria for fifty thousand copies—really, given freight costs? The printing and publishing of the new edition appear to have been purely an English operation. Trischler, now trading as the Hansom Cab Publishing Company, issued the first English edition in time for Christmas.[250]

Here he took the opportunity not only of the season, but also the lucky chance of Australians in the news. Melba had just made her European debut in Brussels, as Gilda in *Rigoletto*; sketches of the Lady Loch nugget appeared in the press; and a debate on the existence of Australian literature was ongoing. Some claimed it was non-existent, although Douglas Sladen's centenary anniversary book of *Australian Poets* was heading to a London press. Haddon Chambers, an aspiring playwright, wrote defensively: 'in addition to good cricketers and oarsmen we can produce good authors.'[251]

While the English edition of *Hansom Cab* closely resembled the Australian, with the same cover, there were differences. The text throughout was re-set, with errors corrected. The swearing, which had caused Robertson's rejection, was also toned down, with Mother Guttersnipe's robust language going from the explicit to discreet dashes. Stereotype moulds were made of the text and used for the subsequent printings. Trischler would not make the mistake of distributing the type needlessly again.

Big money backed the Hansom Cab Publishing Company. Obtaining it could have been as simple as Trischler going to his bank manager and asking for a loan. Or since two sources record Hume as working as a bank clerk, it is not impossible he approached his boss. Trischler may have had royalties from the successful Australian editions, shared to some degree with Hume. The Taylors, however, could fund an all-out assault on the English reading market: printing, publishing and advertising. Trischler may have run the Hansom Cab Publishing Company, but they provided the money.

Who were the Taylors, who so boldly underwrote an international bestseller? George Taylor (b. 1830) was from the West Indies, son of an Anglican vicar. Like Trischler he found mobility via the merchant marine, where he attained the rank of second mate. In Melbourne he met Jessie Pearson Dove Cairncross (b. 1843), also from a merchant-marine family, and they married in December 1863.

The Taylors had seven children, five daughters and two sons. At Jessie's instigation George studied accountancy and in 1880 he became manager of the new Land Credit Bank. He was of the type who drove boom-town Melbourne: respectable, Presbyterian and sober about everything except making money. The banks' clients even included Ned Kelly's family.[252]

In his enterprises, Taylor, like the captain of a ship, had a bosun in Jessie. She had been a teacher, but her real forte was business, beginning with millinery in the early years of her marriage and escalating to large-scale land transactions.[253] Jessie was as fiscally acute, in a lesser way, as Alice Cornwell. The Taylors' business portfolio focussed on land development; their investment in *Hansom Cab* was unusual, but very clever.

In 1880s Melbourne the Taylors lived well, and conspicuously. Her dresses were described by social reporters: pink faille with gold embroidery and a ruby plush bodice; or chocolate silk with more pink faille and rich Maltese lace.[254] Jessie was involved with various charities, sitting on committees with women like Helen (Mrs Henry Gyles) Turner, whose husband managed the Commercial Bank, the largest in Melbourne.[255] But evident was a mercenary streak, directed even towards her own family. In 1884 Jessie's elderly aunt Mrs Dove came to stay with the Taylors in Windsor, probably not entirely at her own behest. The Taylors built extra rooms onto their house for her, but Mrs Dove left after a quarrel. She was billed £150 for building costs and her family plate was placed in the Land Credit Bank, supposedly for safekeeping. Aunt sued niece, ending with the court ordering the return of the plate.[256]

Hume would say, years later, that he sold the copyright to a friend, which could mean Jessie's involvement was personal as well as financial. Although she was a hard woman of business, she enjoyed the theatre. Several newspapers reported literary interests and ability as well.[257] Quite possibly the pages of Victorian journals contain her compositions, if under pen names. She would even be claimed as the co-writer of *Hansom Cab*—unlikely, but it did provide a convenient explanation for her ownership of the copyright and association with the project.[258]

Jessie did not stay long in London, indicating that she was more investor than active partner. Though Trischler would subsequently claim to have merely been 'the managing clerk for certain Australians', the plural suggesting both Taylors were involved,[259] in his interviews with the English press he took centre stage as heroic entrepreneur. Trischler shook up the publishing industry in ways that anticipated book-trade practices of the late twentieth century, particularly in wide and eclectic distribution. His retailers were offered 'liberal' sale-or-return terms and he actively sought new outlets for book sales.[260] As he told the *Pall Mall Gazette*:

> ...the general policy of the London publisher is conservative. He doesn't care about opening fresh accounts, especially in the country, unless he gets a cash remittance. We, on the contrary, take it for granted that if a man has carried on business in a town for a certain number of years he is to be trusted, and we supply him with goods accordingly. We make very few bad debts. It doesn't pay a tradesman to cheat us. He knows that if he fails to pay up honestly he will not be allowed to participate in the good things of the future.

As the records of the Hansom Cab Publishing Company have not survived, information about Trischler's business practices largely comes from newspapers. A friend from Christchurch days, now the London correspondent for several colonial newspapers, used Trischler as copy and Trischler fed him titbits for publicity—ultimately a double-edged sword. But his coverage reveals how innovatively and determinedly Trischler pursued the British market.

He made use of W. H. Smith's for distribution, following the business plan that had been successful in Victoria. And, with more means at his disposal, Trischler could advertise heavily, both with a 'multitude of postcards' and in the press. He would boast that 'if advertisements will sell patent medicines, Pears' soap and Colman's mustard, it will sell a shilling novel'. This citing of the most famous products sold by advertising in his era shows an understanding of the emerging powers of publicity, crude and blatant as they then were, characterised by repetition rather than hidden persuasion. By mid-December 1887 it was being reported that 'a very large sum of money' was being expended on advertising *Hansom Cab*.[261]

Trischler would comment:

> Publishing…is nothing more than an arithmetical problem, which if worked properly, yields a certain definite result. I reckon that if you spend a certain amount of money upon a commodity; it ought to produce a certain percentage of results. We calculate that we ought to sell our books to a half per cent of the community…our first book, 'The Mystery' was sold to 1 per cent.[262]

He began with a prospectus, as if floating a mining concern, for the Hansom Cab Publishing Company, titled *A Message from Australia; a Literary Tribute to the Mother Country*, with the motto *Australia Felix*. It was sent in a yellow envelope with allegorical engraving to newspapers and detailed the product he had to sell. An extract from *Hansom Cab* was included, described as having sold '25,000 copies in three days'—the same claim made in the Antipodes, with an extra zero added. Hume had his age reduced: he was now twenty-two instead of his real twenty-eight. One journalist found the prospectus 'an entirely new departure from the beaten line of custom and routine in literature'. He described it as 'a bold intrusion' that took Hume's peers in England 'by surprise'. The prospectus was newsworthy, not least for being colonial. The PR worked, the journalist professing himself impatient to read *Hansom Cab*. He finished by wondering if the book would be famous to the same degree in England.[263]

Of course it will! said the voice from Ludgate Hill. Trischler, as he had with the Australian publication, sought a major review. Labouchère would have got a copy, but he did not know Hume. Someone who did, if only by correspondence, was Clement Scott, who had published Hume's poems. Trischler sent him a copy of the book and boasted of *Hansom Cab*'s Australian success, casting himself as good angel. Clement Scott responded in print:

> But let me begin at the beginning, and tell my little story, for it is an encouraging and a hopeful one; it is a helpful lesson to all beginners, and it shows the value at the outset of any career in this life of a helping hand. We all need it, we all know and appreciate the value of it, we none of us should have been where we are, or been able to do what we do, without it. It appears then, that this young fellow, a colonist, a resident of Melbourne, a poet—and not at all a bad poet, either—a dramatist, and clearly an observer of men and manners; a writer of wide sympathies, with a strong dramatic fervour, wrote a brochure, a shilling book, a *'shilling shocker'*, as these nervous clever sketches are often called, and styled it 'The Mystery of a Hansom Cab'…A murder case whose details, incidents, and circumstantial evidence bring out the firm faith of women, the loyalty of friendship, and all the best and finest qualities of human nature. It is a pure book; it is a good book; it is, unquestionably, an interesting book. Sensational it may be called, if by sensation one means sustained interest, artistic treatment and dramatic glory. But it is not sensational in any

tendency to shock to thrill, or to cause a shudder. It is a drama of real life, with men and women of to-day as the actors and actresses. They all wear modern dress. They all speak colloquial English. But there is no attempt to over-colour, no desire to exaggerate, no tendency whatever towards vulgarity and coarseness, no unnecessary striving after blood and murder at the expense of what is truthful, tender, and human.

…Every incident in the book is natural; every scene and every chapter as worked out, makes you think better, and not worse, of your fellow creatures. Of course there are bad men and bad women, as well as virtuous members of society; the hags and harridans, the dissolute and the drunken of lower Melbourne life speak with their accustomed coarse-ness, and act with their conventional brutality, but the tendency of the book is to show that truth is great and will ultimately prevail, so that love that is strong will last, that sin of whatever kind will be ultimately found out, and that honour and honesty and loyalty are preferable, after all, to degradation, debauchery, and deceit.

Not only a good read, but with the all-important Victorian moral-ity. Scott went on to analyse the book's Australian success:

The book was clever, and it sold on its own merits. When it was well received it was found that the reviewers were correct. When it was well spoken of, those who subsequently read it under advice discovered that all that had been said about it was true. For a book of the kind I really do not see how it could be better. It is a tale of accusation, of doubt, distrust, and the complications of evidence, and those who take the book up, be they lawyers or laymen, are not likely to put it down until it has been finished.

Scott hastened to add that his glowing words have nothing to do with Hume, whom he knew only through his poetry:

> Why, then, do you ask me, do I go out of my way to do
> all this? What is my motive? What is my idea? I have not
> been asked to dramatise the book, for I have been told it is
> already in the hand of a 'well-known London playwright'
> [here he quotes Trischler]. Good luck to him! He has an
> excellent plot to work upon. Will it be believed that my sole
> and wholly conscientious object is to do a clever young man
> a 'good turn', to get his capital story read and talked about.

Scott took his review to *Echoes of the Week*, a paper whose editor,
Augustus Sala, would have been naturally interested in tales of
'Marvellous Melbourne'. It appeared on 3 December, in time to spur
the Christmas sales.[264]

But success would need more than one good review. Trischler
would use the same techniques that were successful in Australia: the
book became a bestseller because it was puffed as a bestseller. With
the Taylors' funds, he could fully exploit the power of advertising,
making innovative use of what we would now term the advertorial:

> THE MYSTERY OF A HANSOM CAB
> The one topic of conversation in London literary circles is
> the phenomenal success that has attended the publication in
> England of the Australian novel, 'The Mystery of a Hansom
> Cab'.

Rapid accrued and momentous sales figures were claimed, also
the notion that Hume would be 'a welcome and valuable addition
to English literary circles'. It went on to add: 'Those who have not
read this interesting, clever, and fascinating little work should do so
at once, and the chances are they will feel exceedingly gratified that
their attention was drawn to it.'[265]

These advertisements appeared in newspapers across Britain,
with extraordinary results: twenty-five thousand copies a month
were printed and sold for fourteen months. These figures, unlike the

Melbourne data, are not doubted: 340,000 copies were sold by August 1888. A detailed breakdown supplied by Trischler to a journalist read:

January 3	33,217
February 3	58,304
March 3	103,118
April 3	93,812
May 3	75,418[266]

The *Illustrated London News* commented: 'Persons were found everywhere devouring the realistic sensational tale of Melbourne social life. Whether travelling by road, rail, or river the unpretending little volume was ever present in some companion's or stranger's hand.' The bookstall tables were stacked with copies. Trischler crowed: 'We can't supply the trade fast enough.'[267]

The market was ripe for a crime-fiction sensation, following Vizetelly's Gaboriau translations, Green's *The Leavenworth Case*, *Called Back* and *Dr Jekyll and Mr Hyde*—the latter selling forty thousand copies in six months. To this need Trischler responded, with a perfect example of commodity capitalism at work: find a product, create a mad fad, exploit the market like a sponge, count the money.[268]

Arthur Conan Doyle bought a copy of *Hansom Cab*, curious and not a little envious. Despite his father's insanity, which impoverished the family, he had grown to man's estate successfully. His Doyle uncles, artistic and prosperous, had paid for his education at Jesuit schools. He had attended Edinburgh University and trained as a doctor. Now he was a young married man and aspiring writer. He had written his own first detective fiction, *A Study in Scarlet*, around the same time as Hume had written *Hansom Cab*.

Doyle is not a completely reliable witness: in his autobiography, *Memories and Adventures*, he elides his father's insanity, and claims to have invented the detective-as-protagonist short-fiction serial—a form that had been published for decades, including by Poe and Mary Fortune, among others.[269] He dated the composition of *Scarlet* as

March–April 1886, around the time Hume was busy with localisations and probably submitting *Hansom Cab* everywhere. The two works would have been landing on the same publishers' desks. Payn turned down this first Sherlock Holmes story, as well as Hume's work. Ward Lock in Melbourne undoubtedly rejected *Hansom Cab*, although their London office would accept Doyle around the same time as Hume's book appeared in Australia.[270]

To Doyle's extreme annoyance Ward Lock made him wait over a year for publication, until November 1887. *A Study in Scarlet* finally appeared just as *Hansom Cab* hit the English market—not as a book, but in the magazine *Beeton's Christmas Annual*. Ward Lock had insisted on buying the copyright, for which Doyle received £25. Jealously he read *Hansom Cab*, writing to his mother on 1 March 1888: 'What a swindle "The Mystery of a Hansom Cab" is. One of the weakest tales I have read, and simply sold by puffing.'[271]

Doyle, like Hume, had no intention of specialising in crime. He was simply experimenting, with *Scarlet* intended as a one-off. Here he was as wrong as Hume, but at this point of the literary game, Hume was ascending the wheel of fortune high, while Doyle languished among the aspiring authors, published but largely unknown.

ACROSS THE FOOTLIGHTS IV

'The people about here do not approve of the stage.'
'People who lived before the flood never do,'
retorted Benke coolly.

ACROSS THE FOOTLIGHTS[272]

While Hume had some involvement in *Hansom Cab*'s colonial push, the overseas sales were not his business, but Trischler's. Hume was, as he always had been, more intent on the theatre. The problem was that the ploy of writing a novel to draw attention to his dramatic skills had not so far been successful, in contrast to the book itself. Still he kept busily writing plays, and networking with the visiting theatricals.

The year 1886 had seen *Hansom Cab*'s publication, his localisations, the writing of light opera with Alfred Plumpton and the approach by Rignold. Hume plainly expected his theatrical fortunes to improve now his book was out. But all he got was a nibble, and from a rather small, if English, fish. A visiting manager, Mr Calthorpe Mallaby (in real life William Calthorpe Deeley, whose well-connected father had insisted on a stage name), was putting together a touring company for New Zealand. His intent had been to sign Beck, but he found Hume instead.[273] A playwright with a reputation across the Tasman was exactly what he wanted.

Mallaby requested farcical comedy and Hume obligingly provided *The Bigamist*, which in his early days in Melbourne had been roundly rejected by the theatre trade. It was written too early to have been part of the deal with Beck. The two talked their theatrical business not with Beck, who was busy all October acting in light comedy, but a new friend of Hume's, Brough-Boucicault actor Walter Everard. Hume thought the play needed a rewrite, but he and Mallaby agreed on terms.[274]

Mallaby's company staged the play successfully in New Zealand, in Dunedin in November and in Christchurch the following month:

THE BIGAMIST,

A Farcical Comedy in three acts, by Fergus Hume.

The Amorous Scotchman

The Mercenary Jew

The Blighted Irishman

The Bewildered Englishman.

'I want my wife!!!'[275]

In the play, the Hon. Teddy manages to get three women claiming him as their lawful husband at once. But at the end 'everyone is satisfied,' the *Oddity* commented, witheringly, 'except, perhaps, the audience.' *The Bigamist* did briefly please Hume, who compiled a file of its New Zealand reviews. Mallaby then offered terms for taking the play to London. Hume agreed, provided the manager return via Melbourne so that a proper agreement could be signed.[276]

Mallaby was not a man of great theatrical-business skills, and his New Zealand venture failed. He returned to London hurriedly, leaving his troupe behind. The voyage was spent profitably for him, playing poker with the ship's officers and another saloon passenger, a lawyer—who would unsuccessfully sue Mallaby over unpaid IOUs, despite the latter winning £200–300 during the voyage.[277]

Another theatrical annoyance for Hume was that J. C. Williamson had proved impervious to the flattering mention in *Hansom Cab*. It was not Hume, Fergus that Williamson would sign, but Hume, Mary. The Humes loved Gilbert and Sullivan, and now, in February 1887, Mary would appear with the Royal Comic Opera Company in *The Pirates of Penzance*. For the first time she would professionally act as well as sing, indicating how far she and her brother had come from respectable Dunedin and the all-male performances on the madhouse stage.

Hume kept writing: a comedietta, 'Dolly', for his Prince Masher Amy Horton, which she proposed taking to England, and a play for Carrie Swain.[278] Then Mallaby provided a bombshell. When the manager scarpered from New Zealand, he took with him the manuscript of *The Bigamist* and two other Hume plays. In March, now using the name Calthorpe, he staged the play at London's Vaudeville theatre as *The Mormon*, and as his own work. Hume had not received any money from the New Zealand production and on opening a copy of the *Era* that May saw a review of his play, recognisable as such despite the change of title and (almost) all of the characters' names. He immediately sent an angry letter to the magazine, citing Walter Everard as a witness.[279] The letter was published, useful exposure for his playwriting.

Trischler had taken the dramatic version of *Hansom Cab* to London. Although the novel had been a huge success, to the theatre managers of London Hume was still an unknown, and worse, a colonial, with all the baggage of cultural inferiority. Hume's script was not acceptable without revisions from an English, and more established playwright. Arthur Law (1844–1913) a former military man and actor, got the job, although the closest he had come to adapting a mystery was *The Great Tay-Kin* (1881), a libretto for music by Gilbert and Sullivan baritone George Grossmith. It had little in common with Hume's work. Given the geographical distances, a collaboration by mail or the expensive telegraph was unlikely—Hume may not even have had power of veto.

In early 1888 the play was staged at London's Royal Princess's theatre, leased by actress Grace Hawthorne, who played the plum role of Sal Rawlins, 'a poor storm-tossed waif upon the sea of life'. Brilliant marketing was again in evidence: it was claimed a genuine Melbourne hansom cab had been imported for the production. Posters appeared on walls and shopfronts, showing characters from the play. Then a spectacular publicity stunt occurred. London hansom cabs drove around the streets carrying effigies of the murderer and the victim,[280] with the theatre manager personally starring in a special disruption of Fleet Street:

> He organised an army of one thousand sandwich-boardmen, who marched down Fleet Street displaying vivid posters. At the end of the procession came the hansom cab. In the cab sat the manager dressed to kill in silk hat and frock coat with a nosegay, while at his side dropped a dummy representing the victim with a gory gash across his throat. The procession absolutely disorganised the traffic. The police took a hand and chased the sandwich men into the side streets, but the manager had reserves, who took up the boards and carried on. The police called for reinforcements, and there was renewed excitement and arrests. The advertising genius was fined heavily, but he had achieved so marvelous a degree of publicity for the play that he regarded the fine as a veritable bargain.[281]

A copy of the first night's programme, 23 February 1888, has the handwritten annotation: 'In the drama it was indispensable that the audience should be let into the secret from the very first.'[282] Here the contemporary limitations of adapting the whodunnit plot to the stage are evident. Now plays with shock endings, such as Agatha Christie's *The Mousetrap*, are commonplace if not conventional. But in Hume's era the villain, like Beck, melodramatically announced his stage career of evil from the opening scene, the suspense being not who had done the deed, but how he would be caught. It was virtually impossible to keep the secret of a murder-mystery drama, particularly since newspaper reviews would give the plot in full. Hume and Law's *Hansom Cab* was less of a mystery than an action melodrama, and not of outstanding quality either.

Clement Scott, who had praised the novel, saw the play when it opened. As was his innovation, he completed his review for the *Daily Telegraph* on the same night. It was a classic of negative, witty reviewing:

> The story is nervously and cleverly written; the drama turns out to be a tottering edifice, shaky and ill-constructed. That which should have been clearly and concisely told in a prologue meanders over the best part of two acts; the scent, once fairly strong, becomes fainter and fainter, and ultimately those who were anxious to follow give up the chase in despair…In this instance the actors and actresses can render very little assistance. Their parts are as feeble and invertebrate as the drama is involved and misty.

Others were more magnanimous, with the correspondent of a colonial newspaper only taking offence at the backdrop: 'the Collins street scene is a libel on one of the finest thoroughfares in Christendom.'[283] Despite these cavils, the play would have a successful run in London. It was the signal Hume needed to make his move to England. He had left England as a small child, the son of a lowly madhouse attendant. Now he was a conquering literary hero, who could afford a first-class passage Home.

Before Hume left he arranged with Kemp & Boyce for a further colonial printing of *Hansom Cab*, of ten thousand copies. Both parties seem to have been unaware that the English copyright, owned by Jessie Taylor, had global effect. She promptly sued for infringement, in what must have come as rather a shock to the printers. The firm lost substantially, and the business was sold at the end of the year.[284]

Even before Hume arrived in England, he would have known that the play was not bringing in all the revenue it could, due to theatrical piracy. A dozen touring companies presented different versions of *Hansom Cab* outside London—unauthorised, and for which Hume received no pay. Not surprisingly, theatrical piracy figures in *Madame Midas*, for it was much on Hume's mind. A touring theatre troupe, the Wopples family, are minor players living off their dramatic wits.

The Wopples survive because of Mrs Wopples, wife, actress, mother of a large family. She is also a stage pirate, attending the latest plays in a modest seat, 'between a coal-heaver and an apple-woman', where she transcribes the latest dramas as they are played. The troupe gets the newest London dramas, merely changing the title, just as Mallaby performed Hume's *The Bigamist* as *The Mormon*. The Wopples act *Called Back* (performed by Rignold) as *The Blind Detective*, and *The Silver King* (J. C. Williamson) as *The Living Dead*, a title which at the time did not suggest zombies. Another in-joke here, at the expense of some big theatre names: 'thus do we evade the grasping avarice of the Melbourne managers, who would make us pay fees for them.'[285]

Fergus might personally have deplored stage piracy and certainly suffered from it. But he made the Wopples clan likeable and kindly, even Christian. Here he showed his sympathies for those considered raffish and disreputable by society—the theatricals like Amy Horton who had welcomed his works, as opposed to the 'unco guid' like Robertson, who had rejected *Hansom Cab*.

The likes of the Wopples did certainly exploit Hume. After the success of the London *Hansom Cab* production, enterprising colonial theatricals suddenly saw the potential of the play. Some of these had rejected Hume's original dramas, but were happy to benefit from a play version of his bestselling novel. In Melbourne, first cab off the rank was the H. C. Sidney company, which in August 1888 presented their version. A journalist who knew Hume from New Zealand went to the opening night. He thought the play good, but poorly acted. Also present were some other faces familiar to him: Hume's 'people', James and Mary Hume, proud siblings at the theatre production of their brother's work, even if pirated. They boasted that '300,000 copies of the "Mystery" had been sold in England'.[286]

Fergus Hume had licensed the Australian theatrical production of the novel to S. F. Travers-Vale, who rewrote it. But this company was not quick enough off the mark, although they would tour the production in rural Victoria. They did benefit in Melbourne from a happy accident. John Orange, a hansom cabman, drunkenly drove over a seventy-foot cliff into the flooded Yarra. Riverside wattle trees broke the fall, with Orange and his horse suffering only bruises and scratches. The cab was pulled from the river undamaged except for broken glass windows—and was promptly dried out and repaired to play a starring role onstage.[287]

In the meantime H. C. Sidney took his version interstate, only to fall foul of the law. In Brisbane, where 'they are more severe on advertising novelties than Melbourne', the authorities were scandalised by an idea borrowed from the London production: a hansom driving around the streets with fake corpse. A disgusted magistrate suspended the cabman's licence for a fortnight, with the threat of a permanent cancellation.[288]

Several other touring companies pirated the play in Australasia. George Darrell wrote a version with the alternative title of *Midnight Melbourne*. Reviewers commented that the play had more of Darrell in it than Hume. He changed Sal Rawlins' name to Kate, giving the role to his young second wife, Cissie. In the play both aesthete Felix Rolleston and detective Calton compete for Kate, the latter winning: despite her slum upbringing, the young lady is 'of innate purity of mind and uncontaminated'. Again, a real horse and hansom were driven onto the stage.[289] Darrell even took the play to Dunedin, but whether James Hume ever saw it is unknown.

Fergus Hume by this time had departed the colonies. Dunedin, and subsequently Melbourne, had nursed his talent, given him the inspiration for a bestselling novel and finally a play, performed in London. Good things had come from *Hansom Cab*, for he had even become, belatedly, a contributor to the *Argus* newspaper.[290] But the colonies were too small for him now and international success was his for the taking.

Hume was farewelled from Melbourne in some style, with a dinner party. Host Dr William Maloney, a friend of Tom Roberts, was a dapper dresser and aspiring politician, his interests progressive: the following year he would introduce the first bill for women's suffrage in the British Empire. In the one account of the event, poet Victor Daley recalled Hume as 'a small, dark man with a voice like corduroy. But he had a great heart and great confidence. "I know what they want," he said, "and they shall have it." He did know.'[291]

Hansom Cab ends with the married lovers, Madge and Brian, taking the steamer to London under a blood-red sky. They stand on deck, watching the tall landmarks of Melbourne, the Exhibition and Law Court domes, as well as Government House's tower, slowly recede. The ship 'bore them away into the placid beauty of the coming night towards the old world and the new life'—the last words of the novel. It also expressed Hume's aspirations. The colonial dream was to make enough money to return triumphantly to England, although once there the returnees could find themselves less conquering heroes than, in the words of Macmillan's reader, a nuisance. Aspiring writers, musicians and artists found themselves competing fiercely with the best of the Empire. The streets of London could be mean, with the expatriates coming to seek their fortunes, but instead finding penury, far from family and friends.

In a nineteenth-century novel, conventional in its structure and expectations, this story would have ended, as in *Hansom Cab*, with the triumphant departure for England. Hume had become famous in the literary world, his sideways strategy to achieve a career as a playwright having yielded results beyond his wildest dreams. When Hume arrived in London, the doors to the theatre were open to him—or so it seemed.

20

ALADDIN IN LONDON
Consequences

'You can't elevate the drama out of a dustbin.'
WHEN I LIVED IN BOHEMIA[292]

Hume and Beck took the steamship *Oceana* to England in April 1888. On board they were a popular pair—both were now famous, Hume a 'great favourite' and Beck described as the 'irresistible'. They also put on amateur theatrics for the passengers, including a comedietta called 'A Rainy Day', which Hume reportedly wrote in a few hours.[293]

In Hume's novel *The Girl from Malta*, a young Australian man travels to England. The authorial voice comments: 'Can there be anything in the world more pleasant than sea life on a steamship with jolly people?' It seems a rare autobiographical reflection. The cliffs of Dover may have looked dingy under a grey English sky, the Thames as dirty as the Yarra, but a great city still beckoned. Hume: 'Without doubt London is an ugly city; still it is London, and there is a fascination about its miles of bricks and mortar which none can resist.'[294] Melbourne might be marvellous, but London was the centre of the Empire.

In *The Girl from Malta* the heroes head for a hotel, the Tavistock:

'the Australian cricketers generally stop there, so it will feel home-like.'[295] Here Hume inverts a common usage, for 'home' in colonial parlance meant England. Yet the homeland, once reached, could seem profoundly alien: sunless, cold and conservative. In the late 1800s a substantial community of Australians and New Zealanders lived in London, including members of the British Parliament, musicians (like Melba), mining journalists, artists and literati. They had their own newspaper, the *British Australasian*, which made boast of their success, marking 'the smallest Australian sparrow's chirp in smooth eulogy'.[296]

Beck was a returning hero and Hume the literary lion of the season, which meant for the first time that he gave interviews. But though he told one journalist he was 'just longing to see all the sights', he had work to do.[297] In their first twelve days in London Beck and Hume completed the stage adaptation of *Madame Midas*.

The new novel was destined for the Hansom Cab Publishing Company, with Hume selling its copyright, this time to Trischler alone. His hopes remained primarily with the theatre, and he did not intend that some London dramatist should again rewrite his work. For Beck the collaboration produced a personal star vehicle, with the villain, Gaston Vandeloup, now central character. One review commented on his performance: 'Of villainy, it is the most dangerous kind; it presents vice in alluring forms; it is a well-dressed, well-nourished, jewelled kind of wickedness.'[298]

The play of *Madame Midas* finished, Hume and Beck can be imagined sauntering the London streets arm in arm—something unexceptionable for two male friends at the time. They partook of the sights, theatres, and the Savage Club, which had a co-membership deal with the Yorick. Bohemian London was not greatly different from Bohemian Melbourne, with its garrets and merry midnight suppers, but the stakes were higher, with greater promise of riches, influence and fame.

Hume, Beck and Trischler had a strategy to prevent the piracy of

Madame Midas. Book and play were released almost simultaneously in July 1888, with a small performance in Shakespeare's Stratford, to legally secure the copyright for the drama and prevent competing versions being performed.

Again, startling sales figures were claimed for the book. Advance trade orders accounted for most of the printing, as booksellers hoped for another *Hansom Cab*, and nearly eighty-four thousand copies of *Madame Midas* were subscribed before the book was published. The first edition has a claim of 100,000 copies printed on the cover, which Rowan Gibbs believes may be valid. George Robertson, not letting another business opportunity escape, published the Melbourne edition despite the book's immorality: Gaston seduces and lives in sin with pretty Kitty Marchurst. In the play the sensibilities of the theatre-going public were mollified by a fake marriage between the pair.[299]

In the meantime *Hansom Cab* kept giving and giving, to Trischler and Jessie Taylor. George Nicholson Taylor boasted that the book and a family legacy had made his wife £50,000 pounds. Brodzky's *Table Talk* expressed disbelief, but it was true.[300] Now *Hansom Cab* was giving to others as well, for free: the popularity of the book resulted in inevitable piracy in the United States and translations, also pirated, into European and even Asian languages. The extent of their print runs are unknown, but they would have added substantially to the figure of 500,000 copies claimed for England alone.

Success breeds allusion in popular culture, another form of exploitation, and *Hansom Cab* inspired cartoons; a fad for men's short coats, of the sort worn by Brian Fitzgerald in the opening scenes of the novel;[301] a popular song; and a pretty dreadful limerick:

> There was a young man in Dunedin
> Who started a Fergus Hume readin',
> But the spec' didn't pay,
> And he faded away.
> And the verdict was 'died of light feedin'.[302]

Perhaps the greatest compliment was a pulpy 1888 parody, appearing both in London and Sydney: W. Humer Ferguson's *The Mystery of a Wheel-barrow, or Gaboriau Gaborooed* (Walter Scott; Edwards, Dunlop). Its design echoed the cover of *Hansom Cab*, but showing several drunks in charge of a wheelbarrow. Inside, Brian becomes Fitzdoodle O'Brier, as if he was a comic Irishman, and Frettlby, Frecklenose. Perhaps the unknown author had also been rejected by the editor of the *Cornhill*, for James Payn (spelt correctly) is described as an 'obscure English novelist'. It is genuinely funny in places, despite music-hall jokes in the courtroom, as when the cab-driver is questioned:

Q.—'Did you assist him to alight?'

A.—'No, he wasn't smokin', yer honour.'[303]

But other parts of the parody are quite alarming to the modern reader. Frecklenose's fortune comes from inventions, including selling to the New Zealand government the rights to a cattlewash. It is sold to the Māori as a hair tonic: 'An appreciable reduction in the native population having resulted, Frecklenose was honoured with the thanks of the House of Representatives, and a grant of land in Victoria.'[304] The Victorians were casually and unabashedly racist, but genocide was not usually a subject for comedy. Frecklenose is at least inconsistent, for he has an agonising guilty secret: the vital ingredient of his cattlewash/tonic was a black baby, accidentally boiled.

Other consequences of *Hansom Cab*'s popularity were more directly criminal, and even, it was claimed, murderous. Hume's fame in England and his delayed arrival provided an opportunity for impersonation. In his preface Hume recalls that one of these con men threatened to shoot him; another even had a business card printed, with his price for writing a follow-up to the novel.

A third imposter featured in the *Sunday Times*, which had been acquired by Alice Cornwell, playing Madame Murdoch. She had installed as editor her new love interest, journalist Phil (Frederick) Stannard Robinson. An interview with the author of *Madame Midas* would 'boom' both Hume and Cornwell's new mining ventures.

Hume was deemed a suitable subject for the 'Chats with Celebrities' column and a 'distinguished' amateur (an author rather than professional journalist) was dispatched after him. After several days, he reported back to his editor:

'You asked me to interview the author of "The Hansom Cab"?'

'Yes.'

'You said he had arrived in London.'

'Yes.'

'I found tokens of him here and there.'

'Well?'

The journalist reported that Hume had visited theatres and obtained a suit from a fashionable tailor. So far so unimpressive, but then came a bombshell: Hume had left his hotel without paying the bill.

'What! Mr Fergus Hume.'

'That was the name he gave; he said he was the author of "The Mystery of a Hansom Cab," and that he had sold half a million; and he told the box-keeper at one of the theatres that he had a new play in his trunk which would make the fortune of any house.'

'Well, where is your manuscript of the interview?'

'It wasn't Fergus Hume at all; and the police are trying to interview him now.'

'You have written an account of your adventures?'

'No sir.'

'Do, then; you can have a column.'

'But I haven't had any adventures!'

'No! What you have told me does not suggest to me an

interesting column of copy?'

'No sir.'

'Do you think you can remember this present conversation?'

'Yes.'

'Very well, write it out; and when you have finished take a month's salary and go and seek an engagement on the other *Times*.'

'Yes, sir.'[305]

This non-story was still excellent publicity for the real Hume. When he *was* interviewed by the *Sunday Times* a week later, he professed himself most amused by the article.[306]

This unknown fraudster was not the only one to borrow Hume's celebrity. A gang of American swindlers had arrived in England with a clever scam to fleece rich men with hobbies. The trickster would arrive on the doorstep with a (forged) letter of introduction and a specific interest, shared with the intended target. In Birmingham an American gentleman calling himself Mr Ritchie represented himself as an orchid fancier to Austen Chamberlain, a politician and the half-brother of future PM Neville Chamberlain. Ritchie inspected Chamberlain's orchid collection, displaying enthusiastic and convincing admiration. On his departure Ritchie borrowed money from Chamberlain, who also assisted in getting a bill from an American bank cashed, for £250. It proved fraudulent. Ritchie then visited another orchid collector, this time claiming to be Austen Chamberlain, and performed a similar trick.[307]

Then a letter appeared in the *Morning Post*:

A WARNING
TO THE EDITOR OF THE MORNING POST

SIR.—I beg leave through your columns to call the attention of the public, and literary men in particular, to a man who is going around the country calling himself "Fergus Hume." He is of fine physique, height about 5ft 11in, dark hair and complexion, has slight American accent, and appears to have Spanish connections; he sometimes dresses as a tourist carrying a riding whip, he makes very free use in conversation of the names of leading literary men, with the addresses and works of whom he appears to be well acquainted. The man called last week upon me, bringing with him a card of introduction from a well-known publisher in this town, who fully believed him to be the author of "The Mystery of a Hansom Cab." After calling two or three times he asked me to cash a cheque drawn upon a London bank, and signed "Fergus Hume." I have since discovered that the man is in no way connected with Mr. Fergus W. Hume, the author of "The Mystery of a Hansom Cab," and has no account whatever with the bank upon which the cheque was drawn.—

Yours, &c. THOMAS THATCHER[308]

The fraudster had assumed the persona of Fergus Hume in Bristol. In November 1888, he visited the publishers Arrowsmith, then took a hansom cab—appropriately—to visit Thomas Thatcher, a collector of literary autographs. The pair got on well: 'He was very pleasant company, his knowledge of literary men was marvelous; from Land's End to John O'Groats he had their names and addresses at his finger's ends.' To Thatcher he was 'just that jolly, rollicking, good-natured style of man which one might very naturally expect to find in the writer of those racy and stirring novels so popular with the public'.

Also in Bristol 'Hume' took his 'wife', a fortyish, grey-haired, well-dressed lady, to visit a prominent bookseller, and made a purchase of some expensive books with a bogus cheque for £20, pocketing the books and the change.[309] Neither of the victims had apparently read the interviews with Hume that had already appeared in the British press. The *Sunday Times* had described Hume in some detail: he was young, 'of middle height' with a manner 'quiet and unassuming', his accent 'provincial' (probably Scots-colonial, but the wording simply suggests that Hume was not 'one of us'). Dark hair and moustache apart, the flashy American swindler had nothing in common with Hume. The impersonation was ludicrous, but it made for extra publicity, and source material for Hume. The fraudster would operate successfully all over Britain for months before being apprehended in August 1889.

Another crime blamed on *Hansom Cab* was lethal. In February 1889 the elderly John Fletcher, a prosperous paper manufacturer, and Lancaster County Councillor, was found unconscious and dying in a Manchester cab. Shortly before he had been drinking in a pub with an unknown young man. An inebriated Fletcher had been assisted to the cab by his companion, who gave a destination to the cabman. During the journey the young man decamped, leaving the door open.

Fletcher's money had vanished, as had his gold watch and chain, worth £100. The case seemed initially a robbery in which the victim had died of natural causes. However, a policeman had witnessed Fletcher and the young man enter the cab, and later assisted the dying man. He was suspicious and could provide a description of Fletcher's companion.

An autopsy proved initially inconclusive: Fletcher had an alcoholic's liver, but seemed to have died from syncope, a loss of blood pressure.[310] Alcohol alone could not have caused his collapse. Forensic analysis detected chloral hydrate in his stomach contents, then used in medicine as a sedative and commonly available from chemists. It is chemically related to chloroform, used in *Hansom Cab* to kill Oliver Whyte. Chloral added to alcohol increases the effects of intoxication—what we would now term a 'date rape' drug. If too much is used, it can send the victim into a coma, even kill them.

A week before the murder a young man had tried to buy a pound of chloral in a Liverpool pharmacy. The chemist demurred, suggesting a smaller quantity. The customer responded by grabbing the bottle and running away. The descriptions of the thief and Fletcher's companion agreed.

When the teenage Charles Parton was arrested by the Manchester police, he was easily identified in the line-ups. Parton came from a family of prize fighters and had some renown as a lightweight boxer. But he also associated with criminals, having been jailed for 'fencing'. His father had been treated for angina with chloral: the son knew the drug's effects.[311]

The trial proved sensational, with packed crowds outside the courtroom. The prosecution case conclusively proved guilt, with a witness testifying that he had seen Parton at the pub with Fletcher, pouring the contents of a small bottle into a glass of beer.[312] Subsequently it emerged that Parton had used this trick to rob two other men. His mistake with Fletcher, he admitted, had been to administer more chloral than intended. Seeing that Fletcher was a 'gonner', he put him in a cab and fled.[313] Parton was condemned to death, then reprieved after a petition to Queen Victoria. He was, after all, young, and his crime was what we would consider manslaughter.

Journalists in England and Australia made the obvious connection: the case was described as 'A Real Hansom-Cab Mystery'. 'Is Mr Fergus Hume unconsciously answerable for this crime?' asked Australian newspapers. Several sources reported that Parton owned a copy of *Hansom Cab* or had been influenced by the posters advertising the provincial tours of the (pirated) play.[314]

'There can indeed be very little doubt that if Mr. Hume's shilling "marrow-curdler" had never been written the estimable but bibulous Mr. Fletcher would never have been poisoned,' claimed the London correspondent of the Christchurch *Star*. Louisa Lawson's feminist magazine *Dawn* was even more censorious about the case: 'The latent predisposition was evidently excited to activity by the moral disease germ which unfortunately came in contact with it. Into what court will the damages have to be paid for the mischief caused by literary firebrands.'[315] *Table Talk*'s Brodzky had similarly and salaciously claimed Mary Fortune's son George had been led into a life of crime by her Detective Album series. But the *Evening Standard* made the apt point: 'What would not some men give for an enormous advertisement like this?' Trischler would have agreed wholeheartedly.[316]

The irony is that while Fletcher was discovered drugged and *in extremis* in a cab there were otherwise no similarities to the fictional crime in *Hansom Cab*. The motive differed, as did the modus operandi. If Parton had taken anything from Hume's work it was only that the interior of a cab offered privacy for villainous acts: in this case not murder, but robbing a man and leaving him to die. Despite illustrations such as those in the *Penny Illustrated Paper*, which could have advertised Hume's novel,[317] the fact remains that the initial newspaper reports clearly described Fletcher's fatal cab as a four-wheeler. The Manchester case was a media beat-up, as far as Hume was concerned, and not a murder in a hansom cab after all.

A TRAITOR IN LONDON
The End of Friendships

Madame Midas suffered severely from the shocks she had undergone with the discovery of everyone's baseness.

MADAME MIDAS[318]

If Hume's life were compared to a play it would be neither a farce nor a comedy ending in matrimony (he never married). His story resembled the classical form of the tragedy, with an ambitious hero who achieves his aim before the downwards turn of fortune and ensuing disaster. *Hansom Cab* might have been a success, but within a few years the enterprising band behind it would all quarrel bitterly.

The first break was between Hume and Beck. Of their union the major fruit was the *Madame Midas* play. They expected great things of it, after taking such pains to secure the copyright. But though Phil Beck gnashed his teeth and twirled his moustache as Gaston Vandeloup, *Madame Midas*'s run at London's Royal Princess's Theatre proved short.

Beck had introduced Hume to London, the theatre, literary lions' dens and clubland. Now his friend and collaborator was the man of the moment, whom all the society hostesses wanted to meet. The charismatic actor found himself relegated to the background. One issue the pair would have had was that Hume was teetotal, and Beck, though witty good company when sober, did drown adversity with drink. One commentator, who had known the pair in Melbourne, would call Beck Hume's 'old man of the sea'.[319] The literary agreement between the pair became increasingly burdensome to Hume. Professionally and personally, the pair fell out, spectacularly.

Because of the legal agreement, Beck demanded to be paid off. His price? The Australian theatre rights to *Madame Midas*. Beck would tour the production in the colonies, where interest would be guaranteed, given the setting. The stage villain took the steamship to Australia at the end of December 1888, after only six months in England.

Hume did not need Beck anymore, not as a collaborator and certainly not socially. He had other interests now, new friends, a new city to explore. As he had in Melbourne he wandered the seedier parts of London, seeking inspiration and local colour. Hume had enough new ideas for novels to keep him going for years, to say nothing of the theatrical opportunities.[320]

Moreover he was expecting family members in London soon: Mary Hume and her new husband, Charles Willeby. The rising soprano had toured New Zealand, where her accompanist was Willeby, the boy-next-door from Dunedin days. Despite a ten-year gap in their ages, and Willeby only one month discharged from bankruptcy, the pair married in Dunedin in February 1889, the same week Darrell's version of *Hansom Cab* debuted there.[321] It was a quiet occasion due to Bessie Hume's ill health, and would be the only wedding among the Hume children.

The couple followed Fergus to Europe to further their music careers. Mary would continue to perform professionally and teach, despite having two children. Hume found his new brother-in-law convivial and a worthy collaborator. They wrote songs together, a comic opera and even appeared in the same magazine, *Belgravia*, Hume with a reprint of *Professor Brankel*, Willeby with music criticism.[322]

Life seemed good. Hume was reported in London to be:

> enjoying the season, and such distinction as appertains to being the 'man who wrote the Hansom Cab story, doncherknow.' He goes out a good bit into Brompton society [the artists and writers quarter], is made much of by Anglo-Australians as 'one of our rising men', and graciously patronised by the larger literary lions of the Savile Club.[323]

Meanwhile, in Australia, Beck sought out his old theatre contacts. *Madame Midas* was staged first in Sydney with Rignold, from April–May 1889. Beck, in a petty act, deliberately wrote out Hume from the dramatisation—or let the press report it as such—claiming it as his sole production. He played Gaston Vandeloup to acclaim: 'the acting of the principal character is so wonderfully fine, so exquisitely finished, so perfectly complete...' Many thought it his best role.[324]

Beck's Sydney sojourn had one scandalous consequence. In the Brough-Boucicault production of Buchanan's *Sophia*, Beck had played the villain, Blifil. In the same production was Pattie Browne, an actress noted for saucy soubrette roles, who was separated from her husband, William George Baumann. Browne helped Beck, finding him a Sydney billet with her mother during the run of *Madame Midas*. They were colleagues, friends and, in Beck's own words, much more. When Browne's husband visited, Beck, like a villain from a bedroom farce, told him most ungallantly that he had had 'intercourse' with his wife. Though a distraught Baumann offered to forgive Browne, she would have none of it. Their 1890 divorce cited Beck as co-respondent.

Was Beck blurring the line between the cad onstage and offstage? He could equally have had no sexual interest in Browne, rather acting as a beard, to help her get a divorce. This strategy was not uncommon in theatre, especially when an actress had a rich or influential suitor:

in this case Browne's employer, actor-manager Dion Boucicault Jr. In keeping his name out of the divorce courts, Boucicault preserved his impresario reputation. He and Browne were engaged for 'eight years', parting company around 1896. The dating suggests that it was Boucicault, not Beck, who was responsible for Pattie Browne's divorce. But the actor took the blame, either for friendship or for money.[325]

Madame Midas and Beck moved to Melbourne in June with the Alfred Dampier Company. 'Gallery Boy', who wrote a vernacular column for *Lorgnette*, wrote: 'But I must go and gaze upon Phil Beck, who is as lovely as ever...' He found the play less impressive, and also noted strains in Beck's performance: 'What's the matter with Phil Beck? Ain't 'e well, or what? Seemed a bit queer on Saturday night, and some of the audience were of that opinion.' More dramatic was that John Whiteman saw the play about his estranged wife and promptly sued Dampier for libel, claiming £2000 damages—unsuccessfully.[326]

Despite the publicity the production did not become a major success, with no further colonial tours. When the Melbourne run finished, Beck returned to his old role of the Demon in *The Crimes of Paris*, still with Dampier. Back in Sydney by October, he appeared with Rignold in Shakespearean drama, with his best role as Brutus in *Julius Caesar*. But these roles, though good, were not the star, lucrative parts he craved.

Perhaps Beck thought of Hume again as his golden goose. But Hume had wearied of Beck and the 'obligations' of the contract. He complained as much to an Irish nationalist MP and Fleet Street journalist, T. P. (Tay Pay) O'Connor, 'over coffee one night'. The conversation turned to Beck, O'Connor asking if he had ever played Blifil, a character outwardly virtuous but actually devious, conniving and cruel. To Hume, Beck had been a Blifil, and he told Tay Pay the story of their compact.

Hume may have been unaware that Tay Pay wrote a gossip column, 'Mainly About People' for the radical *Star* newspaper. What Hume said would now be regarded as 'off the record', although at the time the rules of journalistic decorum were fluid. Because the pair were not conducting a formal interview, Tay Pay only took mental notes (probably writing them down the same night). He filed the story away—it could have future use, even if it were quite libellous.

Hume not only told Tay Pay about the sickbed contract, but that he had written to Beck threatening to test their agreement in the courts. Beck responded by booking passage home aboard the steamship *Punda*, telling his friends he intended to bring out new dramas from England. Did he anticipate more plays from Hume?[327] Onboard Beck gambled and drank heavily, so much so that the *Punda*'s captain ordered limits on his alcohol supply. Possibly the neuralgia returned, or depression at his debts and the break with Hume. On Christmas Eve 1889, close to the anniversary of his departure to England with Hume, two shots resounded from his cabin. Inside, Beck lay dead, with a revolver and a fatal wound to the temple.

The coroner's jury returned a verdict of suicide with 'no evidence to show any reason for the action'. Gossips at the Savage Club noted that Beck 'had been very unfortunate in his recent enterprises' and seemed 'to have quite lost heart'.[328] A line in the *Madame Midas* play was recalled, something that Beck perhaps wrote, for it was not in the book. Gaston Vandeloup takes poison and dies, his last words being: 'Now for the great conundrum.' Others hinted at more: 'Poor Phil Beck! Those who remember his genial smile, and unflagging spirits find it difficult to realise that life's stage proved too emotional for one who trod so merrily upon the boards.'[329]

Tay Pay, who might have anticipated good copy from a theatrical lawsuit, kept quiet—for the moment. If Hume felt relief as well as remorse, he kept that private. A few others, like Trischler, knew that Beck's suicide was no mystery. Had Beck never met Hume, his career could have been long and distinguished, even extending into the silent-film era. Because he chanced his theatrical fortunes in Australia, throwing everything he had into *Madame Midas*, he paid with his life.

The next quarrel of Hume's was with Trischler. This time indiscreet comments to the press went public, crossing and re-crossing the globe. The journalist concerned was an anonymous foreign correspondent for the colonial papers, a stylish and witty writer, acquainted with Trischler from Christchurch days. He wrote 'Anglo-Colonial Notes' and sent them via mail steamer to both the Christchurch *Star* and the *Adelaide Register*, with slight variations for the two colonies.

For this journalist Hume and Trischler were both newsworthy. He beat up the story of the Manchester murder and also wrote that Hume had to pay a 'stiffish sum' to get out of the partnership with Beck,[330] information that could only have come from someone close to the author, most likely the publisher. Trischler fed him titbits, as part of his drive for publicity.

But this strategy would backfire for Trischler. In early 1889, the journalist 'accidentally met a friend of Hume's and asked what the pride of New Zealand was doing?' He was told the 'energetic little devil Trischler' had Hume under lock and key, busy writing. 'We giggled a little, likewise gargled (as the Americans say), and I believe I was sufficiently amused with the aforesaid remark as to repeat it in a modified form in one of my letters.'

His 'Anglo-Colonial Notes' written in late February, and dispatched by mail steamer to Christchurch, included the headline: 'Fergus Hume Locked Up': 'Mr Trischler (the "Hansom Cab Publishing Company"), says he's got Fergus Hume locked up in his new house at Brixton, and doesn't mean to let him out till he's finished the "shocker" he's at present engaged on. A mad wag is Trischler, yet business-like withal!'[331]

This anecdote appears to have been a variation on a tale told of

Marcus Clarke, when writing *His Natural Life* for the *Australian Journal*. He took longer and longer to file his serial copy, until publisher Alfred Massina took drastic action with lock and key. Mullen's bookseller Leonard Slade records that Massina cheerfully admitted the deed.[332]

The report of the lock-up took two months to reach New Zealand, appearing in April. It was newsworthy, as *Hansom Cab* was still selling well—a local bookseller reported that he would receive a hundred copies at a time, which would disappear rapidly.[333] Somebody in Christchurch seems to have written to Hume, probably enclosing a cutting from the *Star*.

Back in London, far from publisher imprisoning author, Hume and Trischler had been enjoying the social scene. They attended, as the 'Anglo-Colonial Notes' records, an 'Australian night' at the Savage Club, held in early May. Here Hume and 'the irrepressible' Trischler represented colonial 'belles lettres', along with authors including H. B. Marriott Watson, son of the writerly cleric who had married Trischler and his Lucy. The evening was proclaimed 'one of the brightest of the season'.[334] Yet, unknown to either Hume or Trischler on this merry night, a ticking time-bomb was steaming back from the colonies, with explosive consequences.

In July the correspondent wrote in his colonial letter that publisher and author had split, and that he himself was responsible: 'I much regret to learn (I sincerely hope it isn't true) that a little jokelet of mine is a cause of the difference.' He admitted to circulating the report of the imprisonment 'in a modified form'. The crucial change had been to credit Trischler as if quoting him, omitting the anonymous gossiper. Thus hearsay became reportage—and Hume found it insulting:

> You will scarcely credit the truth when I state that Hume, on seeing it, absolutely went furiously to Trischler and asked him what the something something he meant by inventing such scandalous yarns about him. Poor Trischler—taken

completely aback—replied he did not believe he ever had made the remark in question. Surely, however, Mr Hume could see it was merely meant chaffingly. But Hume appears to have felt that the great name of Australia's most famous novelist had been taken in vain, and must have declined to be appeased.[335]

Outraged, Hume took himself off to F. V. White, a major yellow-back publisher. The columnist noted the firm's respectability, with a sting in the tail of his sentence: they had 'quite a large number of mediocre novelists amongst their clients'. He added that Hume's position was 'uncertain' and the move was 'an Irish rise' (that is, not a rise at all). His sympathies were clearly with Trischler.[336]

Hume himself would claim that from White he received the best price ever paid for a shilling book in England, though he did not specify the sum.[337] With the firm Hume released *The Piccadilly Puzzle*, originally intended for Trischler, with a dedication to his new friend, Willeby 'Esq'. George Robertson again published the colonial edition, despite the book being denounced by a New Zealand journalist as immoral and badly written. The follow-up was the sequel to *Madame Midas* and the last book in the Melbourne Trilogy, *Miss Mephistopheles*.[338]

Had Hume received good career advice? Apparently not. Though he had dealings with agents at various points of his career, he appears to have lacked the support of a dedicated literary businessman. He never consolidated his early success into the substantial literary reputation he craved. *Hansom Cab* was a clever literary crime story that became a blockbuster, *Madame Midas*, a fine novel of colonial life. But the works that immediately followed, *The Girl from Malta*, *The Piccadilly Puzzle* and *Miss Mephistopheles*, were hurried. None seem now particularly reprintable and they earned Hume bad reviews.

Hume was a quick and hard worker, but now he was simply producing too much, and of lesser quality. He typecast himself as a writer of 'shilling shockers', a label he found impossible to escape. Hume became a brand name, though not for the dramatic work on which he had set his heart. Much the same would happen to Arthur Conan Doyle, doomed to write more Sherlock Holmes stories despite a valiant attempt to kill off his famous character.

For Trischler, the loss of his star writer presented a calamity. The Hansom Cab Publishing Company had been set up to produce the blockbuster in England and while *Madame Midas* had been less successful it had still done very well. Several more works from Hume had been scheduled, *Miss Mephistopheles* and two others, including *The Piccadilly Puzzle*, which Hume had taken to White. The company had even invested in a 'combined phonographic and type-composing machine'.[339]

Trischler had already begun to branch out, buying and publishing works from other writers. Jessie Taylor and Trischler jointly registered a third copyright in 1888, one month after the registration of *Madame Midas*. But thereafter her name disappears from the firm's history.[340] The demand for *Hansom Cab* had peaked and without Hume the company looked unlikely to generate the sort of profits the Taylors, daring speculators, craved. It seems that Jessie Taylor sold the copyright for *Hansom Cab* back to Trischler. Hume was not given the opportunity to repurchase his copyright (the price by now somewhat inflated by the book's success). The Taylors had done very well from the investment.

Now it was up to Trischler to find new partners in publishing. He called his new venture Trischler and Co. The 'Co.' was one Alfred Perkins Marsden, who joined Trischler in July 1889. He was a solicitor, eager to invest the £20,000 left to him in his father's will, although he knew nothing about publishing. The prospect looked excellent: the Hansom Cab Publishing Company had made £7000 since its inception. Marsden met Trischler's capital of £2200, paying a premium of £5500 and another £4000 subsequently.

Trischler began his new venture cautiously, even astutely. He did not risk his considerable profits on untried authors, like Hume had been in Melbourne—that astounding leap of faith could only happen once in a career. He signed one unknown, the pseudonymous Martius, author of *His Last Passion*, which sank without trace. Otherwise he went for authors who had already proved their commercial worth, with a track record and existing public profiles. He offered very generous terms, luring established authors away from their publishers—something which would have made him even more unpopular among the conservative trade.

The other non-Hume products from the Hansom Cab Publishing Company included a book by Tracy Turnerelli (1813–1896), a Conservative politician and writer on Russia. He had published an 1884 autobiography and for Trischler he provided *A Russian Princess*, comprising two short tales, one being a sensational confession of bloodstained depravity, allegedly factual. *The Crooked Billet* was by Vero Shaw, a journalist specialising in dogs and horses, here providing a novel of hunting and racing society. *Harvest* was by John Strange Winter, in reality Henrietta Vaughan Stannard (1856–1911) a writer with two main strings to her bow, novels of army life and journalism on women's issues. *Harvest*'s advance from Trischler was £300, an extraordinary amount, considering that Hume had sold *Hansom Cab*'s copyright for a sixth of that sum. Of his payment for *Madame Midas*, Hume said he had 'very handsome terms', but did not specify.[341]

Of the Hansom Cab Publishing Company's five publications, the Hume books are the most sought after, and thus highly priced by antiquarian booksellers. Occasionally the three others can be found, quite cheaply. *Harvest*, bought online, proved to be not markedly different from the original *Hansom Cab*. The design is similar, with the line illustration on the cover, the title displayed diagonally and the publisher's address at the bottom. Within the covers is a production of some quality: quite good paper, sewn, with attractive engravings, vignettes. *Harvest* is not crime, but a new-woman novel, and not a bad one, either. Heroine Rachel Power must choose between career or marriage, something of increasing concern with women's growing professionalism. The cover boasts sales of fifty thousand copies. Trischler's journalist friend termed it feeble—it is not, and otherwise seems to have been well received.[342]

The Hansom Cab Publishing Company also produced a 'society novel': *Darell Blake* by Lady Colin Campbell (1857–1911), a figure of recent scandal. Born Gertrude Blood to an Irish landowning family, she had entered elite society through her 1881 marriage to MP and lawyer Lord Colin Campbell, a son of the Duke of Argyll. It made her sister-in-law to Princess Louise, daughter of Queen Victoria. But her husband infected her with venereal disease. Her ladyship, a spirited and intelligent woman, sought a judicial separation, citing the disease as cruelty. In the eventual divorce proceedings Lord Colin blamed his wife—naming four prominent men as co-respondents, including the family doctor. He even called his butler as witness, with keyhole testimony.

The divorce was denied and Lady Colin ostracised. She turned to the arty Bohemia, becoming a journalist. There she found famous friends such as James McNeill Whistler and George Bernard Shaw. When Trischler encountered her she had already published two books. A notorious Lady with a novel manuscript: what glorious publicity! Yet Trischler's journalist friend reported that *Darell Blake* was expected 'to be the best-abused and most-talked-of novel of the season; whereas it has merely fizzled like a damp squib'.[343]

Trischler by nature was a risk-taker, bored with safe bets. His most notorious production was Ernest Benzon's *How I Lost 250,000 in Two Years* (in today's currency, more like twelve million). Ernest Henry Schlesinger Benzon (1866–1912) was known as the Jubilee Plunger, or Juggins (fool, or muggins with a 'J'). He inherited a fortune from his German Jewish industrialist father, which he dissipated in eighteen months, largely through gambling, as when he wagered £14,000 on the Derby, only to have his horse come second.

The notion of the book came from a man named Whittaker, a London tailor who was one of Benzon's many creditors. Benzon was not a writer: while 'very good at "jabber"' he was unable to 'put half-a-dozen words together on paper in decent English'[344] and it would be necessary to 'ghost' the book. Trischler first approached H. B. Marriott Watson, then enjoying commercial success. Watson sensibly declined and Vero Shaw, already a Trischler author, prepared for the task. He, Benzon and a shorthand writer went down to the Isle of Wight. Benzon would tell his story, which Shaw would write into a book. For this he had £100 from Trischler, with the promise of another £100 if the work was a success. Benzon himself received £500 as a retainer.[345]

To Benzon, one of the idle rich, work was foreign, even if it was autobiographical dictation. Shaw found it very difficult to sit his subject down, let alone get information out of him. Benzon preferred driving horses in carriages and running up hotel bills. Shaw, low on funds, returned to London. He did write the book, which appeared under Benzon's name, although Shaw said that the only two words Benzon wrote for it were the signature under his portrait. Just before publication, word got out about the ghostwriting. Trischler asked Shaw to deny it—he refused, and Trischler lied on his behalf.

Despite great expectations, which included newspapers being charged 5d for advance review copies, the 'memoir' did not take off. Shaw sued for his extra £100. He argued the book had two editions, and as such was a success. Trischler was asked to produce his account books in proof, but deliberately delayed as a courtroom tactic. It backfired: a fed-up jury found for Shaw. Trischler was ordered to pay the missing £100, with costs. Remaindered copies were sold by street hawkers for 6d.[346]

Benzon's book was not entirely typical of Trischler & Co.'s

programme. The company would be a brief but important outlet for colonial fiction in England. Trischler bought from friends, such as Marriott Watson père's second futuristic vision, *The Decline and Fall of the British Empire, or the Witch's Cavern* (time-travelling by witch-craft, with a proletarian revolution, climate change and Republican Australia as the dominant power). He bought from writers he had previously known, such as William Carlton Dawe, who had been published by Inglis before the firm's bust in 1886. Carlton Dawe's *The Golden Lake*, an exploration adventure with convicts, appeared in 1891. Trischler published Ben Farjeon's *Blood White Rose* (1889) and *For the Defence* (1891), as well as Rosa Praed's *The Romance of a Station* (1889) and *The Soul of Countess Adrian* (1891)—these last being the most enduring literary productions of the company. Trischler also brought out an Australian anthology, *Under the Gum Tree*, edited by Harriet Patchett Martin, wife of littérateur Arthur Patchett Martin, an important promoter of all things Australian in London.

Some of his non-colonial writers are remembered: travel writer May Crommelin; Julia Frankau, who as Frank Danby had written controversially of London Jewish life for Vizetelly, and would enjoy a long and commercially successful career; Eden Philpotts, similarly successful with novels about Dartmoor; and Robert Sherard, most famous as the biographer and defender of Oscar Wilde. Others have vanished with little trace.

Several of Trischler's books had titles to make the heart sink: *The Romance of a Lawn Tennis Tournament* by Marion Butler, Baroness Duboyne (1890), or *My Weird Wooing: a true story of Australian life* by Thomas Foote (1889). Some were generic crime such as *The Only Witness: what did she see?* (1891) by Edward J. Goodman, which offered readers £50 if they guessed the ending successfully. And there was even a Western, *Golden Face* by Bertram Mitford (1892). Elsewhere Trischler ventured into periodicals with a fashion magazine, *Continental Fashion and English Life*, and the girl's magazine *Atalanta*, edited by the noted writer for girls (and also crime author) L. T. Meade.[347]

In 1889, its first year of operation, Trischler & Co. published six books; in 1890, four times that number; in 1891, nearly forty; in 1892, four. The pace was cruel, the list ill-chosen, and plagued by overproduction and bad debts. When the firm found itself in financial difficulties, a meeting of creditors revealed liabilities of £13,000 and book assets of £18,000. Trischler's journalist friend commented that the publisher's 'judgement as a reader is not equal to his business capabilities, and for some time past he has been publishing shocking rubbish'. The shilling-shocker vogue had ended and the firm's ventures into more respectable literature were 'mostly unlucky'.[348]

Trischler, Marsden and Trischler & Co. filed three separate bankruptcy actions in October 1892. The partnership offered their creditors 7/6 in the pound, which was accepted. In the public examination it was revealed that when the firm tried to become a company 'a balance sheet was prepared which showed the property was worth £22,500'. Marsden discovered that the book stock had been overvalued at 1/6 each, when at best they would fetch fourpence. A second balance sheet halved the value.

Marsden would lose all of his investment, over £11,000.[349] The bankruptcy trustees sold the major asset of the company to the publisher Jarrolds: the copyright of *Hansom Cab*, including stereographs, blocks and plates. The price was £50—the sum that Hume had received in 1887. No wonder that when Jarrolds invited Hume to write a preface, he took a small revenge. He deleted Trischler from the novel's story, though *Hansom Cab* would never have succeeded without the publisher's drive and advertising genius.

Trischler's journalist friend commented:

> Trischler is a man who will always work better for others than for himself. By his energy and hard work he made Fergus Hume. People had to read the 'Mystery of a Hansom

Cab,' because they could not get away from it. The thing was as inevitable as Pear's soap. If Hume and Trischler had stuck together and continued on the same level and basis as they began upon they would probably both be better off than they are to-day. Swelled head is a disastrous complaint.[350]

Trischler, with his colonial push and drive, had shaken up conservative British publishing. The schadenfreude at his bankruptcy would have been huge. Marsden continued on his own for a few years before shutting up publishing shop. Trischler reinvented himself yet again less than a year later becoming the manager of the International Securities Corporation, founded for dealing 'in all those debentures and shares of public companies, which, owing to the prevailing requirements of the London Stock Exchange, are not officially quoted'. Given his record, it was not exactly an encouraging proposition. His salary with the firm started at £250, rising to £1000 a year. By 1898 he was again in trouble, having made both 'a mush of the publishing business' and as a 'financial agent': he owed £4000 and had assets of £180. At the time of receivership he survived on loans and pawning jewellery—the long-suffering Lucy's. Yet he remained irrepressible.[351]

The third quarrel of Hume's in London was with Alice Cornwell. Hume had helped publicise her ventures in *Madame Midas*: perhaps in return he expected more than just an interview in the *Sunday Times*. While the facts behind the novel had been well known in Melbourne, the British were ignorant of how close to the truth *Madame Midas* was. In mid-1889 London news reports of Whiteman's libel suit caused a sensation among the smart set, and the financial movers and shakers with whom Cornwell now dealt. The lady, apparently an eligible catch, was married!

Cornwell, although being discreet with Phil Robinson, had not kept her status a secret: Whiteman was simply a topic too disagreeable and distant to mention. A New Zealand paper commented: 'Still English society does not altogether approve of a married lady passing as single. It seems irregular somehow.'[352] Though society did not shun her, unlike Lady Colin Campbell, it looked ill-bred of Cornwell to conceal her status, even if she were colonial.

Whiteman had sued because of Hume and Beck's play, and the timing was particularly unfortunate. Cornwell, with the help of Lady Maria Spearman, daughter of a Scots earl, had begun a summer programme of lavish party-throwing, as an entree into high society. She held musical 'At Homes' and receptions, at which Hume was a guest.[353] Did she now feel the need to set the record straight? It was reported that a London journalist was writing her biography, 'under the supervision' of Madame Midas herself.[354] A London journalist was not Hume, who had known her well, and for a long time—he might have wanted the job himself. It was precisely the sort of thing that Hume, prickly about his status and still smarting from the Trischler breach, would have found a slight.

In 1890 a spiteful review of Hume's latest book was reprinted in the *Sunday Times*:

> If a superior housemaid were to write a novel, she would write just such a book as Mr. Fergus Hume's 'Man with a Secret' (F. V. White and Co.), crude, coarse rigmarole. A man has an illegitimate son who is engaged to an heiress, a pure young girl, and he, the father, goes to the girl, foully traduces his son, and offers himself as her lover in his place! Could anything be more contemptible than such a 'situation?' Another such book and Mr Fergus Hume had better go back to his clerk's desk in Australia.[355]

The review was not only unfavourable, it was insulting to Hume. Had he and Cornwell been still on good terms it would not have appeared. Fiona Gruber believes she 'dropped him, badly'—Hume had outlived his usefulness. His response was to change the dedication of *Madame Midas*, which was now to his actor friend Walter Everard, 'in token of a sincere friendship'. Implicit in the change was that the original dedicatee had been insincere.

Cornwell and Hume may have had some rapprochement, as in 1892 the paper printed in its 'What to Read and What to Avoid' column a brief notice of *When I Lived in Bohemia*, Fergus's bid for literary respectability, a novel with no murder nor mystery in sight. The review indicated the journalist concerned had not read the book, for it was described as a sensational story suitable for the railway bookstall. Hume must have protested, for two weeks later the same column opened with a review in which the book had been read and enjoyed. 'It is quite one of the best works of the summer season…'[356]

By the end of 1892, Hume had endured the loss of three friends. But he still rode high on fortune's wheel, as did Cornwell, now Whiteman's widow and free to become Mrs Phil Robinson; it was Beck who had died, with Trischler crushed, temporarily. Another old friend had reappeared: Alfred Plumpton's double life with Madame Brussels had been exposed in Melbourne by Evangelical preacher Henry Varley, the story making the papers and destroying his local reputation. He returned to London with his wife, Madame Tasca, working again with Hume on their light opera. Hume still wrote plays, with his *Indiscretion* performed at amateur level in Eastbourne, where he appeared in the cast. His books continued to be published at an extraordinary rate: seventeen had appeared, ranging from crime to literary to futuristic to the occult to children's fiction.

The saga of hubris would continue, with its biggest victim on the other side of the world. It was not only individuals, Hume's friends, who would be affected, but the setting of *Hansom Cab*: the city of Melbourne itself.

22

THE MILLIONAIRE MYSTERY
The Fall of Marvellous Melbourne

This is the age of millionaires,
The Golden Calf is set on high,
We burden life with petty cares,
And know not rest until we die...
'A BALLAD OF ARCADIE'

By moving to London in 1888, Fergus Hume avoided a colonial financial disaster. What happened was part of a larger economic downturn,
but it worst affected the setting of *Hansom Cab*. Within a few years
Marvellous Melbourne lost its defining adjective, not through invading
armies, but from financial speculators, including its most prosperous
and prominent men.

In the Melbourne Trilogy Hume depicted a great city at the height
of its glittering prosperity. His boom town has an undercurrent of
anxiety: the metropolis might not be built on sand, but the reputations
and finances of its inhabitants frequently were. Identities and marital
status were dubious, as citizens remade themselves in a new land.
The past could return inconveniently anytime a ship docked. *Hansom
Cab*'s Mark Frettlby committed bigamy, known in the colonies as
'poor man's divorce'—as did Mary Fortune and also Daisy Bates,

198

whose first husband was Breaker Morant. It seems no accident that both *Hansom Cab* and *Madame Midas* end with images of foreboding, ominous blood-red skies over the city. But neither Hume, nor anyone else, could see from where disaster would come.

To be rich, in the Melbourne Trilogy, is to acquire wealth from wool (Frettlby) or shares and goldmining (Madame Midas). For those on the make with even fewer scruples, there is blackmail, or—as in both *Madame Midas* and an 1889 short, 'The Queer Story of Adam Lind'—bank fraud. In the latter Hume was prescient, but he was, like the rest of Melbourne, blind to another source of danger. *Madame Midas*'s heroine invests her mining 'money largely in land' which renders her 'above the reach of poverty for the rest of her life'.[357] Alice Cornwell did nothing of the sort, moving to England and buying a newspaper while floating new investment ventures, large-scale projects of mining and development. If she *had* bought extensive property in Melbourne, she would have come a cropper.

In the 1880s Melbourne flourished on prosperity and optimism. Business confidence was high, as was immigration, which spurred the city's growth outwards: suburban housing developments followed hard upon massive government infrastructure projects in the form of new tramlines and railways. Parliament, in spending mood, voted itself a new and fancy façade, as the buildings of central Melbourne rose high and ornate as wedding cakes. Conspicuous consumption became the norm, with the appetite for imported luxuries helping to create a yawning trade deficit. *Hansom Cab* was a rare example of the opposite, a Melbourne product lucratively exported overseas—as were Alice Cornwell's gold and speculations.

Money was on display all over Melbourne. But, to borrow a title from Gaboriau, also used for the financial column in Brodzky's *Table Talk*, it was Other People's Money: borrowed, imported capital from the Old Country. Victorian companies and individuals involved in mining, agricultural and urban land speculations spruiked themselves in England, seeking investment. They succeeded, trading on the colony's prosperity by offering a secure return, with attractively high interest rates.

Hansom Cab's export success likely had an effect on investors in England. The book Hume wrote to attract literary attention also publicised his adopted town: a prospectus, in fiction. How many fans of the book speculated in its setting? Given that *Hansom Cab* was a bestseller across English society, such influence cannot be discounted.

George Meudell, a Melbourne man of finance and bon vivant, commented:

> The land boom was encouraged by the excessive influx of British capital into Australia in the form of Government and municipal loans, bank deposits, and money sent by Scotch life assurance companies for investment at 5 per cent. Money was thrown at the Australian banks too rapidly to be absorbed safely, and in order to make a profit on the funds that carried interest, bank advances were made far too freely and without sufficient inquiry. Money was so plentiful that everyone thought land values were bound to rise enormously, and so the future was discounted to an alarming extent.[358]

'The future was discounted'—wise words, but Meudell spoke in retrospect. With the borrowed foreign money, the subdivisions and auctions of Melbourne land speculation took on a frenetic quality. Tom Roberts's *Allegro con brio* became *furioso*. Smaller investors, or those dreaming of home ownership, would borrow heavily—advances on land that were more than they could afford, and at too-high rates of interest. Even for those without securities, or with dubious ones,[359] money could be easily borrowed. The banks competed with each other and also with the cooperative building societies. The latter, through a loophole in colonial law, could even speculate in land. The cumulative effect? Market values, city and suburban, rose unrealistically, creating a bubble.

The chief boom-time players were land investment companies and the mortgage banks. The Land Credit Bank, headed by George Nicholson Taylor, whose wife Jessie had bought *Hansom Cab*'s copyright, was a typical example of the latter. It had been founded in 1876 when Melbourne was still small, with swamps, poor roads and poorer infrastructure, its outskirts not suburban sprawl but orchards and market gardens. In 1880 Taylor became manager, with the bank's directors (and major shareholders) representative of the emerging Melbourne plutocracy: a surgeon, a city merchant, the bank's lawyer. They might be respectable, teetotal men who refrained from betting even on the Melbourne Cup, but the Protestant prohibition on gambling did not extend to their share and land speculations. With Taylor they partook in the real-estate carnival, either overlooking or being complicit in his other, personal transactions.

The nineteenth-century bank manager was not necessarily staid and respectable. Given opportunity and circumstance, bankers could be as greedy and unprincipled as the major players in the Global Financial Crisis, more than a century later. Ellen Davitt's *Force and Fraud* (1865) in its title and narrative shows violent and non-violent crime to be equally reprehensible. Her knowledge was personal: her father, Edward Heseltine, had defrauded his Yorkshire bank to speculate, most likely on the railroads. He only avoided justice by fleeing to the continent and conveniently dying.

Taylor's salary at the Land Credit Bank began at £350 a year, enough to support his large family but not his land speculations. For those he 'borrowed' unofficially from his own bank with some inventive bookkeeping, from 1885 at the least.[360] He, Jessie and his son Harry (who also worked at the Land Credit) had accounts with the bank that amassed huge overdrafts. Taylor told his clerks that the extra overdrafts in the accounts had been officially approved by the board. It was either a lie, or the directors were conniving in his actions.

Taylor also had an accomplice: Charles Ernest Clarke, a share-broker, who after bankruptcy was only permitted a low overdraft. In fact he regularly exceeded his limits, with Taylor's active help. Historian Michael Cannon, whose *The Land Boomers* is the best account of the 1890s crisis, asserts that some of Clarke and Taylor's ruses 'were unique in the annals of financial chicanery'.[361] Each Thursday, for instance, a cheque for several thousand pounds, signed by Clarke, was approved by Taylor. The banker then forwarded the cheque to nearby moneylenders, had it discounted (a cash advance, with interest deducted), paid the money into Clarke's account and thus temporarily reduced the overdraft. Clarke's original cheque would not be cleared until the Friday, when the overdraft would duly rise—until the next Thursday.

This devious process continued without suspicion for years. When Clarke's overdraft approached five figures, Taylor simply removed pages from the ledgers prior to the directors' inspection. The bookkeeping of the bank was unbalanced: the accountant was in Taylor's pocket and the auditor was a convicted fraudster, who had served two years in jail.

What, if anything, did Hume know of this? In 'Adam Lind', the hero:

> felt like Tantalus—he was in a bank in an atmosphere of money—gold and silver and pieces of paper representing gold and silver were all around him, yet he could not take it for his own. The wherewithal of wealth by which he could hope to secure his Letty dangled temptingly before him, yet he dare not stretch out his hand and take it. Dare not? What a word for a lover! Alas, being a lover, he was not wise, not being wise he was foolish, and logically being foolish he made an ass of himself by taking money which was not his own, and speculating. Speculating being risky he failed, and behold the result—Adam Lind, lover and idiot, has to

replace £300, with no chance of doing so.[362]
Hume merely depicted the zeitgeist: Taylor was one of many who
defrauded banks in order to speculate.

When the Taylors withdrew from the Hansom Cab Publishing
Company, following Hume's break with Trischler, the obvious strategy was to reinvest in Victorian property—just as the land boom
became truly feverish. Taylor spent, for instance, '£30,000 worth of his
illegitimate gains' on shares in the Chatsworth estate, a development
in outer Melbourne.[363] One of the Chatsworth directors was also on
the board of the Land Credit Bank. He may well have been complicit
in Taylor's frauds. If not, the manager had a ready explanation for his
wealth: Jessie was worth £50,000 (in today's currency several million
dollars) from an inheritance and investment in *Hansom Cab*. Certainly
her involvement with the book was lucrative. If it was estimated that
Hume should have been paid £10,000, then Jessie Taylor, as copyright
holder, likely earned five times that amount from the book.

The evidence suggests that the inheritance was imaginary, or
inflated. Taylor, like a novelist, embellished his wife's story, who
despite being the daughter of a seaman and a lodging-house keeper,
now gained West Indian antecedents, and immense wealth. A 'picture
of boundless sugar plantations and toiling negroes' was implied. Her
false reputation for independent wealth covered for her husband as he
covered for Clarke. With a rich wife, Taylor had no need for fraud.[364]

The ordure did not hit the fan even when, in early 1890, Clarke
became insolvent again, owing the Land Credit £40,000. He was
not alone: all around Melbourne disaster loomed. Export prices for
primary products had fallen, and there was drought, but the major
factor was the collapsing land bubble. Real-estate prices in the inner
city had reached an unprecedented high: four-figure sums per foot,
with no prospect of recuperating the amount in rent. Out in the
suburbs, the supply of new housing outstripped demand. When the
bottom fell out of the market, it went with an almighty crash. The

building societies failed first and investigation revealed huge amounts of money borrowed for land speculations, bad debts which in turn affected the larger institutions, like a line of dominos. The Land Credit was not the first bank to fall, from mid-1891, but its collapse was inevitable.

Taylor could control his own auditors. He could not, however, hold off the largest bank in Melbourne, the Commercial Bank. As the year ended, news of Melbourne's financial upheaval reached the foreign investors. After seven British life-insurance companies declined to deposit any more money colonially, the major banks in Melbourne decided to act, in self-protection. They investigated their major debtors, seeking culpable speculation. Suspicious overdrafts were called in, including one created by Taylor. The Land Credit's board had just held their half-yearly meeting, and noted nothing amiss, even declaring a dividend.[365] Now, less than a month later, they examined their books properly, to find the coffers bare. On 1 December 1891, the Land Credit Bank closed down. Two more banks shut their doors two days later.

Taylor had a small window of opportunity in which to protect his wife and some of their assets, although he could not hide his own overdraft of £114,000. He drew on his overdrawn account for nearly £15,000 and deposited it in Jessie's overdrawn account, giving her a balance of £7000. Further cooking of the books was hampered by his clerks' mutiny, so he made the entries in the ledgers himself. He gained another £7000 shortly before 'he was deposed'.[366]

One of the bank's directors, J. W. Shevill, shot himself on 10 December, but Taylor would not take that way out. Neither would Jessie, a tough, resourceful, money-wise woman. Their most visible asset was their home, 'Bonnington', in High Street, Prahran, a large house with fine furniture and paintings. It was security for Jessie's overdraft. On 11 December she signed a contract of sale for the property, including furnishings. The following day Jessie left for

Auckland with her youngest daughters, Annie and Georgina, aged ten and eleven, under the name of Mrs Pearson.[367]

Four days later George Taylor was arrested for fraud and taken into custody, with no bail forthcoming. Money was due from the sale of the house, £3000 of which had been borrowed from another bank, but it was intended for Jessie. Through a complicated series of bank transfers, what we would now term money-laundering, young Harry Taylor got the money to a courier, who left for Auckland, also under a false name.[368]

Proceedings became ludicrous at this point. Creditors tried to serve a writ upon Margaret Haldane, a friend of the Taylors and sister of the courier, into whose bank account some of the money had been deposited. She barricaded her house in South Yarra, citing illness, and set her dogs loose. Inside was at least one of the Taylor daughters, creeping around shoeless to avoid making noise.[369]

Jessie hid in Auckland before in January quietly taking ship to San Francisco.[370] Taylor remained in jail and was committed for trial on two minor charges in February. He received a sentence of two years' jail, with a second trial scheduled for July in which he and Clarke would face the charge of conspiracy to defraud. Young Alfred Deakin appeared for Taylor in the July trial. The future Prime Minister had already forged a reputation as a reformist parliamentarian, though here he acted not on the side of the angels. He had close associations with some of the leading boomers, being director or chairman of no fewer than three dubious land-investment companies, all of which crashed. Deakin's legal argument was that Taylor was simply acting under the orders of the board, which may well have been the case. If they did not turn a blind eye, they certainly let him be a scapegoat.[371]

Taylor was sentenced to eight years hard labour, and a fine of £5000; Clarke got four years and a fine of £500. Both these sentences were harsher than expected. Taylor gave a long speech at the sentencing, his voice breaking with emotion, sometimes barely able to speak, and on the verge of tears. He denied fraud, but admitted to 'feverish land-madness'—the same disease that had infected Melbourne like typhoid, destroying the health of the economy. Both he and Clarke 'seemed completely crushed by the terrible prospect laid before them'.[372]

In his Pentridge mugshot Taylor is a balding, greying man, with a wide, thin, frog-like mouth and pockmarked skin. He seems to be staring into the abyss. His prison record notes that he only got in trouble over tobacco, punished with minor penalties such as a day's solitary confinement. But those who had lost money in the banks' collapse—and these included jail warders—would not have treated him kindly.[373]

Outside the jail walls, finance company after finance company teetered and often fell. Shareholders and depositors all lost their money. Even the Commercial Bank, the largest in the colony, suspended trading temporarily. The overseas investors, alarmed by the cabled reports of more financial disaster, withdrew their capital, plunging the colony into its worst depression ever. In 1893 the government declared a week's bank holiday, to try to prevent further runs on the banks. Meudell called it 'The Terror'.[374]

Of the many accounts of misery from this era, one is particularly relevant to Jessie Taylor. She was treasurer of a charity, a crèche for working mothers, whose account was with the Land Credit Bank. The funds all vanished with the bank's closure. The Mayor of Prahran appealed for help and a subscription ball was arranged for its benefit.[375] Many others were not so fortunate. There were no unemployment benefits, so those out of work had to rely on their savings, which often had gone with the banks, or family. Meudell: 'The wages of the bread-winners and the workers were sapped by traitors.'[376] New housing estates stood empty, the occupants evicted for failure to pay their rent or mortgage, and people starved on the street. The population of Melbourne fell by the tens of thousands as those who could left for more stable economies.

Small wonder utopianist Samuel Albert Rosa penned *The Coming Terror: A Romance of the Twentieth Century* (1894). It opens with the words:

> Crash! Crash!! Crash!!! Went the falling timbers of the Austral Bank, while a furious and ferocious mob, drunken with wine and victory, shrieked, fought, and swore in front of the burning edifice. The features of the men and women who composed this mob, rendered savage by want, suffering, and oppression, were distorted by hate, the desire for vengeance, and lust for destruction, while they were lit up by the huge fierce flames which issued from the rapidly perishing but once magnificent building.

The cumulative effect was to make Australian banking staid and careful—something to be appreciated in the twenty-first century, when the overseas excesses of the sub-prime crisis would largely be avoided—because they had already happened in the 1890s. From that period of horror came much social reform, but at a price.

Many of the colony's leading men were culpable, but they avoided adverse publicity due to the process of secret compositions. Theodore Fink, Brodzky's relative, had discovered a useful provision in the bankruptcy laws called 'composition by arrangement': creditors would examine the insolvent's finances privately. It had been designed to protect those whose careers would have ended with publicity of their bankruptcy, such as clerics. As employed by the land-boomers, it not only protected their reputations, but involved some dubious accounting and the concealment of assets. The result was that some of the worst offenders paid little. Benjamin Fink, Theodore's brother, a speculator whose legacy to Melbourne is the Block, owed nearly two million pounds, of which he paid ha'pence in the pound.[377]

Many, like Meudell, were privately incensed at such procedures, but Brodzky went public in the pages of *Table Talk*. He transformed into Asmodeus, fearlessly lifting the roofs off Melbourne's wealthiest finance houses, to the great benefit of his magazine's circulation. It gained him the title of Melbourne's first muckraker and subsequent elevation to the Press Club Hall of Fame. Brodzky was very well informed, almost certainly by sympathisers including Meudell, and he spared nobody, not even the Finks. Cannon states that 'most of the frauds of the boom period would have been successfully covered up had it not been for Brodzky's work.'[378] He simply knew too much, something that probably prevented him being sued for libel.

Court cases came from Brodzky's revelations, though very few actually went to jail. Taylor did, and he had the longest sentence. It was reported that the government had declined to pay 'any portion of the expenses of the recent prosecution of Taylor'. A journalist commented: 'This decision has given great satisfaction to the friends of bank officials associated with other institutions, who are now awaiting criminal prosecutions, which will in many cases now be probably abandoned.'[379]

In the final photo of his prison record, in 1899, George Taylor's hair has gone completely silver but he faces the camera calmly, with resignation. There still remained the fine of £5000. He was released, then rearrested in the street for debt. He pleaded that he had no means of paying. Had he not done his time and been punished sufficiently? The government reluctantly agreed, and Taylor disappeared from the colony.

In the US census of 1900 he reappears with his entire family in Alameda, California. Jessie's flight with what she could grab from the wreckage of the Land Credit Bank enabled the Taylors to be reunited and live comfortably in a place where nobody knew their history. Taylor is listed as G. M. Taylor and has taken ten years off his age. Living at the same address are the rest of the family, including son Harry, his wife and two children. Harry is listed as a lawyer, but the rest have lower-middle-class, small-business jobs, including the five unmarried daughters. Ominously the paterfamilias' occupation is listed as speculator.

What have these dodgy dealings to do with *Hansom Cab*? Quite a lot, for the book was intimately tied to Marvellous Melbourne and its fall. The novel depicted the city at its glorious zenith, but with overtones of foreboding; and the Taylors contributed significantly to the 1890s depression. *Hansom Cab* was only published because those behind it partook of the Melbourne speculation frenzy, from which came the financing for both the local and international editions.

Initially Alice Cornwell was involved, providing sharemarket advice, with the proceeds funding the book's first edition. When Hume sold his copyright, Cornwell was en route to England, as her mining operation struck gold. She was out of the picture, otherwise engaged, and so Trischler sought new financial help for *Hansom Cab*'s onslaught on the English market. He described his partners as 'Melbourne capitalists', which could mean only the Taylors were involved. Jessie owned *Hansom Cab*'s copyright, and putting assets in the wife's name is a well-known financial ruse. Yet Jessie was an active land specula-tor, and that she travelled several times to England on Hansom Cab Publishing Company business shows that she at least checked on her investment personally.

She was not, despite her husband's claims, a woman of major money, such as would be needed for the English edition. The huge sums expended upon the print run of *Hansom Cab* in England, the advertising budget, with multiple advertorials in newspapers, could only have come from George Nicholson Taylor. The board of the Land Credit Bank were most unlikely to have supported a loan for a popular novel with disreputable content. Taylor had a cavalier approach to the bank's funds, dipping into them to support his land speculation habit. Here was yet another speculation, literary but likely to be highly lucrative. While the Taylors were the 'money' behind the

Hansom Cab Publishing Company, it was Other People's, sourced creatively and fraudulently from the bank's accounts. The *Hansom Cab*'s English success was essentially due to bank robbery, by an insider.

There is a curious coda to this tale. Henry Gyles Turner of the Commercial Bank, the Land Credit's creditor, was also a historian and man of letters. His wife Helen and Jessie Taylor served on charitable committees together. Turner would have been aware of Jessie's role in *Hansom Cab*'s publication, and even possibly of her putative co-authorship. In his *The Development of Australian Literature* (1898), co-written with Alexander Sutherland, Turner termed *Hansom Cab* 'one of the worst of Melbourne stories'.[380] That description also applied to how the book was financed for its overseas push. Hume in his preface would deny the book was based on a real murder, but nonetheless *Hansom Cab* was not only crime fiction, but a case of true crime.

23

THE QUEER STORY OF ADAM LIND

Adam Lind, aged 25, handsome, gay, and to a certain degree clever, was a clerk in the Hibernian Bank, Melbourne, a situation of no great responsibility.

'THE QUEER STORY OF ADAM LIND'

'Queer' and 'gay' are words that have changed in meaning over time—like the word detective. The quotation above opens a Hume short story about a bank clerk who for love defrauds his employer. The romance is heterosexual, but title and first sentence suggest something different to modern readers. That these words might describe the story's author is a notion that arose repeatedly in the course of researching this book. It was a question asked by people who had read Hume's works or knew something of his life. They wondered what secrets were concealed by this very private man.

Oscar Wilde was not the only gay in the nineteenth-century village, merely the most famous. When Hume came to London in 1888, a literary lion from the Antipodes, it would have been difficult for them *not* to meet: they were creatures of literature and the theatre, who socialised among London's Bohemians. The extensive scrutinies of Wilde's life do not mention Hume, but that does not prove they never encountered one another. More certain is that Hume's circumstances and circles, from the madhouse onwards, would have exposed him to individuals with same-sex attractions.

The Victorians preached heterosexual virtue, the ideal personified by Victoria and Albert, surrounded by their offspring. Photograph albums and family trees tell a different story: large families had many spinster aunts, many bachelor uncles. Economics might have kept some single, others might have been unlucky in love. Or did they prefer not to marry, seeking alternatives for which, given discretion, an innocent explanation existed? How many people lived at odds with the prevailing heterosexual culture is unknown, but some fascinating traces survive in letters, photographs, archives and even the works of Fergus Hume.

Victorian morality separated the sexes, leading to homosociality: in schools, the army, the clergy and, in the colonies, the Australian convict system and goldmining, from where the term 'mate' derives. Affection between men was manly and unproblematic. It could shade into the romantic, with men posing for photographs arm in arm. Tennyson's 'In Memoriam' mourned a beloved male friend. For women, there were schoolgirl crushes and companions. It was permissible for these friendships to become rather intense; anything else was unthinkable. Thus Agnes Murphy, Hume's co-worker on *Table Talk*, could write the following, from her autobiographical novel *One Woman's Wisdom* (1895):

> 'I can never understand people who are not enthusiastic about girls. Now, to my thinking,' and [Mary's] eyes danced roguishly, 'it must always be more delightful to kiss the fresh soft lips of a girl than the moustached mouth of a man. If I were a poet I should write all my verses to girls, just to show how one of their own sex appreciates them.'[381]

Such lesbian expression was essentially unregulated by law. For men sodomy incurred severe penalty, but was relatively rarely prosecuted. Unless caught in the act, it was hard to prove. Nor did sexual practice define the homosexual identity. However, criminology was beginning to identify a 'type' and activities that would, with the 1885 Labouchère Amendment, be penalised. 'Gross indecency' between men became a criminal offence.

A fine line existed between discretion and expression. Robert Gant, who in Dunedin performed *The Pirates of Penzance*'s Ruth in drag, cross-dressed in the context of amateur and professional theatrics, and took homoerotic photographs. He evaded the notice of the law. Another young man of similar inclinations, Gordon Lawrence, was jailed in Melbourne. The crucial difference was in taking transvestism onto the streets, where it could not be explained away. Lawrence, like Wilde, thumbed his nose at convention at a site of colonial pride: the Melbourne Centennial Exhibition, October 1888. The twenty-one-year-old Sydney-sider paraded in a fetching (and patriotic) ensemble of a red skirt and a tight jacket of blue-and-white-stripes, his accessories a fan, sunshade and coquettish hat trimmed with red. Underneath the hat was a flaxen wig and a face painted with cosmetics.[382]

The use of make-up offstage signified the prostitute: respectable women kept their faces naked. Lawrence was, if not actively soliciting, certainly revelling in the performance, winking at passing men and gaining a train of followers. A watching police detective intercepted him, creating a sensation. In arresting Lawrence the wig was dislodged, revealing a man's cropped hair. An excited, hostile crowd gathered, necessitating Lawrence's hasty removal to the nearby city watch house. His subsequent court appearance confounded spectators, for his garments—the tight-corseted waist, the bulky bustle—were worn with 'the unconscious ease of a person long accustomed to their use. In every look, in every motion, in every line of his figure he was a woman.'

Lawrence was found guilty of 'insulting behaviour and vagrancy', after evidence was presented of 'a long career of nameless immorality'.

He received six months in Pentridge, at which sentence he screamed and fainted. Even this act was performative, it being reported that after being carried out of the courtroom he winked at the constables. Without his finery 'he stood revealed as a sallow faced and unpleasant looking young man of rather vulgar type.'[383]

The press stated that Lawrence was 'a member of a large gang of men who practice loathsome and unnatural offences', both in Sydney and Melbourne.[384] He was also described as 'a companion of the man who went around Sydney as "Carry Swain", and got into trouble'. Carrie Swain was the popular American actress for whom Fergus Hume had written a play, though unperformed.[385] The Sydney 'Carry Swain' was someone entirely different, the alias for a youth otherwise known as George Tremain, or Harrison.

In 1887 'Carry Swain' and several associates faced the court:

> It appeared that numerous complaints had been made against them, and they were watched by police. It was found that they were in the habit of walking the streets at night, impersonating females, and having powder and pearl cream upon their faces. They were in the habit of jostling men in the street and making use of disgusting expressions.[386]

The Lawrence and Swain cases were indicative of a colonial cross-dressing subculture, shading into the rent boy.[387] An English precedent existed, from the 1870s: Ernest Boulton and Frederick Park, who as Lady Stella Clinton and Fanny Park strolled West End London winking, like Lawrence, at likely men. In their letters, used as evidence in their trial, are some of the first uses of the expressions 'camp' and 'drag'.[388] Though charged with conspiracy to commit sodomy they were found not guilty, the reprieve partly due to class: the pair were well connected, with expensive lawyers. In contrast 'Swain' and Lawrence associated with the criminal underclass, vice squad fare.

One intriguing aspect of the Lawrence case was that he knew

Fergus Hume. Indeed, Hume gave him money, for a theatrical columnist reported that Lawrence 'was able to obtain £20 from Fergus Hume in Sydney'. It was not for legal fees, since Hume had left Australia months before Lawrence's arrest. That Sydney was specified indicates the money was not wired from London either. Although Hume was based in Melbourne, he would have visited Sydney to market his literary work, or to accompany Beck in his engagements.

The columnist concerned was Harry Wilby Taylor, a civil servant moonlighting as Scalfax, a reporter of Melbourne theatre for the *Otago Witness*. Hume and Beck frequently appeared in his columns. Scalfax had a fascination with the case, for he kept mentioning Lawrence, noting for instance the 'Carry Swain' association. In Lawrence's prison file his profession is described as actor, a conventional explanation for his transvestism, although his only certain employment is as a page, a servant in Melbourne, from where he stole some of his female finery.[389] It seems more likely that Lawrence and particularly 'Carry Swain' were playgoers, if in the cheaper seats, their subculture intersecting with the theatre.

What Scalfax wrote about Hume and Lawrence would have originated in the playhouse, gossip from an informed and interested party in Melbourne, most likely an actor who knew both men. In turn Scalfax relayed the information, in print, back to New Zealand. To report Hume's gift to Lawrence was not malicious in context, although it has implications: what was it for? And why such a large amount?

Twenty pounds, with modern inflation, does not seem a significant sum, but at the time—when threepence was a tram fare and *Hansom Cab* cost a shilling—it was a considerable amount. Twenty pounds could buy a really extravagant dress, be payment for a legal appeal, or be a deposit on a house. It could also be the price of a ticket to somewhere distant: £20 in 1888 bought an economy steamship fare to England.

Alfred Plumpton is alleged to have started his day by filling his sovereign case at Madame Brussels. If, at the top end of colonial prostitution, a 'shout' cost a 'sov', then £20 was far more than courtesan rates.[390] 'Send money, you wretch,' Frederick Boulton, in his persona of Stella, wrote to an English Lord. Did Lawrence make a similar demand of Hume?[391]

The question of blackmail arises, for Labouchère's amendment was termed 'the Blackmailer's Charter'. Both Lord Alfred Douglas and Wilde were blackmailed prior to Wilde's court case. They paid between £15 and £100 to regain compromising letters.[392] Another nastier means of extortion existed, a gay version of the 'badger game', in which men *in flagrante delicto* would be rudely interrupted by an accomplice demanding money.[393] The rent boys of Sydney would have known all about this trick. 'It was fatally easy to set someone up,' notes writer and lawyer Kerry Greenwood. 'For poor Fergus to pay out such an outrageous sum to a young man of such a profession argues infatuation or blackmail.'

Hume had a reputation as the writer of *Hansom Cab* and if he were to become a successful dramatist he would need to protect it. Another commentator on Hume, *Madame Midas* biographer Fiona Gruber, notes that 'there was always something hanging over Fergus.' The fear of scandal?

Greenwood writes:

> If the putain went back to his profession, then either explanation would still work and they are both tragic: Fergus was desperately in love with him and tried to bribe him out of the life and the Molly took the money and went on with it anyway, possibly spending it on drink or drugs or gambling, or the Molly boy had letters or photographs (tricky at the time, so valuable now) or proof of some sort he could use to extort the 20 quid. Possibly saying that he would sail away. Then not sailing. Either way poor Fergus is cheated and

shamed and possibly has his heart broken, as well.

What a sad story.[394]

Fergus Hume never described Lawrence directly in his writing—the risk would have been too great. In any case he largely kept his life out of his work, though certain motifs recur, such as reincarnation and bossy relatives intent on having a lawyer in the family. What he does is refract himself, with different aspects of his personality given to diverse characters: his playwriting and possibly Christian beliefs to Mr Wopples in *Madame Midas*; Keith Stewart in *Miss Mephistopheles* expressing his writerly aspirations in Melbourne; his mashing and journalism to Felix Rolleston in *Hansom Cab*.

Felix is particularly intriguing, not only for being the one character to appear throughout the Melbourne Trilogy. Firstly the name Rolleston is a New Zealand in-joke. William Rolleston was a New Zealand politician, Minister for Justice in the 1880s, a classicist and friend of the University of Otago's Professor Sale, who taught Hume. As Felix becomes a politician, literary payback seems likely here.

Felix is, like Hume, a dandy: 'His well-brushed top-hat glittered, his varnished boots glittered, and his diamond rings and scarf-pin glittered; in fact, so resplendent was his appearance that he looked like an animated diamond coming along in the blazing sunshine.' He is lively, gossipy, witty, and Hume gives him good lines: 'some fellows are like trifle at a party—froth on top but something better underneath.'[395]

In *Madame Midas* Felix comments that the villain Gaston Vandeloup is a 'deuced good-looking chappie', several sentences later telling him: 'it's a case of we never speak as we pass by, and all that sort of thing—come and look me up.' If spoken by the right actor, as with Nathan Lovejoy in the 2012 telemovie of *Hansom Cab*, this line would be most suggestive. Glen Dolman, scriptwriter of the telemovie, deliberately drew Felix as gay, 'charmingly effete, fingers encrusted with rings'.[396]

Dolman comments:

> Early on in researching the background of the book too, I came across an article that suggested that Hume might have been gay himself, and lived with a partner in the UK. Whether or not that was the case, I felt he was suggesting that in Felix and wanted to include that character and dynamic in the tapestry of the world I was representing.

He adds:

> Re: the character of Felix Rolleston, I just drew what I picked up from the book. I felt like Hume was not only writing about a comical socialite with social ambitions beyond his financial status (hence his opportunistic marriage to Miss Featherweight), but was most likely a gay man playing by society's rules of the time. The images Hume paints of him 'shimmering in diamonds', looking like a peacock, and his flamboyant turn of phrase all seemed to fit.

Philip Bentley, who is writing a graphic novel version of *Hansom Cab*, disagrees:

> What did I think of the TV depiction of Felix R? Well I think they did the most logical thing and made him a bit less of a buffoon and not as gay—I know he ends up marrying, but a modern day reading of the character as written certainly could give you that impression. I'm sure Hume wasn't intending it so, I think he wants him to be read as a fop, but these days that sort of character tends to have melded into a gay stereotype...perhaps we can blame Kenneth Williams.[397]

Felix is an ambiguous character. But ambiguity was one way to write homosexual desire in the 1800s. Various terms were used: Arcadian, Greek, Calamus, deriving from Walt Whitman's *Leaves of Grass*, and Uranian, all words which had coded, hidden meanings. These 'ways of evasion'[398] were pioneered by John Addington

Symonds (1840–1893), a man of letters, specialising in the Classics and Renaissance. He also wrote the first homosexual autobiography, published posthumously.

Symonds had attended Harrow, in his words a den of vice: 'Every boy of good looks had a female name, and was recognised either as a public prostitute or as some bigger fellow's "bitch". Bitch was the word in common usage to indicate a boy who yielded his person to a lover.'[399] As an adult he kept falling in love, chastely but worryingly with men. A doctor advised him to marry, and he did, fathering four daughters, despite finding his wife a good friend but physically unappealing. The poetry of Walt Whitman came as a revelation as it seemed to express so closely his own desires. Finally he visited a male brothel, aged thirty-seven, and achieved erotic liberation.

Symonds sought precedents, beginning with the ancient world. Like many of his era, he sought to reconcile his attractions with his sincere Christian beliefs, the divine with erotic love. He developed a two-level method of communicating his researches and his defence of homosexuality. *Studies of the Greek Poets* (1873) seemed orthodox classicism, but the homoerotic was there for those readers inclined to see it. In the 1880s he began to be more open, producing works printed in small circulations, to be discreetly passed between interested parties. *A Problem in Greek Ethics* (1883) dealt with the Greek institution of 'paiderastia', the relationship between a young man and an older man, socially approved, educative and erotic—which he saw as a cornerstone of the Greek civilisation. *A Problem in Modern Ethics* (1891) argued for the extension of civil rights to gay men.

Fergus Hume, classically educated, knew Symonds' scholarship. In 1892 he gave an interview to a journalist, Raymond Blathwayt, in which he discussed his new novel, *The Island of Fantasy*. Its aim was 'to reconstruct the old Greek civilisation and adapt it to the present day'. His research included:

all the old classics, I super-added the Greek poets of Addington Symonds; I recalled all I knew of the Tragedies; the great pathos and fatefulness of Greek life and history. I studied the whole matter almost as a science, and as a result, I feel I have got somehow into the heart of the old Grecian life.[400]

Hume also showed Blathwayt a verse from his forthcoming book of poetry, which seems never to have been released or else was self-published anonymously in small circulation. It cannot at present be traced.[401] The poem did appear in *The Island of Fantasy*.

Venus Urania

To rose-red sky, from rose-red sea,

At rose-red dawn she came, A fiery rose of earth to be,

And light the dawn with flame; Then earth and sky
triumphantly

Rang loud with man's acclaim. A rose art thou, O goddess
fair,

to bloom as men aspire,

Red rose to those whose passions move,

White rose to chaste desire;

Yet red rose wanes with pale despair,

And white rose burns as fire.

Venus Urania figures in classical mythology, representing spiritual love, as distinct from Venus Pandemos, embodiment of earthly love or lust. The name indicates the origin myth: Venus Urania is of no woman born, arising from the severed genitals of the god Uranus. In Plato's *Symposium*, Uranian love is divine, but also associated with man-love, and superior to heterosexuality. Symonds uses it with precisely this sense; Huysmans' *À Rebours* (1883), a famously decadent and aesthetic novel influential upon Wilde, contains a Miss Urania, a circus acrobat with ambivalent sexual appeal, both masculine and feminine.

Earlier in the century, Dickens and the Baroness Coutts opened a hostel for fallen women known as Urania House, signifying divine love rather than lust. By the end of the century the meaning had changed. Wilde wrote in an 1898 letter: 'To have altered my life would have been to have admitted that Uranian love is ignoble. I hold it to be noble—more noble than other forms.'[402] Significantly, a group of classically minded and pederastic poets, operating semi-clandestinely from the 1850s–1930s, are known as Uranian poets. Poet Chris Wallace-Crabbe, seeing the word Urania in the title of Hume's poem, immediately asked me if Hume was gay.

Fergus Hume was very well informed, even in distant Dunedin aware of London literati. Once in England, he would partaken more closely of the late-century zeitgeist. To mention Symonds, a reconstruction of Ancient Greek civilisation and Urania in the same interview suggests that he is aware of 'the ways of evasion', and is using them to communicate. Arguably Blathwayt is knowingly part of this process. It is the latter who describes 'Venus Urania' as 'a very dainty little lyric'—with implications of the feminine. Since much of the interview is a plea from Hume for acceptance as a serious writer, is it also a plea for something else?

What does Hume mean by saying his intent is 'to show how a life such as that led by the ancient Greeks, and that nurtures the genius under every possible advantage, ought to be encouraged and not discouraged'? Hellenism might then be intellectually fashionable, but at the time it was also a code word for homosexuality. 'Encouraged and not discouraged' hints at much.[403]

The Island of Fantasy is a utopia, in which an eccentric millionaire recreates ancient Greek civilisation on an Aegean island. It is also astoundingly homoerotic. Consider Count Caliphronas:

> I can tell you that his figure was as perfect as the Apollo Belvedere, and say that his face was as flawless in its virile beauty as the Antinous of the Vatican [a beautiful boy, lover of the Emperor Hadrian], but this will give you no idea of his physical perfection. His body seemed to be instinct with

the lawless fierceness of wind and wave; he moved with the
stately grace of a nude savage unaccustomed to the restraint
of clothing.[404]

Caliphronas poses naked for sculptor Maurice, as Endymion
(another classical figure who has become a gay icon). Maurice almost
despairs 'of being able to mould the soft clay into a perfect representation of this virile perfection'. The tactile act reads like sublimation, or
a transferred caress. Elsewhere a sequence of nude bathing features
Caliphronas, about to dive: 'As he stood there with his arms raised
above his head, the first yellow ray of the sun flashed on his white
body and enveloped him in glory, as though he were indeed a stray
Olympian.' The scene culminates in Caliphronas galloping on a
horse and Maurice 'thought of the frieze of the Parthenon, where
nude youths ride fiery steeds in a long serene procession of marble
figures'.[405] Hume thus anticipates some notable gay icons.

Certainly the authorial gaze appreciates the physique of
Caliphronas. However, the commercial publication of *The Island
of Fantasy* in the 1890s precludes an erotic consummation. Instead
Hume's characters travel to the millionaire's island, a sanitised
recreation of Ancient Greek culture. Maurice and the Count conventionally fall in love with the same, colourless maiden. It reads like an
instance of the love triangle concealing the attraction between men, as
identified by queer theorist Eve Kosofsky Sedgwick. Pirates attack—
and the island's volcano erupts and destroys this earthly paradise.

The novel predated Freud, yet the symbolism of the volcano
indicates extreme repression, finding vent in melodrama. The book
was not a critical success and it did not enable Hume to escape from
what had become his personal, if unwanted brand: the shilling crime
shocker. But what it suggests about him is significant.

Fergus Hume was a lifelong bachelor. Women liked and helped
him professionally, but newspapers never mentioned any romance.
His female friends were all older women such as his sisters, Janet

Michie, Alice Cornwell and the actress Ellen Terry.[406] Otherwise his closest associations are with men, including the charismatic, doomed Beck.

His 1885 poem 'My Lady Disdain' might seem autobiographical, with its reference to law books, but is in the Gilbert and Sullivan style, and probably intended for a comic opera. Little else in his oeuvre suggests heterosexuality. His young lovers seem curiously passionless, his gaze upon attractive women brotherly rather than lustful—and nothing like the depiction of Caliphronas. Compare, for instance, the opening of Francis Adams' *Madeline Brown*, a leisurely and quite lascivious description of a semi-clad woman bleeding to death.

In the 1900 UK electoral roll Hume is listed in Elm Park Gardens, Chelsea, in the same street where Australian writer Rosa Praed rented a house. The location proved too expensive for the Praeds, and probably also for Hume—by the 1901 census he was living with the Willebys in Kensington. The following year he moved to Thundersley in Essex, cheaper and quieter living, but with convenient access to London trains and the Continent. It is likely no coincidence that the move came in the same year as Tay Pay O'Connor's belated circulation of the Philip Beck story in print (August 1902), taking advantage of Hume being newsworthy due to a court case over theatrical pay.[407] Those who remembered the actor fondly from the English theatre or the Savage Club could well have cut Hume, for blackening a favourite's name.

In Thundersley the local Rector, Thomas Noon Talfourd Major, was a friend, and had a cottage for rent. In the 1911 census Hume is shown living quietly with a housekeeper, Ada Louise Peck, a widow of sixty-nine. After Major's death in 1915, Hume was obliged to move. He remained in Thundersley, living with John Joseph Melville, a colourful character. Melville, though trained as a metallurgical chemist, practised alchemy: on at least four occasions he persuaded rich capitalists that he could extract gold from base metals. Did he also persuade Hume to invest his writing money with him?[408]

An article by Jeremy Parrott, with information from Marie Dalton, a distant Hume relation, described Melville as Hume's 'companion'.[409] It is this article that informed Glen Dolman's reading of Felix Rolleston. Yet Melville had a wife: in 1904, aged forty-one, he had married Florence Amelia Wright, in London. She was part of the household in Thundersley and, when he died in 1928 after yet another alchemical scandal, Melville left all his small property to her. Hume moved out, to lodgings.

Of Hume's gay contemporaries, Wilde paid the price for public exposure; Gordon Lawrence served his time in Pentridge and afterwards disappeared. Others lived more discreetly. Robert Gant would retire to Wellington with a male partner decades his junior, the pair quiet suburban bachelors. He created for himself an antipodean domestic idyll, where homosociality shaded into passion undreamt of by the wider, censorious world. Agnes Murphy and her partner Aimee Moore had a lifelong union. They became militant suffragettes and Murphy was secretary to Nellie Melba, also writing the diva's first biography. Family historian Ian Moore has proudly added Murphy to the family tree as the wife of Aimee, his great-great aunt.

In 'Venus Urania' Hume talks of chaste desire, a burning white rose. It suggests a safe option: celibate love, allowing companionship and manly affection, if not sex. Thus might Hume have lived with the Melvilles. He and John Melville had similar interests, in the Classics, languages, alchemy and theosophy. Reincarnation had fascinated Hume since Dunedin and he dedicated his *A Son of Perdition: An Occult Romance* (1912) to 'Eloquent, Wise, Patient' Annie Besant, a major figure in the theosophy movement.

Theosophy could provide another means for the expression of same-sex desire. For those who felt ill-fitted for their times, reincarnation was an explanation for a 'lost soul', a coded statement similar to the 'ways of evasion'. Hume, though he would novelise the occult, never expressed anything openly autobiographical about his lovelife. In contrast Rosa Praed wrote up her intense relationship with the medium Nancy Harward in *Nyria* (1904). It revealed that the pair believed that they had met in ancient Rome, with Harward a slave girl and Praed an Imperial noblewoman.

Yet reincarnation appears repeatedly in Hume's novels, in conjunction with love: two souls are twinned through time. His first novel for F. V. White, *The Man Who Vanished: A Psychological Phantasy*, concerns astral travelling, with strong theosophical aspects. For a male character, the chief attraction of the heroine is 'the strong masculine spirit which inhabited her feminine body'.[410]

From Hume's relative Marie Dalton comes the information that John Melville believed that he was the reincarnation of philosopher Roger Bacon, a famous alchemist. Hume, in turn, was the reincarnation of a French nobleman, guillotined in the Revolution, something he 'remembered' vividly. It represents a curious link to Robert Gant: 'I wonder what it would feel like?' is the caption in one of Gant's albums, below a photograph of a young man gazing at the axe and block. Though Freud's superego and id had yet to gain currency, a coded meaning seems likely here: with the head and heart separated, carnal desires could be expressed, in death and beyond.

It is possible to speculate about Hume's private life. He gave money to Lawrence, suggesting infatuation or blackmail. Beck suicided from the loss of Hume, an association that was as much professional as personal. Certainly Hume used forms of communication and expressions associated with same-sex love. *The Island of Fantasy* is either consciously or unconsciously homoerotic. 'Venus Urania' suggests he took the option of chastity, prudent in the era of Labouchère, which allowed companionship with Melville without danger. Ultimately, though, Hume hints at but never reveals his personal mystery.

HAGAR OF THE PAWN SHOP
Hansom Cab's Collectors

Sir Gilbert Harkness was a bookworm. In his youth he had loved books passionately, and this love, increasing as he grew older, the one tyrannous passion of his heart soon mastered all the others.
PROFESSOR BRANKEL'S SECRET[411]

Fergus Hume's life is not an open book, which is why a conventional literary biography could not be written about him. Instead *Blockbuster!* is the story of Hume and *Hansom Cab*—a work so successful that it permanently typecast him as a pulp writer. He was more than that, and so was the book, which had a significant afterlife.

One aspect of *Hansom Cab*'s story remains to be told, about the book as a physical, bibliographical object: the surviving early editions, and the people who owned them. There are rare editions of *Hansom Cab*, worth thousands of dollars. They represent a story that Hume could have written, full of obsession, mystery and the thrill of the chase.

And also hidden treasure. Over a decade ago, someone visited Young's Auction House in Camberwell, and spotted 'an unconsidered trifle'[412] in a box of books from a deceased estate. Young's is not a place for the book collector, specialising as it does in bric-a-brac, artwork and china. Book dealer Bill Mathews imagines what might have occurred:

> Young's haven't advertised any books, so the book trade won't be coming to the auction. But by chance a book collector wanders into the viewing, and spots the only books for sale, a box lot, shoddy and dull, in tattered brown paper covers. He examines them and finds *Hansom Cab*: obviously an early edition, maybe even the first. He repacks the box, placing *Hansom Cab* carefully at the bottom, in case somebody else investigates. Then he makes a mistake: in going out for a coffee, he leaves the viewing before closing time. Now he broods: in the meantime, has someone seen or even stolen *Hansom Cab*? It is a size to fit easily in a jacket pocket. Anxiety rules: could an expensive bidding duel ensue?
>
> He hurries back, but the auction has already started, and he has no opportunity to check if the box is intact. 'Win or lose,' the poet John Forbes once said of horse-racing, 'the faces tell you nothing.' All around him are hardened dealers, who give nothing away.
>
> He is still anxious, but pulls himself together, and makes the opening bid: $10. Someone else, alert at his interest, or aware of *Hansom Cab*, also bids: $20. Heart in mouth, he bids again: $30. This time no counterbid is made, and the hammer comes down. Still anxious, our dealer pays, and a staff member brings the box out to him. In his car, he checks his purchase, to find *Hansom Cab* still at the bottom of the box. Only then does he permit himself a smile, then a moment of laugh-out-loud joy.[413]

What the bidder got, at a knock-down price, was a first edition, from the initial Melbourne print run in October 1886 of *Hansom Cab*. The find brought the known total of the surviving first-edition copies to four, the others held in libraries: two at the Mitchell at Sydney, the other at the Baillieu at the University of Melbourne. Nearly fifty years had passed since anyone had definitely sighted another copy. There had been rumours—something that makes the edition seem like a near-extinct bird, a *rara avis*. It has been termed a 'daydream', and a 'mythical creature'. The first Melbourne edition of Hume's book is an ultimate collectable for detective-fiction buffs.[414]

The copy concerned had first been sold for one shilling in 1886, bought or given to young Maudie Manton. The price at Young's is unknown, but it was a bargain. When offered for sale by Australian Book Auctions in 2011 the reserve was a five-figure sum, the book worth tens of thousands of dollars, even in imperfect condition.[415]

How, if you were at a garage sale or clearing out a cobwebbed attic, would you recognise *Hansom Cab*'s first edition, this nugget of bibliographic gold? It is quite unimpressive in appearance, a cheap Victorian pulp paperback. As the years have passed the surviving copies have generally been rebound, something that lessens the value for collectors, who prize mint condition. The pages of advertisements were generally lost in the process, bookbinding practice being to sell such ephemera back to the paper manufacturers as waste. The Melbourne University copy lacks even the title and author's name on the new binding, as if the owner thought the book was naughty or notorious, in need of a plain wrapper.

The rebinding has occurred because the original cover was soft paper, liable to tearing. That, and the fact that the novel was so popular it was circulating from one person to another, meant it was quickly damaged. The cheap price made it disposable, undoubtedly a factor in why so few copies have survived from the early print runs. Only one copy of the first edition, in the Mitchell, preserves it as it originally appeared, with the advertisements a fascinating snapshot of 1880s Melbourne. To find another copy of the first edition in such good condition would be extraordinary, and most unlikely. But the book collector can always dream…

Open the hypothetical book at the garage sale. Inside, the paper will be slightly foxed—referring to tawny stains, like the liver spots of age. In Ronald Searle's guide to the jargon of the rare-book trade, *Slightly Foxed—But Still Desirable* (1989), 'slightly foxed' is illustrated by a foxy lady in a library, complete with fangs and brushy tail. A copy of the first edition of *Hansom Cab* will not only be foxed, it will be 'utterly desirable', in Searle's definition: 'just about worth the money, if you *must* have it'.[416]

The easiest way to tell an *editio princeps* or first-edition copy of *Hansom Cab* is the pagination. The first edition has 242 pages, with the printing type being redistributed after the pressing was completed. The edition selling out, the text had to be hastily re-set, with a small but crucial difference: the book now comprised 230 pages.

The second edition of *Hansom Cab* is even more of a mythical beast, with no copy known to exist. The situation is only marginally better for the third (or second impression of the second edition). One copy of *Hansom Cab* labelled third edition does exist. In September 1997 New Century Antiquarian Books listed a copy of this edition for sale.[417] Australian crime collector John Loder, the first person to do a textual bibliography of *Hansom Cab*, missed out on this most desirable item—although he did try to contact the buyer, unsuccessfully.

Loder recalled the buyer's name, which was a little uncommon. It appeared online, in connection with the history of the Chinese in Australia. *Hansom Cab* has scenes of Melbourne's Chinatown—someone collecting in this specialist area might find the novel 'desirable', if not as utterly desirable as it would be to a crime buff like Loder. It seemed likely this person was the third edition's owner.

As in Hume's Melbourne, minimal degrees of separation can exist between people. Through a useful intermediary, I learned that the collector had recently died, but that his widow might still have the book.

A week later the phone rang: it was the collector's widow. Yes, she had the book, though she thought it a most unprepossessing object. I asked her to count the pages, which numbered 230 in all. It was clearly labelled as a third edition. I took a deep breath: 'You almost certainly have a unique item, very valuable.'

When she responded I could hear the grin in her voice, the pleasure of the collector with a nugget safely in their grasp.

Would a unique copy of the third (let alone the elusive second edition) be more valuable than the first edition? Even the first English edition, with its huge print run, has rarity value. Book dealer and collector George Locke acquired his copy in the 1970s. His interest was Hume's science fiction and fantasy, but he knew a desirable crime collectable when he saw it. The price? Fifty pence. The book showed some signs of wear, but was 'generally a very good copy'.[418] That Locke got a bargain is shown by a quick perusal of Via Libri, the major rare-book collecting website. Of the several hundred copies of *Hansom Cab* listed for sale, the rarest and most valuable is the first English edition. The price listed in 2013 was US$11,000 for a copy not in first-rate condition: the gradations of excellence being mint, fine and very good. The third edition might possibly be worth more, for its rarity value. But the real kudos in book collecting remains the first edition of *Hansom Cab*.

'People of the book' is a term applied to the religions deriving from the Bible: Judaism, Christianity, Islam. But it can also be applied to the wider fandom of book-industry professionals, writers, librarians, booksellers and, beyond that, consumers, collectors, reading groups, attendees at writers' festivals—all those for whom reading is habitual and a book a good companion. In a time of rapid technological change, as momentous as when Gutenberg's printing press superseded the medieval scriptoria, it might seem the book is fated for obsolescence. Or perhaps not. The ebook might be used for the disposable, 'beach books' that are downloaded, read and quickly forgotten. What people most prize they want in hard copy. The book as physical object, the smell and silken feel of its paper, excites passions that the ebook cannot.

Among the most obsessive people of the book are the collectors. Like trainspotters they tend to be male. Mostly they begin as passionate readers, who buy the books they love. Then they begin to collect, say, the complete works of a favourite author, including variant editions. Next they move beyond acquiring a book for reading to owning the book as an object in itself. The words become secondary to their format, its rarity and condition. The collector now has the first stage of bibliomania, the thrill of the continuing chase, in which the fix is acquisition. The final stage, notes Bill Mathews, is to buy the books, but never remove them from their packaging.

In *Professor Brankel's Secret*, Fergus Hume described an obsessive bibliomaniac, the wealthy Sir Gilbert Harkness:

> He spared no cost or personal trouble in securing any rare book, and, on his frequent visits to London, would be constantly found turning over the dusty treasures of the old book stalls with reverent and eager hands. The nature of the man could be seen in the way in which he smoothed and caressed his books. Oh how tenderly did he brush the dust off the back of some antique folio, and how gloatingly did his eyes dwell on its yellow, moth-eaten pages as they displayed their rich store of black-letter type.

The description makes Harkness's books seem a fetish. Hume continues: 'He never went out, save on some bookish expedition, from whence he returned a glorious victor, and with famous books captives at his chariot wheels...' Hardly surprising then that Harkness was:

> ...a tall, thin man, with a stoop, owing to his incessant bending over books. His skin was like a snake, wrinkled and loose, and, clad in his faded velvet coat, with his thin,

white hair scattered over his bent shoulders from under a black skull cap, he looked a singularly striking figure.[419]

Such an eccentric is not out of place in the modern world of book collecting. On a cold, wet winter night in Melbourne, the opening night of the ANZAAB 2012 Antiquarian Book Fair drew a well-heeled crowd, tending to the middle-aged, men wearing hand-knitted jumpers beneath their tweed jackets, moving between the stalls, inspecting the wares. An organist played Mendelssohn as an assortment of the finest antiquarian books, prints, magazines, even a framed white waistcoat once owned by the first man to sight Antarctica, tempted the buyers. Australiana featured, as did children's books, natural history prints, crime pulps and pages dispersed from illuminated manuscripts. I perused through protective glass a proof copy of Alan Garner's *The Moon of Gomrath*, beyond my means. Eventually I bought an early 1900s pulp copy of *Hansom Cab*, published by Pearson, once sold for a shilling and now worth $75. It seemed a small price to pay for the experience.

Given that an ocean of desirable books exists, most collectors sensibly choose to specialise. Harkness had chemistry. His counterpart in Australiana was David Scott Mitchell (1836–1907), the greatest book collector of the nation's history. Like Harkness Mitchell was wealthy, cultured and leisured, becoming ascetic and reclusive with age. His one known consuming passion was for books. Initially he sought English literary works in fine editions. In the 1880s the anniversary of European settlement in Australia brought a change in direction, said to have been fanned by the Melbourne George Robertson.

Mitchell's ambition became to own a copy of every printed document relating to Australia and its environs, from the first explorers onwards: a national history in books. So dogged was his pursuit that the State Library of New South Wales found itself competing with Mitchell in the arena of book auctions. He had the superior means, and so they lost out on rare Australiana. H. C. L. Anderson,

Principal Librarian, wrote in exasperation that Mitchell was a 'dreadful human bogey'. He added:

> This hated rival got the first choice of everything rare and valuable, gave extravagant prices, kept his treasures locked up in his 'dungeon', refused access to visitors, was a mere bibliomaniac who collected without knowledge and discrimination, for the mere pleasure of owning, and generally left the State Library lamenting and resentful.[420]

If the Library could not beat Mitchell, then they could possibly join his collection with theirs, posthumously. Anderson courted Mitchell and succeeded: Mitchell's memorial, the wing of the State Library that bears his name, opened in 1910, with a collection of sixty thousand books and manuscripts. It is now more than ten times that size.

In this collection are two rather unprepossessing objects, which make up half of the surviving copies of *Hansom Cab*'s first edition. One of these is the only complete copy known to exist. Mitchell definitely owned the other, as it bears his bookplate, with the family arms and motto 'Eureka'—appropriate for a collector. Traces remain of an even earlier owner, the mysterious Edith, her name half-erased. She may have been the only reader, for the book, although rebound, is inside clean and fresh. Mitchell would have certainly been more interested in its condition than its content. Bill Mathews comments that he would have only 'riffled the pages for vermin, dead or alive, taken a sanding block to any gunk on the edges, glued any loose bits on the spine—basically cleaning it before it went on his pristine shelves'.

The second copy, the complete one, has been repeatedly read, the pages slightly dog-eared. Nobody added their name to it, but on the index page along the spine is an annotation in pencil: *Robertson & Mullen 24.9.40*—its provenance. This copy was discovered during World War II in the second-hand division of Robertson's firm, now amalgamated with that of the former rival Mullen. The finder was

John Holroyd, a legendary bookseller with a formidable memory and a sharp eye. He wrote the firm's history, recording for posterity Robertson's low opinion of Hume's novel. Holroyd collected editions of *Hansom Cab*,[421] but recognised that this book was something he had never seen before, an *editio princeps* in original condition, and too valuable for him to keep. He is recorded as personally conveying the book to Sydney, where it entered the collection of Sir William Dixson, a tobacco heir and another bookish bachelor. Dixson, in turn, would leave his books to the Mitchell upon his death in 1952. Thus a Sydney library owns the only complete copy of possibly the most famous book ever produced in Melbourne.

A third copy of the *editio princeps* also surfaced in the 1940s. Sixty years had passed since the novel's publication, and those who had bought it when it first appeared were in their dotage or dying. Slowly their personal collections—made up of Dickens, Adam Lindsay Gordon, *Cole's Funny Picture Book*—began to disperse. Family members kept some as mementos, but other books scattered in deceased-estate sales, jumble stalls, pawn shops (a favourite locale of Hume's) and the many second-hand bookshops of wartime Melbourne.

In the twentieth century, book collecting was no longer reserved for the wealthy, such as Mitchell and Harkness. Otherwise Cyril Goode (1907–82) could never have amassed his collection. He was a working man and a poet, radicalised by the Great Depression into a devout Communist. A photograph of him as a young man shows him as dapper as Hume: in a pinstriped suit, clean-shaven, square-jawed and handsome. Goode kept a diary, in which this Australian Pepys records a very full life, both political and social, with his nationalism, book collecting, and love of literature intertwined. He married, begot an adored daughter, kept a photograph of Stalin (referred to sardonically as the 'Worker's Christ') on his wall—but his overwhelming passion was book collecting.[422]

Goode's bookplate, in contrast to Mitchell's armorial bearings, is Norman Lindsay's Bunyip Bluegum from *The Magic Pudding*, with his name and the phrase 'Bear in mind his book'. He would therefore forgive the terrible puns on his name happily perpetrated by librarians: 'Oh, you're here for the Goode collection. We have lots of good collections', or 'The Goode book? Go to the 200s, the theology section.'

Goode, as a bush balladist, collected first editions of Australian poets. He built up his collection constantly, at low cost and on layby from small second-hand bookshops. In his diary he wrote: 'a month or so ago I had books aside at twelve different shops in & around Melbourne'. His dedication extended to small but significant economies: 'If I walk up & down to work everyday and go without milk in my tea I save 3/- a week—to put into first editions.'[423]

Goode, rejected for war service on physical grounds, was drafted into work at a munitions factory. In his spare time he hunted books incessantly. Within his first edition of *Hansom Cab* is a typed note: 'This copy was purchased in a secondhand furniture dealer's store for 6d'—half the 1886 price.[424]

Where Goode actually found his copy is sadly unrecorded, but a rough fix can be put on the date: 1944. Goode had a local rival in rare Australiana, J. K. (Jack) Moir (1893–1958), an accountant and political conservative, who funded his book habit through canny investing. He was bald and gnomish, with hooded, wary eyes. Moir was the convivial host of the Bread and Cheese Club, which met at his home in Richmond. It was a broad church, for men of the book (and some women) devoted to 'Mateship, Art and Letters'. Writers like Alan Marshall and Miles Franklin would visit (Moir lent Franklin his copy of *Hansom Cab*); Goode frequently attended. In a late 1944 article in the *Argus* Moir wrote: 'Recently a Melbourne collector bought a copy at a jumble sale for sixpence. However it has been rebound and the original cover is missing.' He can only be describing the Goode copy.[425]

Goode did not record the 'Eureka!' moment of his find, probably because he had the habit, as a busy man, of writing his life on any paper available, later transcribing these scraps into a series of notebooks. So the note concerning the find may have been lost. In any case Goode's life then was dominated by the chaos of a preschooler and the project of preserving Adam Lindsay Gordon's Brighton home. 'Australia's most important literary landmark,' he called it. Ultimately Goode would dismantle the Gordon residence brick by brick, the raw materials being preserved in his backyard in hopes of re-erection.[426]

Goode wrote on 24 March 1944: 'he [Moir] is the kind of thing that doesn't want anyone else to have something if he can't have it himself.' The 'something' could be Gordon's cottage, but it could also be the fantastically rare copy of *Hansom Cab*, a book that Moir, who sought every novel or book of verse by an Australian writer, coveted.

Goode was too much in love with the word to forgo any reading, usually by the light of a log fire, a pleasure often referred to in his diaries. The following diary entry of 31 May 1944 suggests that having read his copy of *Hansom Cab* he went to visit its locales: 'Away along Lt Latrobe Street & numerous winding alleys in what was even up to the beginnings of this trade war, the Chinese and brothel quarter of Melbourne—until I come out up at Spring Street.'

Note the mention of trade war. On 11 February 1944 he wrote: 'Russia must be the only really civilised country in the world (as the people there are free of the fear of starving to death).' Naive in retrospect, but he believed it passionately. He would have been the subject of scrutiny by the security services. Jack Moir informed on his left-wing literary guests, listing them as 'bloody Communists' and 'bloody fellow travellers'. He 'proudly admitted' what he was doing, so not to break the rules of hospitality.[427]

Moir and Goode both left their collections to the libraries of Melbourne, Goode's books to the University of Melbourne, his manuscripts to the State Library of Victoria. The latter was where Moir bequeathed his books, the most important donation in that institution's history. He never found a first-edition copy of *Hansom Cab*, although other Hume titles were in his collection. He did own a copy of Mary Fortune's 1871 *The Detective's Album*, the first detective-fiction book published in Australia, though it is now lost, probably stolen. His granddaughter is the true-crime writer Robin Bowles.

Other book collectors go one step further, not only amassing substantial personal libraries, but compiling catalogues of them. The greatest in this category enter into their area of choice when it is a Terra Incognita, largely unknown, in the same spirit as explorers map coastlines. George Locke produced *A Spectrum of Fantasy: A Bibliography and Biography* (as if the collection were a living thing). Sir John Ferguson was the greatest bibliographer of Australiana. John Loder chose Australian crime fiction as his special subject. In 1994 he published *Australian Crime Fiction: A Bibliography 1857–1993*. The frontispiece shows the cover of *Hansom Cab*.

On a stormy Anzac Day I took my copy of Loder's bibliography to his South Yarra house. There I proffered it for his signature, and we sat in his library to 'yarn books', as Goode would put it.

I asked Loder why crime fiction. He grinned like a small boy. 'For the fun of it. The escapism, being a scientist.' He gained a PhD in Chemistry then worked for CSIRO, becoming Principal Research Scientist in the Division of Chemicals and Polymers. Loder's collecting began in his schooldays. He had to buy crime fiction in paperback, because he couldn't get hold of it otherwise. 'Crime was the hardest thing to find. Lending libraries didn't have good collections of crime fiction'—because it was considered downmarket, disreputable. Little did he know that crime fiction was just beginning to be seriously collected, by such notables and fans as Ellery Queen and Graham Greene.

Loder would retain every book he acquired, all the while

considering himself more of a keen reader than a collector. As he rose in his profession, with more ready money, he began to visit antiquarian book dealers. He built up an impressive collection of early Australiana and modern editions of writers such as Virginia Woolf in original dust jackets, but what set him apart was the subject of his bibliography: Australian crime, particularly pulp.

Like Goode, Loder fossicked in second-hand shops for his books. As a Sydney-sider relocated to Melbourne, Loder frequently drove up and down the Hume Highway on family visits. He noted the book exchanges on the way, breaking up the long trip: a 'huge shed' at Wodonga and another at Goulburn. In this way he amassed an extraordinary collection. It did, though, lack the very rarest items in Australian crime fiction: Mary Fortune's *The Detective's Album*, of which only two copies are known to survive,[428] and the first edition of *Hansom Cab*.

In time Loder decided to sell his collections. The crime and his literary first editions went to auction in 2011, via Australian Book Auctions, whose showrooms in the Melbourne suburb of Armadale comprise a temple of the book. Much to Loder's surprise, the sale included two icons of crime fiction, much coveted, but elusive for him. The first was *Beeton's Christmas Annual* for 1887, which includes the first Sherlock Holmes story, *A Study in Scarlet*. Only thirty-three copies of the magazine are known to have survived.[429] The other was a first edition of *Hansom Cab*, the Maudie Manton copy found at Young's. Australian Book Auctions had both items in stock, but held them back until they could be complemented, like precious stones in a setting, by Loder's crime fiction collection. Both of these rarities were imperfect, the *Beeton's* lacking its original wrappers, but still priced in the thousands of dollars.

The auction was important to the trade in establishing the prices of crime Australiana: 'the value of an old book is the highest price someone is prepared to pay for it.'[430] However, with the effects of the Global Financial Crisis still being felt, neither the Hume nor the Doyle sold on the day—'no money around,' commented a dealer. A rare-book librarian commented to me that the *Hansom Cab* was overpriced for its condition. It did subsequently sell, and is now in private hands.

John Loder is philosophical about the early editions of *Hansom Cab* eluding him. 'Booksellers all have these stories. It's like a mythical beast—everybody claims to have seen it…Miss Berry was supposed to have one.'

I nearly fell off my chair at this zero degree of separation. I knew Miss (Elizabeth) Berry, from a family of antique dealers: her mother, Mrs Frances Berry had premises in a cavernous basement in Flinders Lane, and her brother Richard had a sideline in books. Miss Berry had a tiny treasure chest of a shop near the Victoria Market. I fossicked in her trays of goods and bought from her wonderful trifles, beads, baubles, china and a battered but still beautiful lacquered wooden Chinese doll.

Miss Berry, with her pastel cardigans and her hair piled high—she owned a first edition of *Hansom Cab*?

Loder: 'So Richard said. He didn't like crime fiction much. I once got some signed copies of Ngaio Marsh from him. Inexpensively.'

When I repeat this anecdote around the second-hand book trade, the consensus is that it is not something that Richard Berry, an introverted man who knew his business well, would have invented. Loder went several times to the shop, but never found it open, because Miss Berry kept Victoria Market hours.

'Elizabeth had a good eye for books,' comments a dealer. 'She probably looked at it, decided she didn't know how to value it and so held onto it.'

Elizabeth Berry predeceased her brother Richard, who was her executor. Even if he didn't like crime fiction, would he have held onto *Hansom Cab*? His collecting focus was quite different: ephemera, mostly printed objects that would otherwise not be preserved. When he died in 2000 he left what became known as the Berry collection, a huge assortment of saucy Victorian postcards, sheet music, colonial banknotes, theatre programmes and more, stored in tea chests within an Ascot Vale lock-up. Nick Dawes of Australian Book Auctions had the job of sorting through it prior to auction, a process that took months.

'If there was a copy of *Hansom Cab* it wasn't in the Berry collection,' Nick said. He commented that Miss Berry 'probably sold it for $50'—a rarity, but not an extreme rarity price. 'The Berrys were never greedy,' he recalled.

Should the Maudie Manton copy be the same as the Berry copy, the possibility exists that the owner died without leaving any indication of the book's worth. The heirs not knowing better, the book ended up at Young's. However, two separate book dealers have expressed disbelief to me that such a rare item should emerge serendipitously. As Jonathan Wantrup states in his guide *Australian Rare Books (1787–1900)*, 'a book worth a few cents will stay hidden, one worth a few hundred dollars will not.' Bill Mathews, however, disagrees: 'In the trade, yes, but out in the wider world rare books get pulped everyday.'

Wantrup also writes that collectors acquire books in two ways: 'purchase and theft'.[431] Stories abound around the trade of collectors so keen that they help themselves to items not for sale; one was said to be David Scott Mitchell himself. If Maudie Manton's copy was at some stage stolen, then it seems entirely appropriate for a crime fiction book to be the subject of a crime itself.

My mind keeps returning to the book in Miss Berry's shop. Did I ever tell her I was a researcher for Professor Stephen Knight's history of Australian crime fiction? Had I but known (a catchphrase of crime fiction from the early twentieth century), she could have unlocked the glass-fronted case for me and I would have bought it. Oh for a time machine! I wonder, too, if it really was the Manton copy. If not, then there are five, not four surviving copies of the first edition. Somewhere out there is book gold, the *rara avis* of crime collecting.

After I concluded my interview with John Loder, we stood on the doorstep chatting. In his front garden my attention was caught by a brilliant globe, hanging high, the colour of a yellowback book: a ripe persimmon in a tree, being pecked by anything but a rara avis, a garden wattlebird. It brought to mind an image from Hume's one attempt at children's fiction, *The Chronicles of Fairy Land* (1892). In it a writer, with some faery blood in his ancestry, falls asleep by his fireside. He awakes to find himself in a moonlit glade, where he meets the faery Phancie, librarian to King Oberon—a job several more mundane librarians have said they covet.

Phancie tells the narrator he stands in the royal library. At the response 'I don't see anything except leaves', the scene transforms like a Victorian pantomime. The glade becomes a palatial interior, where the trees are pillars of white marble, upholding an azure ceiling, inlaid with gold. Under the glow of a globe, the moon-lamp, are green velvet curtains, behind them the books, their covers brown as withered leaves.[432] They comprise fairy stories, non-fiction in this library, but also the lost books of this world, and the works that authors never wrote (but completed in fairy land, as if writers in residence).

In Oberon's library might be found Hume's lost playscript for Henry Irving, never performed before the actor died in 1905, and kept by Hume until he died. Here also would be the book that Hume never quite succeeded in producing, which would have rendered him respectable to the literati, more than just an author of shilling shockers. Had Hume not encountered Trischler, an additional item in the library would have been *The Mystery of a Hansom Cab*. Without that book, Hume would have been forgotten completely, an unsuccessful dramatist, probably a provincial lawyer, like the hero-poet of *When I Lived in Bohemia*, an unobtrusive bibliophile. Instead, with *Hansom Cab*, Hume became one of the few antipodean authors of his generation with a worldwide circulation, continuously in print, with the book now marketed as a classic—enduring literature, his ultimate memorial.

Phancie's loss is our gain.

POSTSCRIPT

It was a changeable Melbourne spring day, almost 127 years precisely after *Hansom Cab*'s first publication. I had travelled far for *Blockbuster!*, even had my plane struck by lightning, and now the researches were nearing an end. I sat with W. H. Chong, designer of this book, in the State Library of Victoria, awaiting a bulk delivery. In came a trolley loaded with every edition of *Hansom Cab* in the library's collection— which is by no means all that were published. The library did have a deposit copy of *Hansom Cab*'s first edition, which has vanished, probably stolen. It missed out again on the elusive first edition when Cyril Goode's books went to the University of Melbourne. Belatedly, and retrospectively, the library has responded by acquiring every edition of *Hansom Cab* it can. Librarian Des Cowley recalls thinking, 'Oh my God! What have we done?' as more and more copies of the book arrived, bought inexpensively by book aficionado John Arnold for the collection.

Forty to fifty different editions of *Hansom Cab* were wheeled out for our delectation. Here were copies of the 'fourth' Melbourne edition, by Kemp & Boyce, which caused the court case over copyright with Jessie Taylor. Here also was the first English edition by the Hansom Cab Publishing Company, a cheaper production, with pulpy paper sheets stapled together. Inside, showing the appeal of *Hansom Cab* across class lines, was a bookplate with the arms of the Honourable Charles Russell.

Many copies of the book have been rebound, either by fond owners or book dealers, but enough survive in their original form to show a fascinating variety of cover designs. Here be pirated American editions, along with translations into French, German and various Scandinavian languages. The images tend to the unashamedly pulpy, with various permutations of horses and hansoms, but pretty misses also feature: 'for the Romance market!' commented Chong. One book shows a horseriding couple, an illustration that has little to do with the content and is most likely a stock image, or one intended for another book. One cover derives from stills from Arthur Shirley's lost 1925 film. Occasionally different images appear, of a man with a handkerchief tied over his face and, most luridly, the death of Frettlby, with Madge and Sal gazing on, horrified.

The cover of the most recent foreign translation, the Chinese of 2009, is in comparison tasteful and restrained. Hume was among the earliest Australasian writers to be translated into Chinese,[433] but as he walked through Melbourne's Chinatown in the 1880s he would never have anticipated *Hansom Cab* being read in China eighty years after his death. Other twenty-first-century translations have appeared, in Dutch, French and Japanese.

Cowley opened one of the earlier editions, carefully because of the fragile paper, and showed the pages of advertisements. Chong was struck by Kemp & Boyce using the spine to advertise Chipperfield's Ironmongery—'We could do that!' However, he commented that of all the covers on show the most effective was the original, used for the earliest editions: the engraving showing the moment of the murder, with Government House in the background.

Not many authors succeed in publishing a book. Even fewer create something of enduring value, a classic. A very small number succeed in producing a writer's dream, a book so popular it creates sales records.

The consequences of *Hansom Cab* were legion. Hume had said he 'would hate to be known as a "one book man"', but that is what happened.[434] *Hansom Cab* changed Hume's life, making his name, even if shilling-shockery was not the reputation he craved. It killed Phil Beck, though probably had little effect on the death of drunken

John Fletcher of Manchester. The book made Trischler an international publisher, if briefly, and also made his backers, the Taylors, a pile of cash before the fall of Marvellous Melbourne.

Hansom Cab showed the Australian book market that a local product could become a raging bestseller, locally and internationally. It paved the way for Angus & Robertson in the 1890s, with their successful stable of nationalist, *Bulletin*-puffed authors. *Hansom Cab* also proved to overseas publishers that there was publishing gold in the colonies, not only as an export market for their books, but as a source of new writing talent. After *Hansom Cab* was published the number of Australian authors with book contracts increased. Ward Lock, for instance, did very nicely with Ethel Turner in the 1890s and beyond.

Above all, the work consolidated detective fiction as a publishing genre, one with a mass readership of avid fans. Vizetelly with Gaboriau, Anna Katherine Green and others had shown that the market existed for tales of crime, but it took the blockbusting success of *Hansom Cab*, achieved by Trischler's brilliant marketing, to prove how lucrative crime fiction could be. Publishers took note and, over a century later, detective fiction is still a market leader.

Hume had not wanted to write crime in the first place, though it was something for which he was perfectly fitted, with his taste for melodrama, his legal experience and his ability with dialogue, honed from writing theatre scripts. It would be the regret of his life that he never made it as a successful dramatist in London, unlike his rival Doyle, who had Sir Henry Irving perform his one-act play in 1894. It was not for want of trying, either, with Hume described as a 'pushful New Zealander'.[435] Yet he was never as brilliant at self-promotion as dramatist Haddon Chambers, who famously followed impresario Beerbohm Tree into a Turkish bath, play in hand, and read it aloud to his captive audience. Chambers' dramas are never performed now and he is hardly recalled, except as Nellie Melba's lover. Fergus Hume's conventional Victorian dramas similarly faded from view, lacking the groundbreaking, enduring realism of works by Ibsen or Chekhov.

Hume also dabbled in futuristic writing, literary fiction and the occult. As he complained bitterly in *When I Lived in Bohemia*: 'There is nothing so much hated by the public as a versatile man.'[436] But the public knew what he did not; that his greatest talent was for crime fiction. Although he resented the restrictions of the label, he was conscientious about his craft. It wounded him that the skill of his productions was not recognised:

> Look at all the work, observation, logic, analysis, and memory involved in the writing of such a book, and yet when it is done and presents a perfect picture of a difficult criminal case, then critics dismiss it with the contemptuous remark 'that it is a shilling shocker!'[437]

Like many colonials in London Hume appealed to the English market by writing 'Home' settings. In the process he lost what had made *Hansom Cab* so different and distinctive: the Melbourne background, a European city familiar but strange.

He made one crucial mistake at the beginning, in not following Gaboriau or Fortune closely, and making the detective the central character. Instead he followed the practice of Sensation fiction, where the functions of detective were shared between a number of characters, from Madge to Calton and Gorby. Nor did he stick with his police detectives, even throughout the Melbourne Trilogy. *Hansom Cab* has Gorby and Kilsip, *Madame Midas*, Kilsip, *Miss Mephistopheles*, Naball. He did not have one detective as protagonist, which was becoming a characteristic feature of the emerging crime-fiction series. In the 2012 telemovie of *Hansom Cab*, Hume's multiple detectives were retained, although a spin-off series was posited to feature Calton and Kilsip (which did not eventuate). Bill Garner, who wrote an earlier commissioned script for a feature film that was never produced, took a different tack:

> As you know, the detective novel was in an embryonic
> condition at the time Hume wrote it, so the story did not
> naturally fall into the shape of a modern murder story, in
> which the detective is usually the main character...in the
> book the detectives are secondary characters and there are
> two of them so I got rid of Kilsip...I made Sam Gorby a
> larrikin detective which opened up the class differences
> between him and the people he was investigating and I
> made him attractive as an outsider, someone the audience
> could identify with...Madge, enraged that the men will tell
> her nothing because she is a woman, secretly approaches
> Sam to keep investigating. He becomes her guide to the
> underground...this created an opportunity for a trans-
> gressive love affair between Gorby and Madge.[438]

Hume did later have a single series detective in Octavius Fanks of
Scotland Yard, who appears in several novels of the 1890s. But Fanks
did not gain public acclaim, unlike Sherlock Homes. Doyle had also
intended his venture into detective fiction to have been a one-off. *A
Study in Scarlet* was an experiment, one rejected repeatedly and only
selling belatedly and under poor terms to *Beeton's*. Doyle had tried to
negotiate a royalty, but Ward Lock refused. Like Hume with *Hansom
Cab*, Doyle never earned any more from the work. But he had created
Sherlock Holmes, a classic character. Doyle returned to Holmes in
another novella, *The Sign of Four* (1890). The favourable reaction,
when published, led him to think of continuing the character in a
short-story series. Furthermore he put his business dealings in the
hands of A. P. Watt, the man who coined the term 'literary agent'.

In 1891 the new *Strand* magazine began its series of Sherlock
Holmes stories, and Doyle struck gold, enduring fame and fortune.
He might have had a low opinion of *Hansom Cab*, but it played a
major role in creating his market.

DRAMATIS PERSONAE

Maudie Manton, the twenty-one-year-old owner of a first edition of *Hansom Cab*, was married to Joseph Tompson for fewer than two years. In May 1888 their daughter, Dorothy Maude, was born. Thirteen months later Joseph died, only a few months after Maudie's mother, Caroline. On the first day of November 1889, on Cup Day eve, the *Argus* reported that the young widow was putting all her 'extremely valuable furniture' up for auction before quitting the colony. When Mrs Tompson left Melbourne, she may have taken her copy of *Hansom Cab* with her as a memento of her marriage, so intimately tied to the novel's settings. She remarried within eleven months (May 1890) to Arthur Blachford Cox, a surveyor, in NSW. The following year her father died, his profession given as 'mining speculator'—allegedly just before going insolvent again.

In a five-year period Maudie married twice, gave birth, and lost both parents and her first husband. Her later life was less eventful, with four more children born, including twins. Maudie and her family returned to Melbourne in the new century, when it became prosperous again. She died in Caulfield in 1936. Despite the sorrows of her early life, she is recalled as never having had a white hair.[439]

James Hume died in 1896, of a stroke. At the time he was under a cloud after a patient at Ashburn Hall committed suicide, with a subsequent public enquiry. None of his children were in Dunedin when he died. Sarah and Bessie Hume were probably visiting Fergus and the Willebys in Europe, and James Hume Jr was working as an engineer in Western Australia. His will had two main concerns: to maintain Ashburn Hall and to provide income for his unmarried daughters. Lawyer George Mondy was bequeathed Hume's partnership in Ashburn Hall, and his sister-in-law, Matron Janet Fergusson, received almost all of his personal effects and furniture. A trust set up for Sarah and Bessie would produce £300 a year, to be shared between the sisters. After their death, the money was to go to the surviving children in equal shares, with Mary's share on her decease going to her children. The trustees had the discretionary power to withhold James and Fergus's shares, an unusual provision suggesting that James Hume had doubts about his sons' grasp of money.

George Robertson retired from bookselling in 1890, suffering ill health, and died in 1898 still a wealthy man. The 1890s Depression had affected his business, which in the new century would concentrate on retail. In 1921 the firms of Robertson and Mullen merged, uniting postmortem two businesses created when friends bitterly fell out. His rival **Edward Cole** similarly survived the hard times, semi-retiring in 1911 and dying seven years later. His business was wound up in 1929, the site of the Bourke Street Arcade bought by Coles (no relation) and demolished. The 1890s Depression ended Melbourne's dominance of the Australasian book trade.

Charles Willeby is listed in the 1901 UK census as living in Chelsea, described as a 'music composer working from home'. He and **Mary Hume-Willeby** kept four live-in servants—a sign of prosperity. Willeby would have a considerable career as a music writer and a composer of songs, ranging from classical to ragtime. Mary continued her public singing, teaching and frequent travel. She was in New Zealand when Fergus died in 1932. Her last visit there was in 1939, presumably avoiding World War II, and she died in October of that year. Willeby died in 1955.[440]

James Hume Jr travelled to Malaya in 1902. After a few letters to his family he vanished, leaving no trace. Steps to have him declared legally dead were not undertaken until 1930, when Fergus needed James' share of his father's legacy.[441]

Alfred Plumpton died in London in 1902, his musical collaboration with Hume unperformed and lost. After he left Melbourne **Caroline Hodgson** briefly reunited with her husband. Following his death she would make a second marriage, ending in divorce. She continued her brothel trade in Melbourne until a clean-up of the red light district in 1907 forced her premises to close. She died the following year.

Maurice Brodzky also met with disaster in 1902: the brilliant gadfly was finally swatted. A new political force, the Labor Party, had arisen and an article in *Table Talk* libelled the state leader, F. H. Bromley. He sued successfully; the case made Brodzky insolvent again, and he lost control of *Table Talk*. He moved to San Francisco and new journalistic fields—only to encounter the great earthquake of 1906. Brodzky continued to work as a journalist in England and New York before dying in 1919.

Sara Hume died in Auckland in 1904, where she had been living with Bessie in the seaside suburb of Devonport. **Bessie Hume** had spent her life, post-accident, as a teacher of music and elocution. She had a further setback in an 1890 accident when milk cans, shining bright in sunshine, caused the ponies drawing her carriage to shy. The Hume family sued the milk company, engaging Sir Robert Stout for the prosecution.[442] After Sara's death Bessie returned to Dunedin, where she was noted for charity work, also jingoistic poems and songs, written during World War I.

Marcus Hume died in 1906 in Bega, New South Wales. A press notice stated that 'he was a cultured gentleman, was for years a capable journalist, and as a musical critic stood in high repute.' He was described as a 'remarkably keen businessman', ending as a successful hotel-keeper.[443]

Frederick Trischler was listed as a stockbroker in the 1901 UK census. His Lucy was stated to be blind. Four years later, a widower, he made business trips to New York, where he stayed at the Waldorf Astoria. The passenger lists described him as a financier. He died in Sussex in 1909, at the age of fifty-six. His brother **Walter Trischler** outlived him by decades, dying in 1931, with **Minnie Trischler** following twenty years later.

Alice Cornwell was involved in mining and harbour speculations in Australia, but lost money in the 1890s. She sold the *Sunday Times* in 1893 and the following year married Phil Robinson. Gradually she faded from public view, though she was known under her married name as a breeder of pugs and founder of the Ladies' Kennel Association. She died of cancer in 1932, the same year as Hume. Her biography is being written by Fiona Gruber.

Fergus Hume's life in England, post-*Hansom Cab*, was busy. A glimpse was provided by 'Tay Pay', in a 1903 full-page profile— written possibly to compensate for the Beck article of 1902. He noted '…the genial warmth of his manner and unfailing wit. A Celt, with all the fire, imagination and the innate poetry of his race.'[444]

What evidence survives of Hume's later life indicates a quiet rural existence in Thundersley, with periodic literary lunches at Fleet Street's Green Dragon inn, and trips to the Continent, particularly Cannes and Switzerland.[445] He gained a knowledge of Romany life, of which he wrote with great affection in his books. In addition he was said to have been part of a group of informal readers who critiqued the manuscript of Bram Stoker's *Dracula*.[446] Yet on the whole Hume failed to be mentioned in the memoirs of his literary contemporaries, perhaps because as a shilling-shocker writer he was not considered worthy of note.

Although he never gave up his theatrical dreams until old age, even venturing into the music hall with a comic tale of anarchists,[447] increasingly his life revolved around his writing desk, at which he kept office hours. He could make a living, but only by incessant work. Ill health stopped Fergus after 140 novels, including some fine detective novels such as *The Silent House in Pimlico* (1900). His productivity surely left time for little else than meeting deadlines. In his busiest years, a novel was produced every few months, the busiest year being 1900, with eight novels. His work was serialised, particularly in Australia, providing extra income.

The genre Hume helped create moved into the twentieth century. His work, as the Golden Age and a little later the hardboiled era commenced, would seem increasingly old-fashioned. A new medium, the silent film, did adapt his works: *Hansom Cab* (thrice), the 1909 novel *Top Dog* in 1919, and (in Dutch) *The Other Person*, 1921. None of these films has survived.

A glandular operation brought Hume's career to an end, for it apparently destroyed his ability to create fiction. It did not stop Hume writing entirely, for he contributed reviews to the *Bookman*, naturally of detective fiction, by the younger writers who had benefited from the market created by *Hansom Cab*.[448] He tended to be an appreciative rather than destructive critic. Several more novels, previously unsold manuscripts or newspaper serialisations, were published before his death.

When filmmaker Arthur Shirley wrote to Hume in the mid-1920s he learned that the writer was 'in want of money to keep going'. Shirley started a subscription fund, but though Hume was grateful he refused it 'with quiet dignity, saying that he loved what was imagined to be his poverty'. His *The Fever of Life* had opened with a poem and paean to English writer Mortimer Collins, who led a 'Horatian life' of quiet intellectualism in the countryside. The phrase was also used of Hume, with the comment made that he was 'quite content'.[449] He took part in debating societies, and lectured to youth groups.

In his childhood bookseller Ben Weinreb (1912–99) knew Hume, accompanying him on weekly walks in the countryside, during which the master storyteller exercised his art. They would pass a coffin-maker, and Hume would invent stories behind the burials: 'Only later in life,' said Weinreb, 'did I wonder how the sleepy village of Thundersley managed to bury so many lovelorn ladies and noble adventurers during that short span of my childhood years.' The former dandy sported a bedraggled moustache and trousers frayed at the hems.[450]

At the end of his life Hume lived alone, in one rented room in a bungalow, surviving on a regular income of £2 (approximately $150) a week, probably from his father's bequest. Hume died of heart disease on 12 July 1932, aged seventy-three. Among his possessions at his death was found a typescript of 'The Vestal', with annotations by Henry Irving. After probate Hume's effects were valued at £200, not a small amount at the height of the Great Depression.

Hume's story had been as sensational as any he had told to young Weinreb: a man who had written a major international bestseller and not become rich. Of his contemporaries and rivals, Doyle had died two years previously, and Anna Katharine Green would die three years later. A new crop of crime writers were busy: Agatha Christie, Dorothy Sayers and Dashiell Hammett from the early 1920s, Marjorie Allingham from 1926, Ellery Queen and, in Australia, Arthur Upfield, from 1929. All these newcomers had read or owed something of their success to *The Mystery of a Hansom Cab*.

Fergus Hume may not have died rich in worldly goods, but he had the goodwill—even the word love was used—of his community, the villagers of Thundersley, who followed his coffin to the graveyard.[451] Since he deserves the last word, what comes to mind is something he wrote in *The Chinese Jar* (1893) about one of his favourite haunts, a curio shop: 'And over all lay the grey veil of dust, trying to hide from the modern world these pitiful wrecks of the past. What sermons did that shop preach, of folly, of sorrow, of crime, of tenderness!'

REVIEWS AND OPINIONS OF
THE MYSTERY OF A HANSOM CAB

'A perusal of this fascinating story will serve at least one useful purpose, and that is to convince the most sceptical that a colonial writer can produce literature of the "shilling shocker" type at least as realistic, sensational and entrancing as any that Hugh Conway or his imitators have evolved. There is genuine ability in the book. It exhibits imagination, constructive powers of a high-class and a gift of easy dialogue that many a French novelist might envy.' *British Australasian*, 2 December 1887

'A more clever, fascinating or interesting little volume has seldom been issued in such a cheap form...Although it is a sensational romance, yet it is so blended with curious and interesting studies of human nature in all its phases that it bids fair to rank with the famous character tales of the immortal Charles Dickens...' *York Herald*, 14 January 1888

'Where is the great Australian novel? Hansom Cab Mystery is the very best.' Letter to the *Herald*, 26 October 1893

'Mr Fergus Hume's literary career has been a strange and hard one. He made a reputation with a tawdry and worthless book, and now seems to be losing it with a lot of really passable and (in some cases) meritorious ones.' *South Australian Chronicle*, 18 February 1893

'Mr Hume is in the unfortunate position of having written his best book first. He should have led up to it gently by such books as are now published from his pen. In the stead whereof he consistently lets us down.' *Sydney Morning Herald*, 21 April 1906

'Fergus Hume…was an unknown colonial; his first book was purely a colonial production; but so decisive was his bid for recognition that the British public stood aside while he laid his scarlet literature on the table. There was no question of where he came from, or who he was—the man was there beside the book, and it was accepted without demur.' John Maclennan, 'Colonial Literature in Britain', *Otago Witness*, 24 March 1909

'Speaking entirely from memory, and subject to correction, of course, I should say "The Mystery of a Hansom Cab" was the first book written by an Australian which dealt with a first-class murder mystery. I was a very small boy when Fergus Hume's book was first published, and I well remember the sensation it caused. Despite parental injunction I read it, and have done on several occasions since.' 'Orestes', *Morning Bulletin* (Rockhampton), 27 September 1926

'For some unfathomable reason this shoddy pot-boiler received vastly more contemporary attention than Doyle's *Study in Scarlet*… by the time of its author's death it had sold more than half a million copies—making it, according to Willard Huntington Wright and other authorities, the greatest commercial success in the annals of detective fiction. Scarcely readable to-day, *The Mystery of a Hansom Cab* belongs among the famous "freak books" and is mentioned here for its historical interest only.' Howard Haycraft, *Murder for Pleasure*, 1941

'…our valiant old cab.' Miles Franklin, *Bulletin*, 17 December 1952

'One of the hundred best crime novels of all time.' *Sunday Times*, 1954

'...ranks as the most successful detective story of all time.' *Everyman's Dictionary of Literary Biography*, 1960

'Like all village lending libraries, this one had not bothered much about keeping itself up to date, and I was hesitating between *By Order of the Czar* and *The Mystery of a Hansom Cab*, which seemed the best bets...' P. G. Wodehouse, *Aunts Aren't Gentlemen*, 1974

'Without the example of Fergus Hume, Ngaio Marsh would never have written crime fiction. He was inspirational for her.' Joanne Drayton, biographer of Ngaio Marsh, 2012

'I absolutely hated it.' Kerry Greenwood

'I absolutely loved it.' Sandra Nicholson, Former Assistant Commissioner, Victoria Police

'I always have a copy of the Arrow edition in stock, for someone is bound to ask for it.' Kay Craddock, rare-book dealer

'...critically overlooked under the stunningly professional assumption that colonials can't write.' Adrian Harrington Rare Books, viaLibri website, 19 July 2013

'What book has best captured your sense of the city?'
'*The Mystery of a Hansom Cab* by Fergus Hume. Every time I walk through Little Bourke Street I can't help but imagine what Melbourne was like in the 19th century.' Adam Bandt, interview in the *Age*, 26 October 2013

SELECT BIBLIOGRAPHY

SOURCES

Works by Hume Cited

Manuscripts

Letter to [Sampson and Low?], San Remo, 7 July 1891. Collection of
  Elizabeth Paton, transcription by Kay Craddock and Lucy Sussex.

Published Texts

Across the Footlights. London: F. V. White, 1912.

Aladdin in London: A Romance. London: Black, 1892.

Answered. London: F. V. White, 1915.

'A Ballad of Arcadie'. *Gags*, 1889: 89.

'A Ballad of Fortune'. *The Theatre*, 1 May 1886, 290.

The Chronicles of Fairy Land. Philadelphia: Lippincott, 1911.

'A Colonial Banshee'. 1893. In *Australian Gothic: An Anthology of
  Australian Supernatural Fiction 1867–1939*. Ed. James Doig. Mandurah:
  Equilibrium, 2007.

Crazy-Quilt. London: Ward Lock, 1919.

The Dark Avenue. London: Ward Lock, 1920.

'Dreams to Sell', *Bookman*, Nov. 1926, 128–9.

'Fact and Fiction', *Bookman*, July 1927, 235–5.

'Farcical Comedy', *Table Talk*, 3 July 1885, 3–4.

The Fever of Life. London: Sampson Low, 1892.

'Four Novels'. *Bookman*, Dec. 1927, 168.

The Gentleman who Vanished: A Psychological Phantasy. London: F. V.
  White, 1890.

The Girl from Malta. London: Hansom Cab, 1889.

Hagar of the Pawn Shop. London: Skeffington, 1898.

The Island of Fantasy: A Romance. London: Griffith Farran, 1892.

Lady Jim of Curzon Street. London: T. Werner Laurie, 1906.

Madame Midas. 1888. London: Hogarth, 1985.

The Man With a Secret. London: F. V. White, 1890.

The Millionaire Mystery. London: Chatto & Windus, 1901.

Miss Mephistopheles. London: F. V. White, 1890.

Monsieur Judas: A Paradox. London: Warne, 1896.

'My Lady Disdain', *Table Talk*, 26 June 1885, 8.

Not Wanted. London: F. V. White, 1914.

The Piccadilly Puzzle: A Mystery Story. London: F. V. White, 1889.

Professor Brankel's Secret: A Psychological Study. Melbourne: Baird's, c. 1887.

'The Queer Story of Adam Lind'. *Manchester Times*, Supplement, 5 Oct. 1889, 5.

Review of *The Martyrdom of Madeline* by Robert Buchanan. *Otago Daily Times*, 10 Mar. 1883, 1.

'Richard Wagner'. *Evening Star*, 17 Feb. 1883, 2.

'Satirical Opera'. *Table Talk*, 26 June 1885, 2.

The Secret of the Chinese Jar, Or the Loot of the Summer Palace. 1893. Cleveland: Westbrook, 1912.

The Silent House in Pimlico. London: Long, 1900.

A Son of Perdition: An Occult Romance. London: Rider, 1912.

A Traitor in London. London: Long, 1900.

Tracked by a Tattoo. London: Warne, 1896.

When I Lived in Bohemia. Bristol: Arrowsmith, 1892.

The Unexpected. London: Oldhams, 1921.

With Philip Beck

'A Centennial Song'. *Argus*, 26 Jan. 1888, 5.

ARCHIVES AND MANUSCRIPTS

Ledger Book, Angus and Robertson records, Mitchell Library, ML MSS 3269/11.

Dolman, Glen, script for *The Mystery of a Hansom Cab*, 2012.

Goode, Cyril, Diaries. State Library of Victoria. MS MCFB 1 (EX MC 1, DR 1).

James Hume. Will. Dunedin Regional Office, Archives New Zealand: DAAC D239 9073 Box 120.

——Diary, Dunedin Regional Office, Archives New Zealand.

Pyke, William. Diary. State Library of Victoria MS 9429.

Register of Proprietors of Copyright of Literary, Dramatic and Musical Productions. NAA: A2389, 3.

Reports on Lunatic Asylums in New Zealand. Appendix to the Journals of the House of Representatives. AtoJS Online.

Requests to Register Under Copyright Act 1869—forms requesting entry of proprietorship, v. 18, nos. 3000B to3199B. NAA: A2387, 18/3000B-3-3199B.

Taylor, G. N. Prison Record. Victorian Public Record Office VPRS 515/P1 25270.

Tremain, George (Carry Swain). Prison Record. NSW State Records. Digital IDs: 2232_a006_a00607_13804000067r; 2138_a006_a00603_6053000168r.

PRIMARY SOURCES

Alison, Jennifer. *Doing Something for Australia: George Robertson and the Early Years of A&R, Publishers 1888–1900*. (BSANZ Occasional Publication: 9). Melbourne: BSANZ, 2009.

Altick, Richard. 'Nineteenth-century English Best Sellers'. *Studies in Bibliography*, (22) 1969, 197–206.

Angus, John. *A History of the Dunedin Hospital Board and Its Predecessors*. Dunedin: Otago Hospital Board, 1984.

Bell, Eric Sinclair. 'The Publishing History of Fergus Hume's *The Mystery of a Hansom Cab*'. Appendix, *Victorian Detective Fiction: A Catalogue of the Collection made by Dorothy Glover & Graham Greene*. Bibliographically arranged by Eric Osborne. London: Bodley Head, 1966, 123–6.

Bell, Ian. 'Alchemist of Kosmoid Hall'. *Herald Scotland*, 16 Sept. 2013.
http://www.heraldscotland.com/sport/spl/aberdeen/alchemist-of-
kosmoid-hall-1.396953'-of-kosmoid-hall-1.396953

Brickell, Chris. *Manly Affections: The Photographs of Robert Gant, 1885–
1915*. Dunedin: Genre, 2012.

'Campbell, Margaret' [Ethel Anderson]. *Music in Dunedin*. Dunedin:
Begg, 1945.

Campbell, Ronald G. *The First Ninety Years: the Printing House of Massina,
Melbourne, 1859 to 1949*. Melbourne: Massina, 1949.

Carr, John Dickson. *The Life of Sir Arthur Conan Doyle*. London: Murray,
1949.

Chambers, Haddon. '30 Years of Playwriting'. *New York Times*, 13 Oct.
1918.

Chesser, Lucy. *Parting with My Sex: Cross-Dressing, Inversion and Sexuality
in Australian Cultural Life*. Sydney: Sydney University Press, 2008.

Clarke, Patricia. *Rosa! Rosa! A Life of Rosa Praed, Novelist and Spiritualist*.
Melbourne: Melbourne University Publishing, 1999.

Coghlan, T. A. *A Statistical Account of the Seven Colonies of Australia,
1897–8*.

Cook, Matt. *London and the Culture of Homosexuality, 1885–1914*.
Cambridge: Cambridge University Press, 2003.

Davenport, Sarah. In *No Place for a Nervous Lady: Voices from the
Australian Bush*. Frost, Lucy (ed). Melbourne: McPhee-Gribble, 1984.

Davies, Suzanne. 'Sexuality, Performance, and Spectatorship in Law: The
Case of Gordon Lawrence, 1888'. *Journal of the History of Sexuality*, Jan.
1997, 389–408.

Dixon, Robert. 'Closing the Can of Worms: Enactments of Justice in *Bleak
House*, *The Mystery of a Hansom Cab* and *The Tax Inspector*'. *Westerly*,
37.4 (1992), 37–46.

Downes, Peter. *Shadows on the Stage: Theatre in New Zealand—the First 70
Years*. Dunedin: McIndoe, 1975.

Doyle, Arthur Conan. *Arthur Conan Doyle: A Life in Letters*. Lellenberg,
Jon; Stashower, Daniel; and Foley, Charles (eds). New York: Penguin,
2007.

Drayton, Joanne. *Ngaio Marsh: Her Life in Crime*. Sydney: HarperCollins,
2009.

Ellmann, Richard. *Oscar Wilde*. New York: Vintage, 1988.

Feece, Ignatius. 'The Great Cryptogammon: showing the real authorship of the 'Hansom Cab'. *Otago Witness*, 14 Sept. 1888, 15.

'Ferguson, W. Humer'. *A Blood-Curdling Romance: The Mystery of a Wheelbarrow, or Gaboriau Gaborooed*. London: Walter Scott, 1888.

Fletcher, Brian H. *Magnificent Obsession: The Story of the Mitchell Library, Sydney*. Sydney: Allen & Unwin, in association with the State Library of New South Wales, 2007.

Frame, James. *The Philosophy of Insanity, By a Late Inmate of the Glasgow Royal Asylum for Lunatics at Gartnavel*. Fromm-Reichmann, Frieda (intro). 1860. New York: Greenberg, 1947.

Fredman, Lionel. 'Follow that Cab.' *Quadrant*, 21 (4) Apr. 1977: 63–66.

Gardner, P. D. 'Brief Notes on Some Fraudulent Aspects of the Secret Compositions of William Lawrence Baillieu and Friends 1892'. *Victorian Historical Journal*, June 2009, 61–75.

Glass, James. *Chats Over a Pipe*. London: Simpkin Marshall & Co, 1922.

Hallmann, Robert. 'Thundersley: Mysteries of a Quiet Man: Fergusson Wright Hume.' The Hadleigh and Thundersley Community Archive. http://www.hadleighhistory.org.uk/

Harvey, Norman K. 'Towards a Bibliography of *The Mystery of a Hansom Cab*.' *Biblionews*, Sept. 1958, 29–30.

Harvie, David. Information from David Harvie, mostly reports from the *Daily Mail*, concerning the activities of John Joseph Melville.

Hawthorne, Stuart. *No Humbug: The Life of Pioneer Educator Stuart Hawthorne MA*. Brisbane: Boolarong, 2013.

Holroyd, John. *George Robertson of Melbourne 1825–1898: Pioneer Bookseller & Publisher*. Melbourne: Robertson & Mullens, 1968.

James, Gwyn. 'A Literary Mystery'. *Age*, 30 Oct. 1965.

Johanson, Graham. In *Books for Colonial Readers: The Nineteenth-Century Australian Experience*. Kirsop, W. (ed). Melbourne: BSANZ, 1995.

Jones, Julia. *Fifty Years in the Fiction Factory: The Working Life of Herbert Allingham*. Sokens: Golden Duck, 2012.

Kaplan, Morris B. *Sodom on the Thames*. Ithaca: Cornell, 2005.

Kellow, A. H. *Queensland Poets*. London: Harrap, 1930.

Knewstubb, Elspeth. 'Respectability, Religion and Psychiatry in New Zealand: A Case Study of Ashburn Hall, Dunedin, 1882–1910'. A thesis submitted for the degree of Master of Arts in History at the University of Otago, New Zealand, 2011.

Law, Graham. 'On Wilkie Collins and Hugh Conway "Poor Fargus"'. *Wilkie Collins Journal*, 3 (2000) http://wilkiecollinssociety.org/on-wilkie-collins-and-hugh-conway-poor-fargus/#identifier_0_379/

Locke, George. *A Spectrum of Fantasy*. 3v. London: Ferret, 1980–2002.

Meudell, George. *The Pleasant Career of a Spendthrift*. London: Routledge, 1919.

Moore, Jerrold Northrop. *Edward Elgar: A Creative Life*. Oxford: Oxford University Press, 1984.

Murphy, Agnes. *One Woman's Wisdom*. London: Routledge, 1895.

Ouyang, Y. 'A Century of Ozlit in China: a Critical Overview'. *Antipodes*, 25, no. 1, June 2011, 65–71.

Parrott, Jeremy. 'Fergus Hume: Mystery Man'. *Book and Magazine Collector*, 232, July 2003: 39–50.

Pittard, Christopher. 'The Real Scandal of 1887: Fergus Hume and *The Mystery of a Hansom Cab*.' *Clues*, 26 (1) 2008: 37–48.

[Royal Princess's Theatre Programmes, 1888] Rex Nan Kivell Collection, National Library of Australia.

Ryan, John. 'Melbourne's Century Old Mystery—Who Was Fergus Hume?' *Margin*, 14, 1985, 17–20

Searle, Ronald. *Slightly Foxed—But Still Desirable: Ronald Searle's Wicked World of Book Collecting*. London: Souvenir, 1989.

Selby, Isaac. *Hinemoa and Memories of Māori Land*. Melbourne: Tytherleigh, 1925.

Scull, Andrew, MacKenzie, Charlotte and Hervey, Nicholas. *Masters of Bedlam: The Transformation of the Mad-Doctoring Trade*. Princeton: Princeton University Press, 1996.

Shirley, Graham and Adams, Brian. *Australian Cinema: The First Eighty Years*. Sydney: Currency Press, 1989.

Sladen, Douglas. *My Long Life*. London: Hutchinson, 1939.

Smith, Timothy D'Arch. *Love in Earnest: Some Notes on the Lives and Writings of English 'Uranian' Poets from 1889 to 1930*. London: Routledge, 1970.

Somerville, Alan. 'Ashburn Hall and Its Place in Society 1882–1904'. MA thesis, University of Otago, July 1996.

Stashower, Daniel. *Teller of Tales: The Life of Arthur Conan Doyle*. London: Allen Lane, 1999.

Stitz, Charles. *Australian Book Collectors*. Bendigo: Bread Street, 2010.

Sussex, Lucy. 'Collecting Books and Intelligence: The Curious Case of Jack Moir.' *Overland*, 155 (1999) 16–18.

——'Madame Midas and Henry Lawson'. *Notes and Furphies*, 21 Oct. 1988.

——*Women Writers and Detectives in the Nineteenth Century: The Mothers of the Mystery Genre*. Houndmills: Palgrave, 2010.

Symonds, John Addington. *The Memoirs of John Addington Symonds*. Grosskurth, Phyllis (ed). London: Hutchinson, 1984.

'T. F.' [Frederick Trischler?] 'The Palace Hotel San Francisco'. *Once a Month*, Feb. 1886, 129–31.

——'The Underwriters' Fire Patrol'. *Once a Month*, Mar. 1886, 239–242.

——'William H. Vanderbilt', *Once a Month*, Apr. 1886, 320–3 and 372–374.

Topp, Chester W. *Victorian Yellowbacks & Paperbacks 1849–1905*. 8v. Denver: Hermitage Antiquarian Bookshop, 1993–2005.

Trischler, Frederick. Letter. Qu. in *Tuapeka Times*, 3 May 1888, 3.

Torrance, J. A. 'Public Institions'. In *Picturesque Dunedin*. Bathgate, Alexander (ed). Dunedin: Mills, Dick & Co, 1890, 183–242.

Turner, E. S. *The Shocking History of Advertising*. London: Michael Joseph, 1952.

Turner, H. G. and Sutherland, A. *Development of Australian Literature*. London: Longmans, 1898.

Turnley, Cole. *Cole of the Book Arcade: A Pictorial Biography of E. W. Cole*. Melbourne: Cole Publications, 1974.

Vizetelly, Edward. 'My Life and Publications.' *Queanbeyan Age*, 2 June 1888, 1.

Wantrup, Jonathan. *Australian Rare Books 1788–1900*. 1987. Sydney: Hordern House, 2001.

West, John. *Theatre in Australia*, Sydney: Cassell, 1978.

Wilde, Oscar. *Complete Letters of Oscar Wilde*. Holland, Merlin and Hart-Davis, Rupert (eds). New York: Holt, 2000.

BIBLIOGRAPHY

INTERVIEWS AND COMMENTS FROM:

Philip Bentley

Ewan Burnett

Mimi Colligan

Nick Dawes, Australian Book Auctions

Glen Dolman

Joanne Drayton

Bill Garner

Kerry Greenwood

Fiona Gruber

Nick Hudson

John Hunter

Stephen Knight

Elisabeth Kumm

John Loder

Jeff Prentice

Henry Rosenbloom

Bob Sessions

Rory Sweetman

ACKNOWLEDGMENTS

Thanks are due to many people, firstly Hume's bibliographer Rowan Gibbs, ever a source of helpful information. Without him this book could not have been written. Also the People of the Book: Bill Mathews, Kay Craddock, John Loder, Jeff Prentice, John Arnold, Nick Dawes and Gavin de Lacy at Australian Book Auctions.

Librarians at the State Library of Victoria, in particular Des Cowley; Special Collections, Baillieu Library; Richard Overell, Monash University; Alison Belcher, Athenaeum; Helen Harrison, State Library of New South Wales. In Canberra: William Edwards at the National Archives of Australia. In New Zealand: Lorraine Johnston, Dunedin Public Library; Rory Sweetman, historian of Otago Boys' High School; the Dunedin Regional Office of Archives New Zealand; at the University of Otago, Donald Kerr and Shef Rogers; in Auckland, Graham Beattie; Joanne Drayton; in Wellington, John Quilter. In New York: Joshua McKeown, New York Public Library, Moshe Feder. Publishers: Nick Walker, Bob Sessions, Henry Rosenbloom, John Hunter, Nick Hudson. Family historians: Marg Kaan (the Mantons), David Green, Christchurch (the Trischlers). Readers: the Maclachlan family, Kylie Mirmohamadi, Mimi Colligan and Elisabeth Kumm, Damien Barlow, the Supernovans. For musical history, Therese Radic, Polly Sussex, Timothy Anderson. Blogger, anthologist and crime historian Curt Evans; crime historian Stephen Knight; Fiona Gruber, biographer of Alice Cornwell; Kerry Greenwood; Tim Richards for Wodehouse; Chris Wallace-Crabbe, for opinions on Hume's verse; Kristen Headlam, for opinions on Irvine's painting of Park House; Verity Burgmann; Meg Tasker. In London, Ilse Woloszko, Royal Academy of Music; in Essex, Robert

ACKNOWLEDGMENTS

Delderfield; in Scotland, David Harvie; Graham Peters and Judy Edmonds, for the loan of a rare book; Philip Bentley, Erica Wagner, Marcus Niski; Paul Poulton; Robyn Bowles. The Hansom Cab and Film: Ewan Burnett of Burberry Productions; Glen Dolman; Bill Garner.

ENDNOTES

INTRODUCTION AND CHAPTER 1: THE DARK AVENUE

1   The radio serials appeared in 1954, from the ABC; and in 1950 and 1958 from the BBC. In 1961 Channel Seven broadcast a stage production by the Union Theatre Repertory Co., dramatised as musical theatre by Barry Pree, the cast including Frederick Parslow. The 1911 film was produced by the Tait brothers, Millard Johnson and W. W. Gibson, dir. W. J. Lincoln, and is said to be the first Australian film with a mostly urban setting. *The Great Hansom Cab Mystery* was a 1917 US animated film, either an adaptation or a parody. Arthur Shirley also tried to raise the money for a talkie version of the book, but failed. The 2012 telemovie, written by Glen Dolman, was a joint production by the ABC, Film Victoria and Burberry Entertainment. Austlit; the *Mail* (Adelaide) 23 Oct. 1954, 67; *Australian Women's Weekly*, 23 Aug. 1961, 19; Shirley and Adams, 41, 82.

2   Hume, *Madame Midas*, 211.

3   Hume, *The Piccadilly Puzzle*, 38. In a later novel, *The Chinese Jar*, he notes that 'Asmodeus, uproofer of houses, is a peculiarly detestable fiend', 20.

4   Frame, *The Philosophy of Insanity*, 55.

5   Frame, 60.

6   Doyle, Mary, in *Arthur Conan Doyle: A Life in Letters*, 307.

CHAPTER 2: CRAZY-QUILT

7   Hume, *Crazy-Quilt*, 7.

8   Hume, *The Fever of Life*, 13.

9   *Inquirer & Commercial News* (Perth), 24 Aug. 1888, 3.

10   Information about James Hume from *ODT* obit., 31 Aug. 1896, 3.

11   Torrance, 222–3.

12   Information about the asylum from Angus, 48.

13   Hume, *The Silent House*, 220.

14   *Otago Daily Times*, 2 Sept. 1873, 2.

15   Angus, 47.

16   *Otago Daily Times*, 5 Dec. 1868, 6.

17   *Otago Daily Times*, 5 Dec. 1868, 6.

18   Reports on Lunatic Asylums in New Zealand, 1871, 13.

19   *Free Lance*, 30 Jan 1909, 4.

20   James Hume, Diary, 3.

21   1879, [14].

22   Angus, 50.

23   'Men With Brains', *Birmingham Daily Post*, 6 Apr. 1889; Hume, *Across the Footlights*, 107.

24   Doyle, Mary, 308.

25   Angus, 49.

26   James Hume, Diary, 6.

27   James Hume, Diary, 81; Torrance, 224; 'Campbell', 13.

28   Frame, 50.

29   *Otago Daily Times*, 5 Dec. 1868, 6.

30   'Gossip', *Sydney Stock and Station Agent*, 23 Dec. 1913, 3.

31   *Otago Daily Times*, 5 Dec. 1868, 6; Edward Hulme, in Reports on the Lunatic Asylums in the Colony, 1872, 16.

32   *Otago Witness*, 5 Aug. 1882, 24; *Otago Witness*, 6 Sept. 1905, 68.

33   *Otago Daily Times*, 24 Feb. 1873, 2.

34   *Otago Daily Times*, 2 Sept. 1873, 2.

35   *Otago Daily Times*, 26 Dec. 1872, 6; *Otago Daily Times*, 23 Dec. 1869, 3.

36   Painter Kristin Headlam considers that, the composition needing some foreground focus, Irvine added the figures of the children, probably basing them on an earlier image from his sketchbooks, which would account for the girls being dressed in 1860s fashion, with wide skirts, unlike the women in the painting background, who wear the narrower 1870s skirts.

37   Selby, *Memories of Maori Land*, 74.

CHAPTER 3: A COLONIAL BANSHEE

38   Hume, 'A Colonial Banshee', 180.

39   *Otago Witness*, 13 Nov. 1875, 17.

40   *Otago Witness*, 7 July 1877, 7.

41   Quoted in Somerville, 20.

42   Torrance, 227.

43   *Otago Witness*, 13 Nov. 1875, 17

44   *Otago Daily Times*, 12 June 1869, 3.

45   Information on OBHS comes from Rory Sweetman, interview, and his history. Quoted in Sweetman, ch 4.

46 *Auckland Star*, 13 July 1932, 6.

47 Ryan, 18.

48 Selby, 74.

49 *Mainly About People*, reprinted in *Table Talk*, 24 Dec. 1903, 24; Newspaper cutting dated 13 July 1932, Hume file, National Library of Australia; Hume, *Bohemia*, 14, 15; Sweetman, ch 4.

50 Quoted in Sweetman, ch 4.

51 Information from Rowan Gibbs; *Evening Post*, 7 Sept. 1933, 5.

52 *Otago Witness*, 12 June 1890, 24; Hume, Preface.

53 *Otago Daily Times*, 2 Feb 1884, 2; Quoted in *Otago Witness*, 30 Aug. 1905, 32; *Land and Sea*, 22 Sept. 1888, 8; 'Gossip'.

54 *Te Aroha News*, 12 Sept. 1888, 4; for Willeby as dandy, *Free Lance*, 22 July 1905, 3; *Otago Witness*, 9 Aug. 1884, 23; 'The Masher' Eliza Lynn Linton, *Otago Witness*, 13 June 1889, 32.

55 *Otago Daily Times*, 31 Dec. 1969, clipping in Fergus Hume file, Dunedin Public Library; Hume, 'Satirical Opera'.

CHAPTER 4: THE FATAL SONG

56 Hume, *Madame Midas*, 200.

57 *Otago Daily Times*, 8 Nov 1878, 3; *Auckland Star*, 20 Apr. 1939, 16—actually untrue, as at least another of Morli's pupils preceded them, though not with the same degree of applause. Interestingly Morli's 1878 productions included a ten-year-old pianist, George Clutsam, who would achieve an international career, even writing opera.

58 *Bulletin*, 3 Nov. 1896, 133.

59 Marcus Hume, *Tuapeka Times* 13 Dec. 1882, 5.

60 *Otago Witness*, 10 June 1882, 18, 22.

61 Torrance, 232; an advertisement for Ashburn Hall on the back of the contents page, *New Zealand Medical Journal*, 8: 1 (1 Jan. 1895), gives the fees. He also increased his salary to £600 a year. Knewstubb, 28.

62 Hume, *The Silent House*, 219–220, 181.

63 Reports on Lunatic Asylums in New Zealand, 1870, 13.

64 *Otago Witness*, 30 Aug. 1905, 32; *Otago Witness*, 27 Jan. 1877, 7; *Southern Star*, 15 Sept. 1906, 2.

65 Information from Rowan Gibbs; *Otago Daily Times*, 5 Jan. 1882, 3.

66 Hume, *Bohemia*, 19.

67 *Bulletin*, 3 Nov. 1896, 133, written in response to a report of James Hume's

death; the boot manufactory was Haig, Bramwell and Co.; *Otago Daily Times*, 24 Sept. 1906, 6.

68   'Feece', 15.

69   *Saturday Advertiser*, 17 Feb. 1883, 13.

70   Hume, *Bohemia*, 19.

71   *Otago Witness*, 22 Feb. 1883, 19.

72   *Otago Daily Times*, 10 Mar. 1883, 1.

73   Bessie's injury and elocution, *Otago Witness*, 12 June 1890, 24.

CHAPTER 5: ACROSS THE FOOTLIGHTS

74   Hume, *Across the Footlights*, 4.

75   Information about Seager and the Marsh family comes from Drayton.

76   Downes, 47, 55.

77   Hume, *Across the Footlights*, 6.

78   *Otago Daily Times*, 29 Aug. 1881, 2.

79   Ryan, 18.

80   *Otago Daily Times*, 8 Oct. 1883, 2.

81   *Otago Daily Times*, 8 Oct. 1883, 2.

82   *Evening Post*, 6 Nov. 1883, 2; *South Australian Register*, 15 July 1895, 6.

83   *Otago Daily Times*, 2 Dec. 1884, 2.

84   *Otago Witness*, 20 Dec. 1884, 23; Scott, reprinted in *Table Talk*, 6 Jan. 1888, 4, 7.

85   *Press*, quoted in the *Otago Daily Times*, 27 Mar. 1885, 3. Hume's farce 'The Bigamist' is also said to have been performed by de Grey, *Otago Daily Times*, 4 June 1887, 2.

86   'A Ballad of Fate', in the April issue of the *Theatre*. *Otago Witness*, 6 June 1885, 23.

87   *Southern Star*, 15 Sept. 1906, 2.

88   Hume, 'A Colonial Banshee', 173.

CHAPTER 6: WHEN I LIVED IN BOHEMIA

89   Hume, *The Fever of Life*, 77.

90   'All Over the World', *Once a Month*, 15 Feb. 1885, 100.

91   Adams, *The Australians*, 26.

92   As reported in *Table Talk*, 26 July 1885, 11. *The Bohemians* is probably Edward Stirling's 1843 adaptation of Eugène Sue's novel *Les mystères de Paris*, as *The Bohemians; or, the Rogues of Paris*.

93   Hume, *Miss Mephistopheles*, 179.

94   As listed in the Sands and McDougall's *Directory* of 1887–8.

95   As reported to the *Bulletin* by its correspondent 'Boheme', 15 Nov. 1902, 13. James was reported as working for the Board of Works, Melbourne *Punch*, 24 June 1897, 2.

96   Hume, *Miss Mephistopheles*, 3.

97   As reported in several papers. It is first mentioned in *Melbourne Punch*, 18 Nov. 1886, 11, and is said to be 'ready' in the *Star*, 8 Dec. 1894, 2.

98   *Miss Mephistopheles*, 7; the dirt on Plumpton is dished out most entertainingly in *Truth*, 31 Oct. 1903, 5.

99   *Argus*, 12 Aug. 1885, 9.

100 *Argus*, 23 May 1885, 16.

101 Blainey, 51.

102 *Otago Witness*, 26 Sept. 1885, 23.

103 *Miss Mephistopheles*, 127.

104 *Bohemia*, 4.

105 *Table Talk*, 25 Mar. 1898, 3.

106 *Miss Mephistopheles*, 8.

107 'Introductory', *Table Talk*, 26 June 1885, 8.

108 *Table Talk*, 14.

109 Hume, *Miss Mephistopheles*, 16.

110 Slade, *Argus*, 31 Jan. 1939, 4. Slade thought Hingston was Hume's uncle, which merely indicates that they were close.

111 Trischler, Letter.

112 *Queenslander*, 29 Mar. 1924, 3.

113 *Colac Herald*, 6 July 1888, 2.

114 *West Australian*, 23 Jan. 1888, 3.

CHAPTER 7: ACROSS THE FOOTLIGHTS II

115 Hume, *Miss Mephistopheles*, 138.

116 Hume, *Miss Mephistopheles*, 22.

117 26 June 1885, 6.

118 *Table Talk*, 26 June 1885, 6.

119 *Table Talk*, 31 July 1885, 13.

120 *Miss Mephistopheles*, 145.

121 As listed on the website 'Theatre in Melbourne: 1885'.

ENDNOTES

CHAPTER 8: 'A CENTENNIAL SONG'

122 For more information on this subject, see Sussex, *Women Writers and Detectives*.

123 *Queanbeyan Age*, 2 June 1888, 1.

124 *Argus*, 31 Dec. 1881, 4.

125 *Table Talk*, 31 July 1885, 6.

126 Hume, *Hansom Cab,* 48.

CHAPTER 9: THE SPIDER

127 Hume, *Bohemia*, 173.

128 *Free Lance*, 16 July 1896, 15.

129 *Star*, 30 May 1889, 2.

130 The Minerva Press was a voluminous publisher of the Gothic.

131 Hume, Letter, San Remo, 7 July 1891. *The Fever of Life* would be published by Sampson Low in 1892. Letter held by Elizabeth Paton, transcription by Kay Craddock and Lucy Sussex.

132 *Bulletin*, 15 Nov. 1902, 13; Masher speech is satirised in an article 'The Masher Poet' in *Table Talk*, 10 July 1885, 3, and in the poem 'The Masher', *Saturday Advertiser*, 24 July 1886, 11.

133 In an article for *Mainly About People*, to be discussed in detail in chapter 11, and an interview, widely reprinted, in the *Sunday Times*, 1 July 1888, 7.

CHAPTER 10: NOT WANTED

134 Hume, *Lady Jim*, 68.

135 Slade, *Argus*, 31 Jan. 1939, 4. It may be that Mullen was the bookseller Hume asked about bestsellers, since one source states Hume consulted a librarian, and Mullen was both. *Table Talk*, 24 Dec. 1903, 24.

136 Coghlan, 98.

137 Davenport, in *No Place for a Nervous Lady*. Frost, L. (ed). Melbourne: McPhee-Gribble, 1982.

138 *Punch Almanac*, Dec. 1886, 12.

139 Pyke, Diary, 22 Aug. 1882; Hume, *Hansom Cab*, 33.

140 Johanson, 75.

141 Quoted in Holroyd, 24.

142 'Gossip', *Sydney Stock and Station Agent*, 23 Dec. 1913, 3.

143 Holroyd, 51–2.

144 Sladen, *My Long Life*, 67.

145 *Australian Journal*, 1 Feb. 1868, 364.

146 Trischler, Letter.

147 Holroyd, 44–5, 56.

148 Qu. in Holroyd, 25–6.

149 'M. M.' Macmillan Reader's Reports, 1st series vols mclxix–mclxxv, 1895–99, 8201/Reel 3, Book xxiii, 232–3.

150 *Illustrated London News*, 6 Oct. 1888, 410.

151 *Sunday Times*, 1 July 1888, 7.

152 Carr, 66.

CHAPTER 11: ACROSS THE FOOTLIGHTS III

153 Hume, *Madame Midas*, 199.

154 *Table Talk*, 24 Dec. 1903, 24.

155 *Argus*, 14 Apr. 1886, 8, and 6 May, 5; interview with Mimi Colligan.

156 'Theatre in Melbourne: 1886' website; *Brisbane Courier*, 12 Mar. 1886, 3; *Australian Town and Country Journal*, 25 Jan. 1890, 32. *Evening News* (Sydney), 1 Apr. 1886, 5.

157 Information about Beck's career comes from profiles or obituaries, in the *Australian Town and Country Journal*, 6 Apr. 1889, 28, and 25 Jan. 1890, 32, and *Lorgnette*, 8 Jan. 1890, 57 and 8 June 1889, 5; *South Australian Advertiser*, 10 May 1880, 5; *British Australasian*, 20 Nov. 1902, 1982.

158 *Mercury* (Hobart), 19 June 1884, 3; *Australian Town and Country Journal*, 29 Aug. 1885, 41.

159 *Brisbane Courier*, 12 Mar. 1886, 3.

160 The article in question appeared first in the English *Mainly About People* and was reprinted all over the world, including the New Zealand *Evening Post*, 24 Sept. 1902, 9. The word romance was at the time subject to several interpretations, as with H. G. Wells calling *The Time Machine* a scientific romance.

161 *Sunday Times*, 1 July 1888, 7.

162 'Theatre in Melbourne: 1886' website.

163 *Sydney Morning Herald*, 16 Aug. 1886, 8.

164 *Brisbane Courier*, 28 June, 5; *Saturday Advertiser*, 26 June, 15.

165 *Bulletin*, 4 Oct. 1902, 15.

166 Something noted by Clement Scott, in the first major English review of the book.

167 *Argus*, 20 Sept. 1886 3.

168 *Star*, 14 Mar. 1890, 2. *Sunday Times*, 1 July 1888, 7.

CHAPTER 12: THE MASTERMIND

169 Hume, *Madame Midas*, 193.

170 *West Australian*, 23 Jan. 1888, 3; *Star*, 18 Sept. 1889, 3; *Advertiser* (Adelaide), 29 Dec. 1898, 6.

171 Information about Trischler from Interview, *Pall Mall Gazette,* 29 Jan. 1889; Trischler, Letter.

172 Information about the Trischler family from David Green.

173 'T. F', 'William H. Vanderbilt'.

174 *Star*, 6 Sept. 1879, 2; *Star*, 14 May 1890, 2. *Star*, 8 Dec. 1892, 2.

175 *Star*, 27 Oct. 1881, 3; *Star*, 18 Nov. 1881, 2.

176 *Table Talk* reports on a luncheon publicising the Inglis firm, 24 July 1885, 5; *Table Talk*, 1 June 1888, 2.

177 Trischler, Letter.

178 Interview, *Pall Mall Gazette,* 29 Jan. 1889.

179 *Maffra Spectator*, 8 Oct. 1888, 3; says that he read the manuscript only after Inglis' insolvency.

180 Hume, *Sunday Times*, 1 July 1888.

181 Trischler, *Pall Mall Gazette*, 29 Jan. 1889; Trischler, Letter.

182 'Gossip', *Sydney Stock and Station Agent*, 23 Dec. 1913, 3.

183 Interview, *Pall Mall Gazette*, 29 Jan. 1889.

CHAPTER 13: MADAME MIDAS

184 Hume, *Madame Midas*, 11.

185 'The Author of Madame Midas'; *Trischler*, Letter; Alison, 39.

186 Campbell, 73.

187 Alison, 34-5, 127.

188 A&R Ledgers, Mitchell Library.

189 Trischler, Letter.

190 Early editions of *Madame Midas* are dedicated to 'Miss Alice Cornwell/The first Victorian Lady Miner'.

191 *Women's Penny Paper*, 19 Oct. 1889, 1.

192 *Argus*, 3 May 1882, 11.

193 See Sussex, 'Madame Midas and Henry Lawson'.

194 Hume, *Sunday Times*, 1 July 1888, 7.

195 Hume, *Madame Midas* 189.

196 Pyke, Diary, 18 June 1888.

197 NAA: A2389, 3; NAA: A2387, 18/3000B-3-3199B.

CHAPTER 14: THE UNEXPECTED

198 Hume, *Tracked by a Tattoo*, 40.

199 Hume, *Madame Midas*, 136.

200 Hume, Letter.

201 *Queanbeyan Age*, 21 June 1888, 1.

202 Information on Cole comes from Turnley, 57–9. Prentice's opinion is that the first print run was small.

203 Comment made by Bob Sessions.

204 *Table Talk*, 6 Jan. 1886, 4, 7.

CHAPTER 15: ANSWERED

205 Hume, *Madame Midas*, 144.

206 Pyke, Diary, 3 Nov. 1878.

207 Turnley, 75.

208 NAA: A2389, 3; NAA: A2387, 18/3000B-3-3199B.

209 *Argus*, 31 Jan. 1939, 4.

210 *Argus*, 29 June 1886, 4.

211 Law.

212 *Punch*, 28 Oct. 1886, 210.

213 *Daily Telegraph*, 1 Nov. 1886, 3.

214 Interview, *Pall Mall Gazette*; *Adelaide Advertiser*, 17 Feb. 1891, 5.

215 *Age*, 3 Nov. 1886, 5. *Punch*, 4 Nov. 1886, 222, 227.

216 'Gossip', *Sydney Stock and Station Agent*, 23 Dec. 1913, 3; *Australasian*, Supplement, 3.

217 *Australasian*, Supplement 6 Nov. 1886, 3.

218 Trischler, Interview; A review appeared in *Press* (Christchurch) on 17 Nov., 2.

219 *New Zealand Herald* (Auckland), 20 Nov. 1886, 1.

220 Altick, 202.

221 Email to Lucy Sussex, 25 June 2013.

222 Holroyd, 61.

CHAPTER 16: THREE READERS

223 Hume, *Hansom Cab*, 187–8.

224 Information about the Manton family from historian Marg Kaan.

225 *Biblionews*, Sept. 1958, 29.

CHAPTER 17: THE YEAR OF MIRACLE

226   Hume, *The Silent House*, 209.

227   *Sunday Times*, 1 July 1888, 7; Trischler, Interview. In his Letter the claims are smaller: first edition of five thousand, another five thousand printed in November, ten thousand in February.

228   *Wanganui Herald*, 16 Feb. 1887, 2; Melbourne *Punch*, 5 May 1887, 1.

229   *Table Talk*, 1 June 1888, 1.

230   *Argus*, 17 Feb. 1887, 4.

231   From an advertisement in the preliminaries of *The Murder of Madeline Brown* by Francis Adams.

232   Melbourne *Punch*, 24 Feb. 1887, 11.

233   The name behind the stage name revealed by Rowan Gibbs. Reviewed favourably in the Christchurch *Press*, 29 July 1887, 2.

234   Kellow, 145.

235   *Bookman*, May 1893, 44; Kellow, 145.

236   *Argus*, 14 June 1887 5; *Euroa Advertiser*, 2 Sept. 1887, 2.

237   *Australian Town and Country Journal*, 6 Apr. 1889, 28.

238   'Gossip', *Sydney Stock and Station Journal*, 23 Dec. 1913, 3. Michie's real-estate business, which included the rural, is mentioned in the same magazine, 9 Apr. 1907, 8.

239   Hume's anxiety, *Sunday Times*, 1 July 1888, 7; lady detective, *Table Talk*, 22 Jan. 1897.

240   *Advertiser*, 19 Apr. 1889, 5.

CHAPTER 18: THE PICCADILLY PUZZLE

241   Hume, *Bohemia*, 261.

242   *Pall Mall Gazette*, 29 Jan. 1889.

243   *Tuapeka Times*, 23 May 1888, 3.

244   Pyke, Letter to *Argus*, 16 July 1932, 20; and Diary, 10 Oct. 1889.

245   *Sunday Times*, 1 July 1888, 7; NAA: A2389, 3; NAA: A2387, 18/3000B-3-3199B.

246   Law.

247   *The World's News* (Sydney), 31 Aug. 1932, 7.

248   Trischler, Letter; Knight, Introd. to *The Mystery of a Hansom Cab*. London: Hogarth, 1986.

249   *Morning Post*, 29 Oct. 1887, 2; Trischler, Letter.

250   Trischler, Letter; James.

251   *British Australasian*, 30 Oct. 1887, 358; 21 Oct., 462, 465; 28 Oct., 495, 496.

252 *Wagga Wagga Advertiser*, 9 Jan. 1892, 4; *Brisbane Courier*, 12 Oct. 1885, 5; Ned Kelly, *Argus*, 16 Oct. 1880, 8.

253 *Table Talk*, 4 Mar. 1892, 3; *Wagga Wagga Advertiser*, 9 Jan. 1892, 4. In early 1886 Jessie was publicly named in the transfer of a large block of land, at the High Street/Williams Road junction in Prahran, *Telegraph St Kilda, Prahran and South Yarra Guardian*, 17 Apr. 1886, 4.

254 Melbourne *Punch*, 8 Aug. 1889, 94 and 12 Dec. 1889, 381.

255 Meeting of the Melbourne District Nursing Society Committee, *Argus*, 6 Sept. 1890, 14.

256 *Williamstown Chronicle*, 19 Jan. 1884, 2.

257 Melbourne *Punch*, 12 Dec. 1889, 381; *Argus*, 16 Dec. 1891, 7.

258 The source was the *Barrier Miner*, 15 Dec. 1891, 2. It was the newspaper of Broken Hill—but as BHP was managed from Melbourne, the paper would have been well informed in terms of Melbourne financial and other gossip.

259 James.

260 *South Australian Register*, 17 Jan. 1889, 6

261 *South Australian Register*, 17 Jan. 1889, 6; *Press*, 3 Jan. 1889, 5; *Te Aroha News* (columnist's copy dated 16 Dec.), 4 Feb., 1888, 5.

262 *Pall Mall Gazette*.

263 *Birmingham Daily Post*, 16 Dec. 1887.

264 Scott, *Table Talk*, 6 Jan. 1888, 4, 7.

265 *Hampshire Telegraph and Sussex Chronicle*, 18 Feb. 1888.

266 Bell, Eric, 123; *Otago Witness*, 13 July 1888, 9.

267 6 Oct 1888, 410; Trischler, Letter.

268 Altick, 202.

269 Doyle, *Memories and Adventures*, 113–4.

270 In *Memories* Doyle cites a letter of acceptance from Ward Lock dated 30 Oct. 1886, 90.

271 Doyle, *Arthur Conan Doyle*, 250.

CHAPTER 19: ACROSS THE FOOTLIGHTS IV

272 Hume, *Across the Footlights*, 42.

273 *Otago Witness*, 1 Oct. 1886, 28.

274 Trischler, Letter; *Era*, 18 June 1887.

275 *Star*, 7 Dec. 1886, 2.

276 *Otago Daily Times*, 17 Nov. 1886, 3; *Era*, 18 June 1887.

277 *Wanganui Herald*, 12 Apr. 1894, 3.

278 Horton, *Otago Witness*, 12 Aug. 1887, 28; *Otago Witness*, 18 May 1888, 28.

279 *Era*, 18 June 1887.

280 *Era*, 25 Feb. 1888.

281 *Auckland Star*, 5 Aug. 1932, 6.

282 [Royal Princess's Theatre Programmes, 1888].

283 *Otago Witness*, 13 Apr. 1888, 28; *Wanganui Herald*, 9 May 1888, 2.

284 *West Coast Times*, 17 July 1888, 2; *Argus*, 21 Apr. 1890, 11.

285 Hume, *Madame Midas*, 92–3.

286 *Te Aroha News*, 12 Sept. 1888, 4.

287 *Warragul Guardian*, 9 Oct. 1888, 3; *Otago Witness*, 26 Oct. 1888, 28.

288 *West Coast Times*, 21 Nov. 1888, 4.

289 *South Australian Advertiser*, 8 Oct. 1888, 6.

290 *Te Aroha News*, 4 Feb. 1888, 5.

291 *Bulletin*, 24 Sept. 1903, Red Page.

CHAPTER 20: ALADDIN IN LONDON

292 Hume, *Bohemia*, 126.

293 *Wanganui Herald*, 14 Aug. 1888, 2.

294 Hume, *The Girl from Malta* 13; Hume, *Bohemia,* 24.

295 Hume, *The Girl from Malta*, 64.

296 'Akenehi', 'Letter', *Bulletin*, 12 May 1904, 25.

297 *Sunday Times*, 1 July 1888, 7.

298 James; *Sydney Morning Herald*, 25 Mar. 1889, 4.

299 Email to Lucy Sussex, 25 June 2013; *Sydney Morning Herald*, 25 Mar. 1889, 4.

300 *Table Talk*, 18 Dec. 1891, 3.

301 *Bulletin*, 9 Sept. 1893, 330; *West Australian*, 5 May 1945, 3.

302 *Observer*, 6 July 1889, 17.

303 'Ferguson', 10, 14.

304 'Ferguson', 35.

305 *Sunday Times*, 24 June 1888, 7, and reprinted widely colonially.

306 *Sunday Times*, 1 July 1888, 7.

307 *Birmingham Daily Post*, 31 Jan. and 20 Aug., 1889.

308 Nov. 16 1888, 6.

309 *Birmingham Daily Post*, 2 Feb. 1889.

310 *Illustrated Police News*, 16 Mar. 1889.

311 *Cheshire Observer*, 23 Mar. 1889, 3.

312 *Star*, 25 May 1889, 2.

313   *Weekly Times, Manchester Times*, 23 Mar. 1889.

314   *South Australian Chronicle*, 4 May 1889, 6; *Penny Illustrated Paper*, 9 Mar. 1889; *South Australian Register*, 2 Apr. 1889, 6.

315   *Star*, 25 May 1889, 2; *Dawn*, 1 June 1889, 8.

316   *Evening Standard*, 1 May 1889, 2.

317   *Penny Illustrated Paper*, 9 Mar. 1889, 151.

CHAPTER 21: A TRAITOR IN LONDON

318   Hume, *Madame Midas*, 277.

319   'Boheme', *Bulletin*, 15 Nov. 1902, 13.

320   *Wanganui Herald*, 6 July 1889, 2.

321   *Evening Post*, 9 Sept. 1887, 3; Hawthorne, 335; *Otago Witness*, 21 Feb. 1889, 33.

322   Hawthorne, 336; *Belgravia*, 70 (1889).

323   *Advertiser*, 8 Aug. 1889, 5.

324   *Sydney Morning Herald*, 4 Apr. 1889 5; *Argus*, 10 June 1889, 6.

325   *Barrier Miner*, 2 Sept. 1890, 2; Information from Elisabeth Kumm.

326   *Lorgnette*, 8 and 22 June 1888, 6; Scalfax in *Otago Witness*, 11 July 1889, 28 and 12 Sept. 1889, 28.

327   O'Connor, *Illustrated Sydney News*, 6 Feb. 1890, 2, 4.

328   *Star*, 14 Mar. 1890, 2.

329   *Evening Post*, 24 Jan. 1890, 4; *Australian Town and Country Journal*, 18 Jan. 1890, 33; *Illustrated Sydney News*, 6 Feb. 1890, 4.

330   *Star*, 14 Mar. 1890, 2.

331   *Star*, 22 Apr. 1889, 3.

332   Slade, *Argus*, 31 Jan. 1939, 4.

333   *Star*, 3 June 1889, 4.

334   *Star*, 1 July 1889, 2.

335   *Star*, 18 Sept. 1889, 3.

336   *Star*, 18 Sept. 1889, 3.

337   *Maitland Mercury*, 19 Jan. 1893, 6.

338   Topp notes Hume is the only White author still in print, v. 7, xi; In *Zealandia*. As Curt Evans has noted, Freeman had his own problems with morality, faking his death to commit bigamy in Australia. *The Passing Tramp*, http://thepassingtramp.blogspot.com.au/2011/12/tale-of-mr-fergus-hume-and-mr-william.html.

339   *South Australian Register*, 17 Jan. 1889, 6.

340   James.

341 *Harvest, Star*, 4 June 1889, 2; Rosa Praed got £225, for the novella *The Soul of Countess Adrian*, qu. in Clarke, 124; *Sunday Times*, 1 July 1888, 7.

342 *Star*, 4 June 1889, 2.

343 *Star*, 12 Dec. 1889, 2.

344 *Star*, 18 Sept. 1889, 3.

345 *Wanganui Herald*, 6 July 1889, 2; Information on Benzon and his court case with Trischler and Shaw from the *Star*, 11 Feb. 1890, 2; 18 Feb. 1890, 2, and 24 Oct. 1889, 4.

346 *Adelaide Advertiser*, 17 Feb. 1891, 5.

347 *Illustrated London News*, 13 Sept. 1890, 327; *Auckland Star*, 21 Nov. 1891, 3.

348 *Star*, 21 July 1892, 2.

349 *Star*, 8 Dec. 1892, 2; *Star*, 10 Nov. 1892, 2.

350 *Star*, 8 Dec. 1892, 2.

351 *Star*, 9 Dec. 1893, 2; *Adelaide Advertiser*, 29 Dec. 1898, 6.

352 *New Zealand Herald*, 19 Oct. 1889, 3.

353 *Sunday Times*, 30 June 1889, 6.

354 *Adelaide Observer*, 3 Aug. 1889, 8.

355 *Sunday Times*, 13 July 1890, 2.

356 *Sunday Times*, 26 June 1892, 2; 3 July 1892, 2.

CHAPTER 22: THE MILLIONAIRE MYSTERY

357 Hume, *Madame Midas*, 154.

358 Meudell, 25.

359 In one infamous case £22,000 was borrowed on little more than a bond warrant on eighteen cases of whisky, Cannon, 140.

360 *Table Talk*, 4 Mar. 1892, 8.

361 Cannon, 138.

362 The story was widely serialised in the US and UK, such as in the supplement to the *Manchester Times*, 5 Oct. 1889, 5.

363 Cannon, 138.

364 *Table Talk*, 18 Dec. 1891, 3; Printed in various papers, including the *Wagga Wagga Advertiser*, 9 Jan. 1892, 4.

365 *Australian Town and Country Journal*, 2 Nov. 1891, 10.

366 *Argus*, 8 Jan. 1892, 2.

367 *Argus*, 5 Jan. 1892, 5.

368 *Evening Post*, 3 Mar. 1892, 4; *Argus*, 20 Feb. 1892, 5.

369 *Argus*, 6 Jan. 1892, 5.

370   *Press*, 12 Jan. 1892, 5.

371   *Advertiser*, 29 July 1892, 5.

372   *Argus*, 1 Aug. 1892, 7.

373   Victorian Public Record Office VPRS 515/P1 25270. Pentridge warder John Hogan, whose life savings evaporated with the liquidation of the Anglo-Australian Bank in 1891, would have been tempted not to treat him kindly. Cannon, 156.

374   Meudell, 58.

375   *Argus*, 21 Dec. 1891, 7.

376   Meudell, 23–4.

377   Gardner, 62; Cannon, 231.

378   Cannon, 91.

379   *Inquirer & Commercial News*, 18 Jan. 1893, 3.

380   Turner, 20.

CHAPTER 23: THE QUEER STORY OF ADAM LIND

381   Murphy, 207–8.

382   For Lawrence, see works by Suzanne Davies and Lucy Chesser; *South Australian Register*, 3 Oct. 1888, 6.

383   *South Australian Register*, 3 Oct. 1888, 6; *Clarence and Richmond Examiner*, 13 Oct. 1788, 6.

384   *Camperdown Chronicle*, 2 Oct. 1888, 2.

385   *Otago Witness*, 12 Oct. 1888, 28.

386   *Sydney Morning Herald*, 7 July 1887, 12. An article on 'The Oscar Wilde's [sic] of Sydney' noted their 'effeminate style of speech, and the adoption of the names of celebrated actresses'. *Scorpion*, 24 Apr. 1895.

387   The 2012 *Hansom Cab* has, in the Lilly Lon scenes, transvestite prostitutes, a possible reference to the Gordon Lawrence case. Scriptwriter Glen Dolman in an email to me stated that it was not in his original script.

388   Kaplan, 35, 54.

389   *Otago Witness*, 26 Oct. 1888, 28; Wilby Taylor identified as 'Scalfax' in *Otago Witness*, 6 Feb. 1901, 29. His obit. *Otago Witness*, 12 Feb. 1891, 28; *Argus*, 2 Oct. 1885, 2.

390   *Truth*, 31 Oct. 1903, 5.

391   Qu. Kaplan, 51.

392   Ellmann, 362, 419.

393   As described by John Saul, a 'professional sodomite', who testified at the

Cleveland Street scandal trial, Kaplan, 202.

394   Greenwood, K. Email to Lucy Sussex.

395   Hume, *Hansom Cab*, 110, 48.

396   Dolman, Email to Lucy Sussex; Hume, *Madame Midas*, 217; Dolman, script.

397   Bentley, Email to Lucy Sussex.

398   Smith, 12.

399   Symonds, 94.

400   Reprinted in *Maitland Mercury*, 19 Jan. 1893, 6.

401   The book of poetry is reported in the *Star*, 30 May 1889, 6, as to be published before the end of that year.

402   Wilde, Letter to Robert Ross, 1019.

403   See Cook, *London and the Culture of Homosexuality*, for Hellenism, 125.

404   Hume, *Island of Fantasy*, 44–5.

405   Hume, *Island of Fantasy*, 85 and 92.

406   Ryan cites Terry as a friend of Hume's, 20.

407   *Otago Daily Times*, 3 May 1902, 11.

408   Hallmann; Bell.

409   Parrott, 46.

410   Hume, *The Gentleman Who Vanished*, 21.

CHAPTER 24: HAGAR OF THE PAWN SHOP

411   Hume, *Professor Brankel's Secret*, 24.

412   Dawes, Interview.

413   Bill Mathews, revised by Lucy Sussex.

414   John Loder describes it as a 'mythical beast', Interview; Locke, as a 'daydream', 231.

415   http://www.australianbookauctions.com/sale_053/sale_053.pdf/

416   Searle, 122.

417   Email from Rowan Gibbs.

418   Locke, 231.

419   Hume, *Brankel*, 24-5.

420   Fletcher, 9.

421   Information from Des Cowley, State Library of Victoria.

422   Goode, Diary re Stalin 27 Feb. 1944.

423   Goode, Diary, 21 July 1944; 14 Sept. 1944.

424   Goode's copy of *Hansom Cab* is now digitised, available online at http://www.apfa.esrc.unimelb.edu.au/objects/D00000710.htm/

425 *Argus*, 2 Dec. 1944, 7.

426 Goode, Diary, on its composition 18 Jan. 1944; on Gordon's house, 18 Mar. 1944

427 See Sussex, *Overland*.

428 Moir's copy has vanished. I was told that the Mitchell's copy went into a safe after I published on Fortune's significance.

429 Wormwoodiana, 5 Sept. 2011. http://wormwoodiana.blogspot.com.au/

430 Wantrup, 7.

431 Wantrup, 5.

432 Hume, *The Chronicles of Fairy Land*, 15–22.

POSTSCRIPT AND DRAMATIS PERSONAE

433 Ouyang, 65.

434 *Sunday Times*, 1 July 1888, 7.

435 *Free Lance*, 16 July 1896, 15.

436 Hume, *Bohemia*, 182.

437 Hume, *Bohemia*, 173.

438 Interview with Ewan Burnett; Bill Garner, Email to Lucy Sussex.

439 That her copy of *Hansom Cab* resurfaced in Melbourne, decades later, could indicate that it was in the possession of Dorothy Tompson, who died unmarried in Fitzroy in 1972. Information from family historian Marg Kaan.

440 *Auckland Star*, 20 Apr. 1939, 16.

441 *Evening Post*, 17 Sept. 1930, 13.

442 *Otago Daily Times*, 12 June 1890, 4.

443 *Bega Budget*, 15 Sept. 1906, 2; *Southern Star*, 15 Sept. 1906, 2.

444 *Otago Daily Times*, 9 Dec. 1903, 2.

445 Victor Daly recorded Hume spent summers in Cannes. *Bulletin*, 24 Sept. 1903, Red Page.

446 Ryan, 18.

447 'The Mystery of the Red Web', with Charles Berte, *Otago Witness*, 29 Apr. 1908, 69.

448 Hume, Obit, *The Times*, 14 July 1932, 17.

449 *Queensland Times*, 14 Jan. 1926, 4; *Daily News* (Perth), 27 Aug. 1932, 10; *Recorder* (Port Pirie), 24 Sept. 1932, 1.

450 Weinreb, 'Books Do Furnish the Imagination', *The Times*, 10 Jun. 1980, 14.

451 *Launceston Examiner*, 1 Nov. 1932, 5.

INDEX

fraud
  bank 199, 202–3
  impersonation 174–8
  murder 178–80, 186
  see also prostitution
Le Crime de l'Omnibus (Boisgobey) 85
The Crimes of Paris (Conquest &
  Merritt) 106, 184
The Crimson Cryptogram (FH) 84
Crommelin, May 193
Crooked Billet (Shaw, V.) 190
cross-dressing 213–4
  see also theatre, cross-dressing in
Crowe, Catherine 77

Daily Telegraph (London) 66, 166
Daily Telegraph (Melbourne) 133
Dalton, Marie 224–5
Daley, Victor 169
Dampier, Alfred 184
dandies 30, 38, 217 *see also* mashers
Dark, Fred 54
Darell Blake (Campbell) 191
Darrell, Cissie 168
Darrell, George 63, 71, 73, 168, 182
Davenport, Sarah 92
Davitt, Ellen 79–81, 201
Davitt Award 81
Dawe, William Carlton 193
Dawes, Nick 240
Dawn (magazine) 179
The Dead Letter (Victor) 78
Deakin, Alfred 59, 205
*The Decline and Fall of the British
  Empire* (Watson) 193
Degas, E. 64
delirium tremens *see* alcoholism
Dennis, C. J. 135
detective fiction
  Australian 75, 78–82
  development 75–83, 252
  etymology and terminology 9, 78
  female detectives 77, 149, 152
  Golden Age 51, 252

hardboiled 252
series detectives: 246; Octavius Fanks
  (FH) 125, 247; Lecoq (Gaboriau)
  77, 83; Mark Sinclair (Fortune) 82;
  see also Holmes, Sherlock
'The Detective's Album' (Fortune)
  81–2
The Detective's Album (Fortune) 81, 96,
  101, 237–8
*The Development of Australian
  Literature* (Turner & Sutherland) 210
El Diablo Cojuelo (Guevara) 9
Dickens, Charles 10, 78, 90, 93, 105,
  220, 234, 255
dime novels 113, 115
Dixson, William 234
Dr Faustus (Farjeon) 104
Dr Jekyll (Stevenson) 93, 115, 132, 160
Dolman, Glen 217–8, 224
Dombey and Son (Dickens) 10
Dorcas Dene, Detective (Sims) 152
Dove, Mrs 154
Douglas, Lord Alfred 216
Doyle, Annette 12
Doyle, Arthur Conan 2, 45, 88, 98,
  101–2, 145, 160–1, 189, 245, 247
  childhood 12, 14–5, 24
  on *Hansom Cab* 161
Doyle, Charles 14–5, 24, 160
Doyle, Mary 14–5, 161
Dracula (Stoker) 93, 252
Drayton, Joanne 257
Drysdale, Robert 20
Dugdale, Henrietta 59
Dumas, Alexandre 36
Dunedin, New Zealand 2, 17–21,
  25–6, 28, 31–3, 37–9, 44, 47, 120, 145,
  163–4, 169, 213
Dunedin Football Club 31

East Lynne (play) 56
Echoes of the Week 159
Eliot, George 73, 93
Elgar, Edward 25